# THE PROFLIGATE COLONIAL

# THE PROFLIGATE COLONIAL

## HOW THE US EXPORTED AUSTERITY TO THE PHILIPPINES

## LISANDRO E. CLAUDIO

CORNELL UNIVERSITY PRESS
*Ithaca and London*

Publication of this book was made possible by a generous subvention from the Southeast Asian Lives and Histories Project funded by the Henry Luce Foundation.

First published 2025 by Cornell University Press

Librarians: A CIP catalog record for this book is available from the Library of Congress.

ISBN 9781501784071 (hardcover)
ISBN 9781501784095 (pdf)
ISBN 9781501784088 (epub)

GPSR EU contact: Sam Thornton, Mare Nostrum Group B.V., Mauritskade 21D, 1091 GC, Amsterdam, NL, gpsr@mare-nostrum.co.uk.

# CONTENTS

# Note on Orthography and Translation

Consistent with contemporary orthography in the Philippines, I have removed accents from vowels in Filipino names with Hispanic origins, except for direct quotations and bibliographic entries. All translations, except otherwise noted, are my own.

# Introduction
## Hidden Empire, Hidden Austerity

William Jennings Bryan, who ran and lost three times for US president, embodied the populism of the nineteenth-century Democratic Party. A politician who claimed to represent common people, he built a career speaking for Southern farmers struggling under a deflationary gold standard. In 1896, Bryan secured the Democratic nomination for president, beating gold advocates in his party and inaugurating a populist revolt. It was a defining moment for the Democrats, breaking the détente between the party's gold and silver factions that had lasted for almost twenty years.[1] For that election and the two that followed, the Democrats would become the party of silver and inflation.

Bryan's populism rested on his belief that the gold standard, which tethered the supply of money to the availability of gold, stifled farmers. The restraint on the money supply resulted in lower prices, notably for agricultural products. Moreover, the gold standard posed a heavy burden on debtors, as it preserved stable or decreasing costs, causing the real value of debts to rise. The gold standard forced austerity on the agricultural South: Farmers had to work harder even as they earned less. Against "hard money" Republicans and bankers who believed that stable money was moral since it prevented price increases, Bryan pushed for the flexibility of silver—a currency whose supply could expand more rapidly.

Bryan lost in 1896 but ran again in 1900. In his second run, he inveighed once more against the gold standard. As before, his campaign continued the struggle of agrarian populists against an establishment of hard money bankers. But events halfway across the globe would add a new, crucial component to his platform. On the campaign trail, Bryan explained that, in the upcoming election, "three questions contest for primacy—the money question, the trust question, and imperialism."[2] If one opposed the gold standard, large trusts, and imperialism in the Philippines, one supported Bryan's challenge to the incumbent Republican, William McKinley.

Though simplistic, Bryan's remarks were a distillation of key debates from the Progressive Era.[3] To him, the first two issues in particular were linked. "The contest between monometallism and bimetallism," he explained, "is a worldwide contest which must go on until silver is once more a money equal with gold, or until the gold standard becomes universal."[4] With England placing India under the gold standard, monometallism was expanding, and a "gold blanket" covered "nearly three hundred million people in Southern Asia."[5] This blanket was a threat to producers the world over because Republican advocates of the gold standard, who wished to raise the value of the dollar, were threatening to cut the world's money supply by one-half. "We cannot afford to throw the influence of this nation upon the side of the gold standard, unless we are prepared to accept universal gold monometallism with all that that means," Bryan added.[6]

As for colonialism, the moral stakes were even more evident. "The Philippine question," Bryan declaimed, "is even plainer than the trust question, and those who will be benefitted by an imperial policy are even less in number than those who may be led to believe that they would share in the benefits of a gold standard or of a private monopoly."[7] Turning Filipinos into colonial subjects would keep them in "perpetual vassalage, owing allegiance to the flag, but having no voice in the government," which was "entirely at variance with the principles upon which this government has been founded."[8] As with implementing the gold standard, narrow economic interests informed imperialism in Asia. "The purpose behind the imperial policy," he asserted, "is the extension of trade."[9] By invading the Philippines, "the Republican party, which boasts that it sprang into existence in the defense of human rights, now coolly calculates the value of human life measured by Oriental trade."[10]

Bryan's campaign highlighted two forms of US power during the Progressive Era, both of which centered on the Philippines. There, the US projected not only its imperial, military power, but also its economic power amid the globalization of a US-style gold exchange standard. Bryan's prescient platform warned of a new era where American imperial power and monometallism would together reorder the world. When Bryan was first nominated in 1896, he declared that the country should not be "crucified on a cross of gold."[11] At the dawn of the next century, this cross was about to be transposed into a colony, with the United States leading Filipinos to a monetary Calvary.

Bryan's second electoral defeat in 1900 allowed McKinley and his Republican Party to continue the occupation of the Philippines and place it under the blanket of gold. If Bryan's loss was thus a blow to Filipino nationalist aspirations, it was nonetheless also a blow to bimetallism in Asia. Republican ascendance would lead not only to American control of the Philippines but also to a new American-designed gold exchange standard, where foreign reserves would be held not in gold bullion but in gold-backed US dollars. Monometallism and imperialism were simultaneously victorious at the turn of the century, and these two ideals would ground the emergence of the United States as a Pacific power. This moment had implications for the colonized and the colonizer. Implementing the gold exchange standard created a discourse of austerity in the Philippines that remains dominant yet hidden today. For the US, this moment would lead to its eventual role as the global guarantor of a gold-based system.

This book is an account of how the US exported the imperial discourse of austerity to and through the Philippines. Its central image is that of the profligate colonial—a figure from the colonies, often feminized, who allegedly thrives on excess, wasting the hard-earned money of the government and investors. Austerity often emerges when governments seek to restrain the spending of or refuse to spend for supposedly profligate, often racialized and feminized, others. Such thinking was at the heart of Ronald Reagan's "welfare queen" rhetoric (a racist dog whistle intended to conjure images of wasteful African American women) in the 1970s. However, well before the fearmongering about welfare queens, the US built a colonial state in the Philippines on the cheap because it thought Filipinos could not be trusted with credit. It constructed the image of a profligate colonial alongside a currency system that tried to limit its supposed excesses.

This construction of a "civilized" economic order in the Philippines had global stakes. Bryan's reference to the US expanding its global influence by covering the world with a gold blanket foreshadowed what would happen early in the twentieth century. Hitherto, the ascendance of the US economy had yet to be matched by the adoption of the dollar as a global reserve currency. By the mid-1920s, however, the dollar overtook sterling as the primary reserve currency, and by the interwar years there existed a "sterling-U.S. dollar duopoly."[12]

This process began in the Philippines, Panama, and Mexico—the exceptional cases in the fin-de-siècle where the dollar served as the reserve currency.[13] The Philippines was the crucible of the emerging system that would culminate in dollar dominance. American "money doctors" used their experiences in their new colony to promote their dollar diplomacy, and based on "the very first patient," they would treat other countries in the Americas, Africa, and Eastern Europe.[14] As Charles Arthur Conant, the economist who designed the gold exchange standard in the Philippines, remarked, it was "greatly to the credit" of the United States that it was "securing throughout the world the same plan which we ourselves have already inaugurated in the Philippines."[15] It is this crucible of monetary and imperial power that concerns our present inquiry. This crucible bubbles to this day.

## Jukebox Economics

US imperialism and hard money were the intersecting themes of Bryan's speech. At the time, the belief in these two ideals was plain to see. Imperialists believed in their manifest destiny—their white man's burden to bring civilization to the rest of the world. Meanwhile, wealthy hard money advocates openly defended their right to prevent a cheap currency from eating away their assets' value.

In today's Philippines, one must squint to see the enduring appeal of empire and hard money. The US empire in the Philippines is famously "hidden."[16] For Americans, its history is obscured by the nation's exceptionalism; the US refuses to view itself as an early twentieth-century colonial power like Britain or France. However, it is difficult to hide this empire in the Philippines—a country with a US-style presidential system, an English-speaking population, and an enduring obsession with basketball. We Filipinos are usually aware of the imperial origins of our traits, habits, and preoccupations. But not always.

In 1994, after the People's Republic of China depreciated its currency by 40 percent, five Filipino economists, mainly from the University of the Philippines (UP) School of Economics, called for a similar devaluation of the Philippine peso. The economists noted that, partially because of high interest rates that raised the currency's value, volatile money flowed into the country, creating the conditions for a real estate bubble. They called for devaluation "to discourage the hot money flows and the property bubble, to protect local manufacturers, to encourage exporters, and to curb banks' reckless lending behavior."[17] Because of their proposal, UP economics professor Raul Fabella (one of the five economists) recalls, "we were treated worse than lepers." According to Fabella, the central bank and the business community criticized them because these groups were content "to party on cheap imports" and accepted that an appreciating peso was a market reality. Not only did the central bank respond with "over my dead body," but one of its allied columnists labeled the group of five "jukebox economists," who sang the tune of businesses that lined their pockets.[18]

The response from the inflation-averse, conservative central bank was to be expected. Surprisingly, however, even the left rejected the jukebox economists (a label some of the five and like-minded economists have embraced). "The business community was firmly on the CB [Central Bank] governor's side," continues Fabella. "But even labor unions whose jobs we were trying to save were calling for our heads."[19]

In the Philippines, left-wing groups often defend the strong peso. Like the central bank, the leading Maoist-aligned think tank, the IBON Foundation, believes that a cheap peso accelerates "domestic inflation which will burden Filipinos with rising prices of basic needs." Unlike the jukebox economists, IBON incorrectly assumes that the Philippine government has had a bias for weak currency because "currency management" has been "liberalized." IBON, therefore, advocates active state engagement to maintain the currency's price without explaining why currency management should favor revaluation over devaluation (cheap currencies, like China's and Vietnam's, are actively managed by the state).[20] In 2022, as global currencies crashed amid a more expensive dollar, IBON called for measures to prevent a further slide, including cuts on government infrastructure spending.[21]

At the time, the jukebox economist Fabella was also concerned. But for different reasons. By September of that year, the peso had reached record lows. Fabella saw the cheap peso as an opportunity, yet he worried that the central bank would commit the mistakes of the past and revalue the peso. For devaluation to work, especially in a country with an ingrained import bias, it must be sustained. But Fabella knew that the Philippine central bank had a penchant for revaluation, and "our history suggests our response will again reprise the same mistakes."[22]

Fabella was right. The following month, the former central bank governor and finance secretary Benjamin Diokno—once a member of the jukebox economist group—announced that the Philippines would step up the defense of the peso by dipping into its reserves—a policy move supported by Diokno's successor at the central bank.[23] After the peso's price bottomed out in October, it would slowly creep back up. The bankers and the leftists had gotten their way.

Empire works in mysterious ways. There is no longer a gold standard in the Philippines, but the ideology of hard, dear money that arrived on Philippine shores through the gold standard is alive and well. This ideology is, in fact, hegemonic, as evidenced by the consensus around it—the way Filipinos treat it like common sense. In the Philippines, discussions about the price of the peso are like discussions about the weather. It is the main economic indicator in newspapers and the topic of everyday conversations: "Say, did you see how much the peso dropped today? Horrible, right?" When the peso drops rapidly, social media pundits turn existential and ask, "What has become of my country?"

Apart from tracing the origins of austerity in the Philippines to imperialist discourse, my goal is to sketch a historical through-line from the Republican imperialists of hard money to the central bank and the Maoists of the present. I first began to suspect that this through-line existed while listening to one of the jukebox economists deliver a lecture in 2015. Cayetano Paderanga had served twice as the government's head of planning and had some insight into why the central bank has been resistant to depreciation. During a lecture at Kyoto University, where I was a postdoctoral fellow, he noted that the bank viewed depreciation as "unmanly." Talking to other jukebox economists in the summer of 2023, I heard the same thing: Philippine central bankers believed they had to be "macho" against inflation and depreciation.[24] Oddly, this was the same rhetoric used by the money doctors who promoted the gold standard in the Philippines and worldwide in the early twentieth century. As the authority on the money doctors, Emily S. Rosenberg, notes,

> Just as manhood implied restraint, self-mastery, and supervision over dependents, uncivilized peoples were marked by feminine attributes, especially lack of planning and weak self-discipline. Against the moral and financial effeminacy of unbacked, inflating paper money could be set the manly, civilizing force of a gold standard, careful regulation by a national banking system, and supervised revenue collection and expenditure. Civilized men conserved

value by restraining and regulating use; whether the currency of potential value was semen or money; civilized men kept control of the quantities produced.[25]

The "manly" hard money advocates believed a strong currency would lead to conserving money and value—which hints that hard money is just the tip of an ideological iceberg. In the Philippines, as elsewhere, hard money is often the pointed tip of the spear that is austerity. Demands to defend the currency are usually followed by demands to shrink public finance. As we saw, IBON proposed a cut in infrastructure spending. As for the central bank, it defended the currency by being the Asian leader in raising interest rates (a way to shrink liquidity by reducing demand for money).[26]

More than a history of austerity in the Philippines, however, this book seeks to theorize austerity in a colonial/postcolonial setting. As we shall see, austerity unfolds in unique ways in colonies. While the history and dangerous effects of austerity in the Global North are well documented,[27] more must be done to theorize it in the Global South and postcolonial settings (apart from critiques of IMF structural adjustment).

In the Philippines, there is a poverty of thinking about austerity. It is not even a word we can accurately translate. When Filipinos write about austerity, they write in English. In Tagalog, which along with English is the language of national policymaking and activism, "profligate" easily translates as *mapagwaldas* or *mapaglustay*. *Pagwawaldas* or *paglulustay* is the act of wasting money. *Waldasero/waldasera* is a slang word for someone who is wasteful, often politicians or compulsive shoppers. All these words come from the root words, *waldas* and *lustay*, which both connote waste, lucre, or something embezzled in the case of *lustay*. On the other hand, the best translation for austere is *matipid*, the adjective used for one who saves. *Matipid* connotes motherly virtue and conjures images of a well-ordered household. The word, therefore, only carries austerity's positive connotations. *Matipid* cannot be used to connote the strangling effect of austerity on society. The noun and adjective versions of *kuripot* (miser or miserly) often connote a lack of generosity. Yet *kuripot* is a much less common way to refer to government than *mapagwaldas* or *mapaglustay*. And few native speakers would translate *kuripot* as "austere."[28]

Despite the absence of thinking about austerity and precisely because of this absence, the Philippines is an ideal case study for our purposes. For one, it was the crucible of the American gold exchange standard. Its story indexes American hard money's globalization in the Progressive

Era. More broadly, it presages the economic logic of our present-day Pax Americana. The Philippines was the colonial laboratory for the US, and the "success" of its experiments there had consequences for the colony and other places within the penumbra of US economic power.

It is also remarkable how hegemonic the theme of austerity has been throughout the country's history. While its neighbors have experimented with various forms of developmentalism and industrial policy, the Philippine state has historically been a weak economic actor except for a few exceptional moments. The reason for this is the almost universal acceptance of austerity's tenets. The Philippines is an extreme example of austerity's victory over other forms of economic thought. Extremes, of course, say little about the mean. But they are helpful as thought experiments. In a place where austerity has the tacit acceptance of almost everyone, we can examine its road to power. Studying how the twin logics of empire and austerity dovetail in the Philippines will allow us to detect these logics elsewhere. I hope this work will help spark research on the history of austerity in other colonial and postcolonial contexts.

In this regard, the story is specific yet universal. It is specific in that not all empires have advocated for hard money like the United States in the twentieth century. Indeed, one of my key observations is that the zealotry of the US for hard money starkly contrasted with that of the British. In colonial India, the British maintained an undervalued rupee because they could successfully sequester the gold value of trade surpluses, unlike the United States, where domestic agricultural interests were in perpetual fear of being flooded by cheap Philippine imports. Later in the twentieth century, neocolonial policy would also move away from hard money, especially in the post–Bretton Woods era when the IMF became more comfortable with currency depreciation.

Yet this early period, when hard money and US imperialism intersect, tells us much about an emerging world order dominated by American thinking on currency. More broadly, this work is an invitation to consider imperialism's crucial role in limiting colonial and postcolonial monetary autonomy and preventing strategic and developmental currency interventions.

## Arguing with Anti-Inflation Zombies

While it is common for left-wing critics to study the economics of the Global South using the lens of "neoliberalism," I contend that thinking about austerity offers deeper insights. Neoliberalism is not only an imprecise concept; its emergence and dominance from the 1980s until the 2000s is also too recent to account for the deeply entrenched economic conservatism of the Philippines. At its most unwieldy, neoliberalism is a blanket invective hurled by contemporary socialists of various stripes against everything they despise.[29] This confusion is especially evident in the Philippines, where left-leaning critics routinely advocate for disinflationary measures like revaluing the currency while labeling their foes "neoliberal." At its most supple, neoliberalism describes an economic rationality that permeates all aspects of social life while degrading the value of collective politics.[30] However, viewing the term in this manner is too analytically expansive and, therefore, vague for a book that aims to narrate a story of macroeconomic thought.

In contrast to neoliberalism, austerity—a related term—corresponds to more specific policies. The term austerity is also more apt, given the historical scope of this book. While neoliberalism is associated with the postwar rise to prominence of figures such as Friedrich von Hayek and the dominance of Reaganism and Thatcherism in the 1970s and '80s, austerity is of an older vintage.

In defining austerity, we do not need to reinvent the wheel. This book's definition of austerity is guided by the pathbreaking work of economic historian Clara Mattei, who notes that austerity takes on three mutually reinforcing forms: fiscal, monetary, and industrial. These faces of austerity are a trinity akin to the triune god, where one form is simply a manifestation of the whole. Fiscal austerity, the simplest form, entails budget cuts, spending limits, and the avoidance of debt, which leads to a reduction in liquidity in the economy.[31]

Meanwhile, monetary austerity / deflation seeks to curtail liquidity and demand, usually by raising interest rates. If interest rates are high, money becomes expensive to borrow, making money dear. Dear money also refers to restrictive currency systems like the gold standard, which requires cuts in public expenditure to maintain. Since, under a gold standard, the money in circulation must correspond to equivalent gold reserves, there is a limit on how much the government can spend. Similarly, suppose a government wants to revalue its currency (for instance, after a depreciation). In that case, it must raise interest rates to make government bonds more attractive (which then makes investors buy more of that government's currency, thereby raising its price), and/or it could remove liquidity by using its foreign reserves to purchase its currency (increasing demand for the currency and raising its value).

This book will pay close attention to monetary austerity because the US introduced austerity to the Philippines through the gold standard. And, as we have seen, the Filipino left and the right sing the praises of dear money. This form of austerity is also challenging for the lay citizen to understand. While the relationship between a budget cut and the amount of money circulating is straightforward, only few noneconomists in the Philippines think about how interest rates affect liquidity and the price of currency. Monetary policy is also distant to Filipinos because it is run by the central bank—a nontransparent government institution whose workings are rarely debated because of its exalted position and the false belief that ordinary citizens should not argue with its experts. Monetary austerity is, therefore, easily obscured. It is in this manner that left-wing critics in the Philippines claim to be anti-austerity in advocating for fiscal boldness while at the same time promoting austerity by defending dear money.

Crucially, as we saw in the case of labor unions that condemned the jukebox economists, Filipinos rarely trace the connection between monetary austerity and industrial austerity. Mattei defines industrial austerity as the imposition of "non-contested, hierarchical relations of production." She notes that increasing the price of money (monetary austerity) "requires downward price adjustments, particularly labor prices (i.e., lower wages), in order to cut the costs of production." And since revaluing the currency creates a loss in competitiveness (a nation's exports become more expensive), lower production costs become more critical. Moreover, by curbing investment (raising interest rates reduces debt and investment), dear money policy reduces employment. With fewer jobs available, laborers lose their capacity to bargain with and defy employers, thereby "killing the political leverage and militancy of labor."[32]

If austerity is a bad idea, why is it so common? Paul Krugman lists austerity as one of economics' "zombie ideas"—ideas "that should have been killed by contrary evidence, but instead keep shambling along, eating people's brains."[33] Krugman's metaphor is only partially accurate. Because zombies are ugly. Austerity is more akin to Dracula or one of Anne Rice's aristocratic vampires—sophisticated, beautiful, and sometimes even hospitable. Its outward beauty and deceptive hospitality stem from its promise to combat inflation. "Austerity," explains Mark Blyth, "is a form of voluntary deflation in which the economy adjusts through the reduction of wages, prices, and public spending to restore competitiveness, which is (supposedly) best achieved by cutting the state's budget, debts, and deficits."[34] During times of inflation, he adds, wealthy advocates of austerity suddenly "express solidarity with the poor *en masse*," claiming that "it mainly hurts the poor since their incomes are low and they are more affected by price increases."[35] This message is powerful in the Philippines, where inflation almost always tops the list of general electoral concerns and is *always* the number one economic priority for Filipino voters, ahead of other issues like jobs or poverty reduction.[36] News outlets, activists, and politicians discuss the anti-poor nature of inflation ad nauseam.[37]

However, Blyth adds, the argument about inflation being anti-poor "is half the story because inflation is perhaps better thought of as a class-specific tax."[38] Inflation primarily erodes the value of creditors' assets (a minority of wealthy people) while making it easier for debtors (the majority) to pay off their debts since less real income is needed to pay these off. "The politics of cutting inflation," Blyth concludes, "take the form of restoring the 'real' value of money by pushing the inflation rate down through 'independent' (from the rest of us) central banks. Creditors win, debtors lose."[39] Similarly, Mattei argues that the fixation on "curbing inflation" contributes to "the subjugation of the working class to the impersonal laws of the market."[40] Most succinctly, the developmental economist Ha-Joon Chang argues, "Inflation has become the bogeyman that has been used to justify policies that have mainly benefited the holders of financial assets, at the cost of long-term stability, economic growth and human happiness."[41] Such arguments are shocking to Filipino readers, leading frequently to the castigation of those who forward them.[42]

## Austerity Matters

Why write—or read—a book about austerity in a colonial and postcolonial context? In diving into the history of austerity in the Philippines, I hope with this book to theorize what austerity has wrought in the so-called margins of the world system. It is, after all, in these obscured margins where global power is most brutish and, thereby, most evident. And, as I hope to show, ideas emerging from the crucible of the marginal quickly gain global traction. In exploring this space, the book also contributes to monetary history, particularly the history of hard money. Works examining the history of the gold standard or even the spread of the American-led gold exchange standard have paid scant attention to the crucible of American monetary supremacy, the Philippines,[43] even as superb historical work has been done on another gold-based economy in Asia, namely Japan.[44]

This work also seeks to contribute to the growing literature on American imperialism in the Philippines. This literature has been a verdant field in Philippine historiography.[45] For example, pathbreaking work has been published on the American-era formation of a legal system,[46] a healthcare system,[47] an educational system,[48] a policing infrastructure,[49] and governance systems for ethnic minorities.[50] And while this is not the first work to examine the American monetary system in the Philippines, it departs from these previous works because it traces the legacies of this economic system across the twentieth century.[51]

Though it may not be directly obvious, I also aim to contribute to Southeast Asian economic history. The Philippines has always been part of regional economic processes. However, its enmeshment in these processes is more evident in certain periods. It was, for example, integral to a Southeast Asian "age of commence," anchored on the trade of spice and silver from 1450 to 1680;[52] it was part of an exploitative region-wide economic system of Japanese imperialism during World War II;[53] and it was drawn into the intense regionalization of economic production after the Plaza Accord of 1985.[54] In the years covered in this book, the Philippines' economy was perhaps more American than Southeast Asian. However, I hope to show that many American and Filipino policy interventions were reactions to tenacious regionalization processes, such as the British-led regionalization of the nineteenth century. I also hope to show that, even when the Philippines was most economically parochial, it remained comparable to its neighbors and experienced similar changes.

Finally, I seek to contribute to discussions that attempt to reimagine economic justice in the Philippines. In this respect, I would like to be read by fellow Filipinos. While the narrative of this book ends in 1986, the book shows that the intellectual legacies of the previous century are ones we grapple with today. Consequently, they continue to limit our imagination, preventing us from exploring alternatives to the status quo. If my observation that monetary austerity remains unchallenged in the Philippines is correct, this book will encounter significant resistance. If you are a Filipino averse to my argument, all I can hope is that you turn the page.

## What—and Who

This book's narrative recounts how austerity remained concealed yet prominently situated at the center of economic discourse. It is less an economic history of the Philippines in the twentieth century and more a history of economic ideas, told mainly through lives. As an intellectual and cultural historian, my concern is not straightforward political economy. For instance, I do not measure how the concentration of capital in specific sectors influences the state's bias for dear money. In any case, rigorous research has already been done to examine this issue.[55] While I am not averse to asking which groups are interested in promoting which policies, I am more intrigued by how those invested in preserving dear money argue for their interests. Naturally, this does not preclude the examination of incentive structures, and I will point out cases where those who defend austerity do so because it directly benefits them. However, the zigs and zags of economic discourse allow us to trace better how we got to where we are—a point where austerity has become a dominant yet concealed ideology.

To trace this discourse, I examine key moments in twentieth-century Philippine economic history that have taught Filipinos the "values" of thrift and so-called financial rectitude. Most of these moments were economic crises. Crises hold significance not only because they disrupt economic progress but also because of the recriminations that ensue in their wake. Amid these recriminations, new orthodoxies arise, or previous ones get reinforced. For many reasons, not least of which are the potency of empire and the complicity of economic commentators in forwarding its logic, these crises have almost always reinforced the orthodoxy of austerity.

The book is structured as a diptych, with the first two chapters mirroring the second two. Chapters 1 and 3 document the creation of two monetary systems—one colonial and another postcolonial. Chapters 2 and 4 document the major crises that these systems underwent. The book also follows a narrative arc in four movements: Americans introduce austerity, Americans defend austerity, Filipino nationalists embrace austerity, and Filipino progressives tacitly articulate it with democracy. The book's two acts—one colonial and the other postcolonial—are separated by an interlude that explores the Japanese occupation during the Second World War.

The dramatis personae are mostly imperialists, intellectuals, and policymakers. These were powerful men who believed in a manly creed. Unfortunately, their opponents have also been powerful men: nationalist politicians, visionary members of a modernizing elite, and even servants of a brutal dictator and kleptocrat. One of the tragedies of this story is that no systematic critique of austerity, especially hard money, has emerged from a grassroots Filipino left. Why and how this happened is another mystery I seek to investigate.

Chapter 1, "Austerity Contracted," examines the implementation of the American gold exchange standard in the Philippines in 1902. Although Mattei posits that modern austerity was "invented" after the First World War, the logic that paved the way for it was already present in the early twentieth century. This sentiment was conspicuous in the Philippines, where Americans sought to establish an empire on the cheap. This opening chapter focuses on the money doctors to see how the Philippines "contracted" austerity through the gold standard. I use "contracted" here like Vicente Rafael, who famously coined the term "contracting colonialism."[56] The Philippines contracted austerity as a kind of economic disease. And it also entered a contract with it—a contract it has yet to break. The chapter additionally introduces multiple American architects of the gold exchange standard. It considers the Philippine careers of Arthur Conant, the primary architect of the Philippine currency system, and Edwin Kemmerer—the implementer of Conant's plan and the economist who would become the US's leading money doctor.

Chapter 2, "Austerity Defended," delves into the Philippines' first major economic crisis in the twentieth century. After the First World War, the world went into a deflationary crisis. This deflation drained the Philippines' reserves and strained the currency system. Despite the crisis being global, American colonial officials and economists blamed the downturn on the profligacy and corruption of Filipinos, particularly those associated with the Philippine National Bank (PNB). Rather than acknowledging the broader deflation, commentators portrayed the global crisis of the early 1920s as a local banking problem and a product of reckless spending. This narrative allowed colonial officials and economists to articulate an early defense of austerity against the profligate colonial. Contemporary scholars have uncritically reproduced this narrative. Central to this chapter is a tension that pit an incipient Filipino developmentalism represented by Speaker of the House Sergio Osmeña and the PNB's first Filipino president, Venacio Concepcion, against the monetary austerity of Republican state builders like William Cameron Forbes and Leonard Wood, both of whom served as governor-general of the Philippines.

The brief interlude turns to a traumatic period for Filipinos—the hyperinflation occasioned by the Japanese occupation. Though brief, this period affected the Filipino psyche in a way similar to the Weimar period in German history, further deepening the fear—already entrenched by imperialism—of a cheap currency.

Chapter 3, "Austerity Nationalized," examines how government officials reconciled austerity with Filipino nationalism during the immediate postindependence period. To distance themselves from the image of the profligate colonial, policymakers like the central bank governor Miguel Cuaderno embraced austerity, turning its "manly" virtues into those of a robust and independent nation. Cuaderno's influence in the 1950s marked the zenith of austerity in the country. During this period, the Philippines even celebrated a national "Austerity Day," a rare instance when officials defended austerity *qua* austerity. This was a period of multiple balance-of-payments crises and the deterioration of Filipino labor conditions. The chapter examines Cuaderno's career, paying close attention to his relationship with President Carlos Garcia, who implemented a comprehensive austerity program designed by the central bank. It also revisits the futile but intellectually courageous resistance to this austerity by revisiting the career of the businessman, bureaucrat, and self-taught economist Salvador Araneta.

If chapter 3 examines how austerity was reconciled with nationalism, chapter 4, "Austerity Democratized," shows how austerity was reconciled with the Filipino struggle for democracy. The dictatorship of Ferdinand Marcos (1965–1986) was brutal and corrupt. But it was not austere. Faced with a profligate dictator, the left adopted a discourse of austerity to challenge the dictatorship. The chapter traces the shifts in economic priorities occasioned by the Marcos regime, the two crises of 1970 and 1983, and the left-wing responses to these. The chapter thus looks at two warring tribes of economic thinkers. On the one hand, it examines the theoreticians of devaluation: Marcos's finance minister, Cesar Virata, and his minister of economic planning, Gerardo Sicat. Against these two figures emerged a left that began to advocate dear money. The lawyer and Maoist fellow traveler Alejandro Lichauco was the most prominent figure representing this tendency.

The book's end thus brings us full circle: from austerity introduced by American imperialists to austerity embraced by Filipinos on both the left and the right. It is a grim ending, revealing how empire's legacy hamstrings economic discourse. My hope, however, is that awareness of this hidden history allows for reexamining its legacies.

CHAPTER 1

# Austerity Contracted

*A Colonial Cross of Gold, 1902–1913*

Filipino tourists rarely travel to Latin America. But when they do, they are often perplexed by the region's most common currency symbol. These tourists, charged in $, assume they are being billed in US dollars, not local pesos. This confusion arises because the Philippine peso is the only peso not abbreviated with the $ sign but with a ₱—a symbol challenging to locate on modern-day word processors.

The $ sign originally referred to the pesos of the Spanish empire, with its two parallel lines symbolizing the vertical portions of the letter *P*, and the *S* indicating the plural.[1] Our association of the $ sign with the US dollar is a testament to its contemporary dominance, or, in words often misattributed to Charles de Gaulle, its "exorbitant privilege."[2]

The exceptional nature of the Philippines' currency symbol is a product of the country's exceptional colonial history—twice colonized, first by Spain, then by the United States. The ₱ sign was a product of a colonial transition between these two empires. In August 1903, after a new coinage act had placed the Philippines on the gold standard, the colony's civil governor, William Howard Taft, ordered the new symbol to "be used by all officials of this Government as the designation for the new Philippine pesos, in contradistinction to the $ mark for United States currency, [or] Pfs. for Mexican or Spanish currency."[3] The order was straightforward. Still, it elided the history of the $ sign by categorizing it as "United States currency" while reducing Spanish currency to Pfs., an abbreviation for pesetas, a peso denomination.

Amid these elisions, the imperialist goal was to differentiate the Philippine peso from the other pesos circulated within Asia in the nineteenth century. Unlike these currencies, the new peso would be tied by the new colonial government to the US dollar and, therefore, to gold, differentiating it from the silver-based pesos of the crumbling Spanish empire. As expected, US colonization altered the Philippines in multiple ways. Yet one of the most profound and lasting changes of US empire relates to Philippine money and how Filipinos think about it.

This chapter has three objectives. First, it documents the Philippines' cosmopolitan trading world before the arrival of the United States. It tells the story of how this ostensibly Spanish colony was absorbed into a wider informal British trading empire in Southeast Asia. Beyond describing the necessary Southeast Asian backdrop, the chapter looks at the Philippines as an early case study, perhaps the earliest, of an imperial transition from Pax Britannica to Pax Americana. Britain was at the heart of the nineteenth-century gold standard. Because it was an unmatched foreign lender and because of its extensive financial markets, the Bank of England was what Eichengreen, Mehl, and Chitu call the "conductor of the international orchestra."[4] Yet its imperial strategy in Southeast Asia was anchored on silver. It was thus a more flexible monetary empire than the emergent gold-based American order. The Philippines offers a case study of the transitions that would unfold globally in the twentieth century: from British to American dominance, from silver to gold standards, and from a flexible and pragmatic monetary empire to one anchored on pro-gold ideology.

Second, this chapter chronicles the debates that culminated in establishing the American gold exchange standard in the Philippines and its initial implementation. Because there had been no monetary policy during the waning days of Spanish imperialism, the formation of the gold exchange system was the birth of modern macroeconomic policy in the Philippines, and many of the assumptions that inform policymaking up to today—from the ills of inflation to the sacredness of a strong currency—can be traced to this moment.

During the early years of US colonization, notions of a profligate colonial congealed in official discourse. In implementing the gold standard, American officials not only created monetary policy in the Philippines but also moralized the language of economics. From then on, economic policy in the colony would be linked to notions of responsibility, righteousness, civilization, and manliness. Austerity at this time had yet to become a coherent ideology. Still, there were, in Raymond Williams's words, "structures of feeling" that signaled a trajectory of thinking and sentiment.[5] The doctrine of hard money was constituted as a civilizational imperative and gauge to assess the colonial polity's readiness for self-governance. Eventually, Filipinos themselves would accept these terms and articulate these ideas alongside modern austerity.

Yet the gold standard would be implemented amid the vagaries of colonial transition. The colonial regime faced two impediments to the implementation of gold-backed currency. First, try as it might, it struggled to disentangle the Philippines from the broader, silver-based world it had belonged to. While the US attempted to Americanize the Philippines, the Philippines still belonged to an Asian trading world.

The second impediment was fiscal: Building a colony required spending, which strained a monometallic system. Recall that a gold standard limits liquidity. But how does an imperialist build a colony on the cheap? Because of the liquidity demands of colonial statecraft, the money doctors' platonic ideal of a gold standard required adulteration. The third objective of this chapter is to examine how the colonial state dealt with these tensions and the discursive moves policymakers deployed to obscure them. In hiding the tensions between the gold exchange standard and the pressures of colonial state-building, the American colonial state laid the groundwork for an orthodoxy that would define Philippine economic policy and thought in the twentieth century.

## Silver Currencies and British Hegemony

American architects of the gold exchange standard in the Philippines often portrayed the new currency as a return to an older gold-backed peso—a restoration of equilibrium and stability. Indeed, gold had once circulated in Spanish-era Filipinas, but this system did not belong to a halcyon period of economic progress. The silver trade had a longer history in the Philippines and Southeast Asia.

Before Spanish colonization, the islands that would eventually form the Philippines were already part of a Southeast Asian "age of commerce" from the mid-fifteenth and sixteenth centuries.[6] During this period, Southeast Asia exported spices and imported silver from the Americas and Japan.[7] After the cobbling together of Spanish Filipinas in the sixteenth century, the new colony took on a central role in this age of commerce. The beginning of the Manila–Acapulco galleon trade in 1571 established the first direct and stable trading route between Asia and the Americas. For Dennis Flynn and Arturo Giraldez, this moment was the beginning of global trade, since from that point on "all heavily populated continents traded with each other directly and indirectly in substantial volume."[8] Silver was central to this global trade, making Manila the entry point of this money from the Americas into China.[9]

Given the islands' centrality to the silver trade, it is unsurprising that various forms of silver currency circulated in the Philippines. Under the Spanish, the colony was mainly on a bimetallic standard, with coins composed of gold and silver from Latin America and Spain, and, from 1861 onward, coins minted from within the colony. A government report on commerce in the islands from 1838 noted the use of various Spanish, Mexican, Bolivar, Puac, Chilean, Rio de la Plata, Central American, and Columbia Cundinamarca pesos of different weights minted in multiple years, all circulating simultaneously. Amid this plethora of pesos, there was a brief attempt to regulate American money, with the general treasury restamping these coins for a fee of 1 percent.[10] But this stamping system proved untenable, and the treasury allowed all coins in the colony to circulate freely.[11] The overall pattern was consistent with that of the rest of Southeast Asia: Mexican currency was supreme within the region despite the circulation of multiple silver coins and attempts at creating local currencies. All money was benchmarked to the Mexican peso, with the different silver currencies being accepted relative to their value against it.[12]

The bimetallic standard held for as long as there was relative price stability between gold and silver. By the 1870s, however, the price of silver declined because of increased silver production and the shift of major economies to the gold standard, which raised the demand for gold.[13] In 1873, the US Congress demonetized silver, occasioning the shift to the gold standard—what William Jennings Bryan and his populists would eventually call the "crime of 1873."[14] Roughly at the same time, Germany introduced the gold-backed mark.

With large economies shifting to gold, silver was unloaded into world markets, decreasing the latter's value. Responding to this decline, the colonial government in the Philippines quixotically decreed parity between the price of the Mexican silver peso and the Spanish-Filipino gold peso. This move led to the exportation of gold to foreign markets, where it could be exchanged for more silver than in the Philippines (this silver could then be reimported into the colony at a profit). By 1881, all gold had been driven out of the colony.[15] Almost as soon as the gold was minted, it would disappear. Of the 9.3 million pesos worth of gold coin exported from 1861 to 1882, 8.5 million went to Britain and its colonies, while only 50,000 pesos' worth went to Spain. Of that amount, 49,000 was sent to Spain in 1861.[16] As we shall see, this exsanguination of gold into Britain and its colonies was not accidental; London was Manila's economic metropole.

The inability to regulate currency showed that the colonial state was weak in the waning years of the Spanish empire, especially in economic governance.[17] There was hardly any fiscal or monetary policy in the last two decades of Spanish imperialism, meaning there were virtually no deficits and no public debt. Expansionary policy was impossible since external markets determined the money supply.[18] The economy was a simple open market with almost no state intervention. This state of economic management aligned with a broader picture of the colonial state's bureaucratic weakness, mainly resulting from the shortage of colonial administrators.[19] However, if Spanish political power was weak because of the lack of officials, Spanish economic power was undercut by something broader.

The absence of Spanish economic hegemony did not mean the Philippines was not part of an imperial trading system. As Takashi Shiraishi has provocatively argued, "toddling leviathans" in Southeast Asia, like the Straits Settlements, the Dutch East Indies, Spanish Filipinas, and the Chakri dynastic states, took shape amid the emergence of an informal nineteenth-century British trading empire.[20] The Spanish in the Philippines began to rely on British capital after the end of the highly profitable Manila–Acapulco galleon trade in 1815 and the shrinking of the Spanish empire after Mexican independence in 1820. Since the Spanish colonial government had limited capacity to enforce forced cultivation and struggled to implement trade monopolies (unlike in the Dutch East Indies), it filled the void left by the expiration of the galleon trade by opening the Philippines to British traders and their Chinese partners, who often spread British capital across the archipelago. As a result, the Philippine economy was brought into a British free-trade zone anchored on the Straits Settlements and Hong Kong.[21] It thus ceased being a Spanish colonial economy,[22] becoming instead a node within a regional network of "Anglo-Chinese" capital.[23] The US at the turn of the century was, thus, not encountering an economic terra nullius but a colony entwined in Asian regionalization and British imperialism. It was this system that colonial officials would try to undercut.

British hegemony was visible in the Philippines. An emergent professional class found employment in the various British and American trading houses in urban centers like Cebu and Manila. British trading houses also fueled exports by tapping into barter markets outside the major cities. In exchange for export crops, these houses gave local producers items such as cotton, agricultural implements, and food.[24] Indeed, there were so many British businessmen in the country that even Manila's drivers of horse-drawn carriages had a rudimentary understanding of English.[25] And the primary conspirators of the Philippine Revolution, many of them employees of the British, would use trading houses as "arenas of conspiracy" to launch the 1896 revolt against the Spanish.[26] Crucially, money was regulated by the British. Of the three major banks operating upon the arrival of the Americans, two were British: the Hong Kong and Shanghai Banking Corporation (HSBC) and the Chartered Bank of India, Australia, and China. The third was the periodically underfunded Banco Español-Filipino.

The extent to which the Philippine economy was tied to Anglo-Chinese trading circuits is also evidenced by the expansion of non-gold currencies circulating in the economy. As we saw above, only Spanish and Latin American coins circulated in the mid-nineteenth century. By that century's close, however, American officials had noted the presence of coins from the former Spanish empire, "Hongkong dollars and fractional silver coins from different Chinese countries, and copper coins from nearly every part of the Orient."[27] Manila had been integrated into an informal common currency zone that included the Straits Settlements, Hong Kong, and parts of China.[28] Because of British capital, the colony had transitioned within fifty years from an afterthought in the Spanish empire to a node in a British regional trading system. British financial power was so entrenched in the Philippines that even after a decade of American rule, Governor-General Francis Burton Harrison was still seeking to "break up the British monopoly of our foreign trade."[29]

The period of British hegemony was one of export growth. In 1825, the colony's export earnings amounted to only 1 million pesos, but this amount grew to 18.9 million in 1875 and 36 million in 1895.[30] Multiple changes led to the creation of this export boom. One was the opening of Manila to foreign trade in 1834 and the lifting of a government tobacco monopoly in 1882.[31] Another was the threefold increase from 1880 to 1913 of the "tropical trade" between the West and tropical countries in Asia, Africa, and Latin America—a result of the decrease in transport costs and increased industrialization demands in the West.[32] Finally, currency depreciation played a role, as a weak currency became a hedge against declines in the prices of tradable commodities. If the silver peso's value declined relative to the gold dollar, more pesos could be obtained for every dollar earned abroad. For as long as the peso was weak or weakening, declines in the prices of exportable commodities could be blunted. For example, from 1873 to 1895, the decline of sugar export prices was lower in peso terms at –2.6 percent compared to dollar terms at –5.1 percent.[33] Export growth occasioned by currency deprecia- tion would only occur again almost one hundred years later, in 1970 (see chapter 4).

Because silver was depreciating relative to gold, the colony primarily exported to countries on the gold standard. When Americans started to collect data on Philippine exports in 1901 (shortly before shifting the country to gold), around 82 percent of exports went to gold stan- dard countries. Of that 82 percent, roughly 60 percent went to Great Britain, with only 14 percent going to the US and the other 26 percent to other gold standard countries.[34] Despite the centrality of Britain, economic historian Benito Legarda has shown that diversification of exports and trading partners allowed the Philippines to weather trad- ing slumps with the UK.[35]

The export boom led to a wealthy local elite. The greatest Filipino writer of the twentieth century, Nick Joaquin, wrote that "from this period date the grand houses of Vigan, the fabled elegance of Lipa, the ornate facades of once-austere town churches like those of Morong and Taal, the great haciendas of Pampanga, Bicol, and Iloilo." So wealthy was the Philippines that "the sons of the Spanish middle class were com- ing to the Philippines in hunt for native heiresses; while the sons of the Philippine middle class were going to Spain to study and, in many cases, marry there."[36] The new middle class and elite not only engaged in bourgeois lifestyles; they also imagined a nation. Indeed, the elite "ilustrados" (enlightened ones) who defined Filipino nationalism in the late nineteenth century emerged as a social class because of native participation in the global economy.[37] At the risk of overstatement, it is reasonable to argue that, in fueling export wealth, currency depreciation helped forge the Filipino nation.

This was the potential beginning of an export-based, industrial econ- omy anchored on an increasingly nationalist elite and an expanding British trading network. As Spain oscillated between protectionist and liberal policy, British and American businessmen hedged their bets by investing in joint business ventures with the local elites. By the end of the century, there were already multiple nascent joint ventures in sugar refining, rice milling, and railroads.[38] For Legarda, these investments "could have been the start of modern Philippine industrialization," which was aborted by American rule.[39]

The dynamic of the British empire in Asia would prove odd to Americans. Although both the UK and the US ostensibly were gold-based economies at home, Britain encouraged a vibrant silver-based free-trade market in Asia, consistent with its proclivity toward supporting trading entrepôts during the belle epoque of the nineteenth century.[40] The dynamic of British imperialist exploitation, unlike what the Americans would develop, was, in fact, more subtle. In India, the British maintained an undervalued rupee because they could successfully sequester the gold value of trade surpluses by manipulating taxation.[41] The overvaluation of British currency relative to colonies, moreover, did not affect its exports, because the British monopolized certain sections of the colonial trade.[42] Meanwhile, as we shall see, the United States was perennially concerned about competition from cheap Philippine agriculture.

When the Americans arrived in the Philippines, they encountered a rapidly changing economy that was growing its export sector while diversifying its trading partners, largely because of depreciating silver. It was also an economy impacted by the changes in its region, Southeast Asia. American colonialism would alter these processes and narrow the horizons of economic change. Dear money policy would be its primary tool.

## Silver for Soldiers

The currency problem began as a military one. During the Philippine-American War, US troops in the Philippines hovered at around forty thousand,[43] and these soldiers were paid in gold-backed US dollars. However, except for the money sent to their families back home, they spent using domestic silver.

For the American military, the currency system was proof of the opacity of their new colonial possession. As an article from *The Manila Times* (founded as an English-language newspaper for American soldiers) noted: "For perversities, complexities, difficulties, and impossibilities, Manila is one of the most wonderful places on the face of the earth, and it would seem that all the natural cussedness of the climate and all the artificial eccentricities of the place and the people are concentrated in the currency."[44] Like their problems with the country's heat, Americans could not avoid the fluctuations of the silver currency circulating in the Philippines. Military regulation mandated that soldiers be paid in dollars, but transactions in the Philippines were primarily conducted in Mexican silver. Currency exchange was necessary, making Americans beholden to British banks and Chinese merchants who sold this silver.

While weak Spanish governance structures were quickly supplanted, the networks of Anglo-Chinese capital were more entrenched. The chief paymaster of the US Army in the Philippines suspected that the two British banks in Manila—the HSBC and the Chartered Bank of India, Australia, and China—colluded in setting the price of gold, making it lower on days when American soldiers received their pay.[45] There was, moreover, significant variability. In 1899, an American dollar received 1.75 Mexican in Cavite (southwest of Manila and a hotbed of the Philippine Revolution) and 1.96 in Manila.[46] Under such a system, added *The Manila Times*, "banks, exchange brokers, and a few clever Chinese and others managed to juggle with the fluctuations" to their benefit.[47] Within this "mysterious system of calculation known only to bankers and bimetallic experts," the fate of economic transactions in the Philippines was dependent on "conditions in China, or India, or Europe, or any part of the world rather than the Philippines."[48]

The currency system intimidated Americans because of its opacity and unpredictability. However, what was opaque to Americans was not the "backward" civilization of Filipinos but the cosmopolitan moorings of their economy, as the colony was a node in a global bimetallic trade that the US military could not domesticate.

The outbreak of the Chinese Boxer Rebellion made currency fluctuations even worse. From 1898 onward, official Manila bank prices were such that one US dollar could always be exchanged for at least two Mexican pesos (despite everyday variability and less favorable prices outside urban centers). However, military demand for silver in China increased its cost, and bank rates in Manila dropped to 1.98. Traders even exploited the situation by exchanging US money for rates as low as 1.5.[49] When the rebellion ended in 1901, silver prices decreased drastically, creating the opposite problem of rapid gold appreciation.[50] This shift occurred just as the Philippines' governance transitioned from military to civilian administration under Governor-General William Howard Taft and an American-dominated legislative body called the Philippine Commission.

One of Taft and the commission's first moves was to fix the two-for-one ratio—the beginning of an official exchange rate that would last until 1962 (with the major interruption of World War II). However, in the spring or early summer of 1901, the price of Mexican currency in Hong Kong fell below fifty American cents (one gold dollar could be exchanged for more than two Mexican pesos). By September of that year, one could hand a Hong Kong banker a twenty-dollar bill and receive forty-two pesos and change in Mexican. Such favorable gold-dollar rates could not be obtained in the Philippines amid the fixed ratio (for the same twenty dollars, one could only receive forty pesos Mexican), so American money flowed out of Manila. Unable to keep its gold within the colony, the American colonial state was at risk of becoming just like the ineffectual Spanish one. With barely any dollars left, the commission was forced to change the peso-dollar ratio to 2.10:1.[51]

British banks devised ways to ease government burdens. When silver prices were up during the Boxer Rebellion, the banks proposed importing the cheaper silver-based Straits dollar, which could be exchanged for 2.01 or 2.02 dollars. American officials rejected this proposal, correctly noting that even the Straits dollar was appreciating because of military operations in China.[52] The British also tried to ease transaction costs by devising an international credit transfer system. HSBC, the bank at the forefront of negotiations between British capital and the US colonial government, proposed a system whereby the US government could deposit dollars with them through the US Treasury in Washington or subtreasuries in New York or San Francisco. The bank would then credit these deposits as Mexican pesos in the Philippines, which troops could use in the colony. Since the system minimized transaction costs, HSBC promised the best exchange rate.[53] Asked by the War Department if it had enough silver currency to sustain such a system, HSBC reminded the Americans of British economic power in Asia by claiming, "It is our business to provide funds to meet all requirements in that part of the world."[54] The military's paymaster general, however, ultimately refused to pay American soldiers in Mexican pesos and decided that shipping American dollars to the Philippines was worth the cost.[55]

While the situation was in flux, British bankers insisted that shifting to gold would harm the colony. According to one of HSBC's Philippine officials, "The native would gain no advantage by the return to the gold standard at this time. Later on, when he gets educated, uses more labor-saving machinery, and can export his produce at good, high prices, in years to come, he may get enough benefit out of the gold dollar to recompense him for giving over the larger amount of money—of dollars—he gets at present."[56]

This language was as paternalistic as the Americans', and it was a blatant defense of British banking interests. But it was also based on sound economic insight. Without an industrial base, it would be difficult for Filipino exporters to compete under the gold standard since they would no longer benefit from depreciating silver. As with the developmental states of the twentieth century (see chapter 4), the Philippine colonial economy relied on a cheap currency while it built its industrial capacity. Against the pragmatic and self-serving position of British banking interests, Americans would push back with ideology.

## Enter the Experts

The arrival of Taft's Philippine Commission would initiate a period of intense civilian-imperial state-building, primarily under Republicans. From 1901 to 1913, Republicans established the basic structures of the Philippine colony that would last until independence and beyond. Because Taft played multiple consequential roles in colonial administration during this period—from governor-general of the Philippines, secretary of war, to US president—historian Bonifacio Salamanca aptly calls this period the "Taft era" in Philippine history.[57]

It was amid this new civilian administration that a more sustained conversation on currency occurred. The issue was no longer the payment of soldiers but the colony's economic future. In this context, civilian officials and legislators began to debate the role of American gold in Asia.

In September 1901, Charles Arthur Conant, special commissioner of the War Department on coinage and banking in the Philippine Islands, arrived in Manila. During his six-week stay, he met with representatives of British banks, leading businessmen, the Philippine Commission, and various army officers.[58] Conant was a self-taught economist who had by then established himself as a prominent public commentator on finance and economics. Because of his public defense of the gold standard, he was a trusted figure within the McKinley administration,[59] and his appointment to the Philippines came with the backing of his friends, Secretary of War Elihu Root and Secretary of the Treasury L. J. Gage.[60]

Conant's imperialist views on the Philippines are well documented.[61] Like the anti-imperialist Lenin, he believed that capitalism's growth required the expansion of markets outside the West. Unlike Lenin, however, he saw this expansion as an unconditional good. For Conant, capitalist development in Asia would center on a competition between gold and silver.

Testifying before the US Senate after his trip, Conant decried the impression "that the East is chiefly on a silver basis,"[62] noting that Japan, Siberia, India, and Australia were all gold-based economies.[63] The most urgent goal for the Philippines, therefore, was to orient toward this alternative world of gold—a world that included the United States. Responding to concerns that the Philippines could be "segregated" from other Asian economies, Conant argued that linking the Philippines to the US and other gold standard nations would "produce the opposite effect of segregation."[64] Against the world of silver dominated by the British, Conant imagined an alternative gold-based Asian trading sphere in which US power, exercised through the Philippines, would play a key role.

The main hindrance to this vision was the British. The continued use of silver, Conant argued, would "keep trade in the hands of the British merchants in Shanghai and Hongkong, and exchange in the hands of British banks."[65] In such a situation, it would be challenging to promote American trade in the colony because "the British houses have almost a complete monopoly of the business in Manila" and because one would not encourage American merchants to invest "by tying up the Philippines on a silver standard."[66] While the British, who operated in gold and silver markets, could hedge their bets amid silver price fluctuations, Americans could not.[67]

For Conant, shifting to gold would benefit exporters based in Europe and, more importantly, the United States.[68] With a gold-based currency, they could send their goods to the Philippines and would no longer have to be concerned with silver depreciation. A strong Philippine currency would also allow Filipinos to buy more of their products. Absent in this observation was any mention of Filipino exporters—the beneficiaries of cheap silver. Instead, Conant asserted that "the gold standard is going to invite American capital there" and that "the people in Manila now do not want anything but the gold standard."[69]

Conant's account was flimsy for an account that supposedly determined the future of currency policy in the Philippines (and, as a result, other places that adopted the American gold exchange standard). Later in his testimony, he would note that Philippine exports were fueled by demand from gold standard countries, notably Britain, prompting

Senator Albert J. Beveridge of Indiana to retort that "there is no diffi-
culty where the silver standard exists in the Philippine Islands of trading with gold-standard countries."[70] Conant was forced to concede that
while such "inference could be drawn to a degree," one needed to "facili-
tate the trade of the islands with a single gold-standard country" (presumably the United States) and to consider the "clerical labor involved
in converting one money into another."[71]

Sensing that Conant was not on solid ground, senators pressed further. When Massachusetts Senator Henry Cabot Lodge asked Conant if
India's trade had increased after shifting to gold, Conant replied that
he did not know. Instead, Conant changed the topic and said, "What
deflects capital in one direction or another is the amount of friction to
be overcome," and that "there is a moral element, the indisposition of
capitalists to go where they are not satisfied with the simplicity of the
conditions."[72]

Still unconvinced, Beveridge continued to press, asking if the silver
standard would deter a hypothetical investor in a Mindanao rubber
plantation. At that point, Conant was again forced to concede that "if
silver continued to fall, they might be encouraged."[73] Similarly, Iowa
Senator William Boyd Allison rhetorically asked, "For example, the
principal products of the Philippines are hemp, sugar, tobacco, and
copra. Now would not the tendency of those articles be toward the
country that consumes them, whatever the standard would be?" Once
again, Conant was forced to concede: "More or less, undoubtedly."[74] It
was a poor showing for Conant, with Beveridge concluding, "I do not
think the conclusions you have drawn, to put it mildly, are the only
conclusions which may be drawn."[75]

The irony was that Conant's interlocutors were not unsympathetic, as
these were hard money Republicans with no ideological stake in repudiating gold. Allison was one of the fathers of the Gold Standard Act, and
Beveridge was one of the leading defenders of McKinley's anti-Bryan/
anti-silver campaign in Indiana. Both men were also firm supporters of
imperialism in the Philippines.

Professor Edwin Kemmerer—who would replace Conant as the
person in charge of Philippine currency—would retrospectively attribute the Senate's hesitancy to adopt Conant's recommendations to
the influence of "partisan witnesses representing English banks with
branches in Manila and business houses interested in the Philippine
export trade."[76] This may have been the case, but Kemmerer's point
obscured the inadequacies of Conant's testimony and inability to

account for the winners and losers under a new currency regime. Even scholarly accounts of Conant's views have failed to note Conant's poor showing in the Senate.[77]

## Following the Flag

Despite the weaknesses of Conant's testimony, the ideological ground was set for the United States Congress to commit itself to gold in the Philippines. Though initially hesitant, it did not take much for Republican senators to change their minds. The continued depreciation of the Mexican peso, which had dropped to forty cents on the US dollar, ended all doubt.[78] Since taxes were payable in silver, this depreciation entailed a loss for the colonial government.[79] This was burdensome for a government that needed to import equipment for a war against the fledgling Filipino Republic. It was also burdensome for colonial officials who were already paid in domestic currency but continued sending money back to the United States. *The New York Times* reported that the colonial government was believed to have lost as much as a million dollars because of the depreciation. The depreciation forced the Senate to respond. As silver continued to drop, a draft bill by Senators Lodge and Allison cleared the Senate Committee on the Philippines on December 18, 1902,[80] passing with little debate in February of the following year.[81] Importation was a prerequisite for colonial state-building, and a strong currency would serve that purpose.

The ideological stakes were more pronounced in the House of Representatives. For most of 1902, free-silver Democrats in the House, still bitter over McKinley's defeat of Bryan, inveighed against the proposed colonial gold standard.[82] But for the Republicans, bimetallism was out of the question in the Philippines because it was out of the question in the United States.[83] Unlike the British Empire, which could countenance various currency systems—from silver in Asia to cowry in Africa—the United States would be consistent. Later into the century, the US would be the great defender of the gold standard globally. It would design gold exchange standards worldwide and even bail out countries like Britain struggling to stay on gold. Such a vision for an American-led, gold-based world economy was rehearsed during debates about Philippine money.

New York Representative Ward Hamilton argued that implementing the gold standard in the Philippines would signal the US commitment to stable currencies. In June 1902, he explained to Congress,

"If the gold standard is a good thing here it is a good thing in the Philippine islands." In the US, he continued, if the government refused "to set up a free open hopper into which every owner of silver may dump his silver and have it come out coined into dollars free of charge and carry the dollars away with him without restriction as to the amount coined and without provision to keep and maintain the dollars so coined at fixed value or parity with gold," the same should be the case in the Philippines.[84]

Hamilton's remarks betrayed an increasing awareness of the dollar's increasing importance in world commerce (recall that this was a period in which the dollar began to compete with the pound sterling as a global reserve currency) and the need to turn the Philippine currency system into proof of the dollar's reliability. "Our dollar," he continued, "is good now the whole world round and our coinage down to a cent is good as gold everywhere." "Even the Chinese rickshaw man knows and prefers our 5-cent piece to the Chinese 10-cent piece, because he knows it will purchase as much, if not more, even on his own soil, and that value is unvarying." Therefore, to "flood" both the Philippines and "the Orient" with "a bastard imitation of our silver dollar" would "be to discredit our money and our flag in the estimation of the world."[85]

Like Hamilton, New Jersey Representative Charles N. Fowler saw the fight against silver in the Philippines as an extension of a domestic struggle. The Republican Party, he explained, had fought the scourge of silver in the US, and he believed the party was responsible for doing the same in the Philippines. For Fowler, continuing the free coinage of silver in the Philippines would be "a complete bar to all progress and prosperity" and subject its people "to the schemes and chicane of the bullion brokers, whose limit is measured by the last farthing of profit." More crucial than this narrow economic goal, however, was the civilization the gold standard represented. "If American civilization is to be the salvation of the Filipino," he continued, "you will lift him farther and faster by the adoption of American money than *by any other force*" (emphasis mine). The gold standard would teach the Filipino "the lessons of the flag and impress upon him the power and the glory of the Republic."[86]

In this instance, civilization was represented by what Fowler continued to refer to as "sound economic principles." And these principles could be achieved by ensuring that monetary austerity led to fiscal austerity. Quoting an article by Conant, Fowler read these principles into the congressional record. For Conant, "The fiscal policy of the Government should stand toward the banking world in much the same position as that of any private firm or corporation." Deficits, as such, "should be covered by loans" if they could not be "promptly met from taxation." If the government issued paper "as a substitute for money," "a disturbing factor is introduced into all business calculations," the result being that "firm commercial credit" would become untethered from price amid "public credit" that was "dragged in the gutter."[87]

Here, then, was the logic of colonial austerity in its embryonic form. For Fowler and Conant, a fixed currency regime constrained deficits by ensuring that money in circulation corresponded to gold or gold-backed reserves. The alternative of introducing more money through a silver standard or printing more paper money would raise the capacity of the government to spend without requiring additional taxation or loans. Such a situation would debase credit, placing it in the gutter of arbitrary value. The quote also distinguished between "firm commercial credit"—virtuous private savings and the fruit of enterprise—and "public credit," which could easily drag the former into the gutter. Not only was this an early version of the common argument that public capital "drives out" private capital, but it was also an argument about the role of the colonial state as austerity police. The US had arrived in the Philippines to secure private capital, and it saw itself as the guardian of "sound money" as it emerged as a Pacific power. To justify this imperial vision of monetary austerity, colonial officials began to turn to what would become the bogeyman employed by all twentieth-century austerity advocates: inflation.

As the congressional debates were underway, credit expansion was slowly becoming associated with consumer price inflation. During the US Civil War, "inflation" only referred to expanding the supply of fiat currency. It was, however, a "professor of economics, committed prohibitionist, proselytizing vegetarian, and first president of the American Eugenics Society," Irving Fisher, who posited an algebraic formula that linked the money supply to consumer prices.[88] Fisher first articulated this mathematical formula in his 1911 volume *The Purchasing Power of Money*.[89] But as early as 1896, he was already arguing that "during a period of inflation the ordinary man conceives the premium of gold as a rise of gold not a fall of money. But if he takes account of rising wages and rising prices he arrives at the same results as if he had thought of falling money."[90] It is unsurprising, then, that in 1903, a *New York Times* headline stated that the gold standard in the Philippines had been implemented to "guard against inflation."[91]

Debates about Philippine currency were developing just as economic experts were beginning to equate expansions in the money supply with rising prices, which would ultimately just be called "inflation." Eventually, the tenor of this association would take on moralist tones. In the following decades, American advocates of the gold standard, like Edwin Kemmerer, would come to view "creeping price inflation" as "a kind of internal burglary."[92] The moralizing rhetoric through which monetary conservatives examined the increasingly interchangeable concepts of an increased money supply and consumer prices was indicative of broader civilizational views about money and credit.

Gold and hard money advocates tied their belief to "natural law."[93] It was self-evident to them that currencies had intrinsic values. But this "scientific" view also encapsulated a civilizational and moral imperative. The bullionist tradition, represented during this period by the mainstream Republican Party, held that gold returned the US to its Christian roots because gold was the currency of Christian Europe, particularly Britain, and it promoted the "Christian value" of honesty.[94] Southern and Western populists who opposed the gold standard were, therefore, outside this civilizational matrix. Akin to them were the "barbaric" and "pagan" Chinese, Japanese, and Indians, who increased their money supply by circulating silver.[95] In its most extreme form, the racialized view of credit dovetailed with social Darwinism, as in the case of Fisher, who viewed eugenics and economics as two mutually reinforcing "sciences."[96]

As we saw in the introduction, there was also a gendered element to this discourse. For Fisher, immorality, prostitution, government corruption and waste, racial mixing, and monetary instability could all be prevented by manly self-control, which he believed was an economic and social virtue. Kemmerer, too, associated the value of money with masculinity. Early in his career, he worried about the emasculating effects of inflation, both on himself and the countries he was studying.[97]

For its American advocates, the gold standard was scientific, civilizational, and masculine. These advocates were lucky in the Philippines. Unlike in the mainland, where Bryan and his agrarian populists were still challenging the gold standard, no such opposition occurred in the Philippines. Even if we assume that certain Filipino exporters were privately wary of the gold standard, there is no evidence that they had established an organized opposition. The concern of Philippine elites who collaborated with American officials during this period was primarily obtaining positions within the emerging colonial government.

Meanwhile, the most anti-American of the Philippine elite did not consider currency, as they were still fighting the Philippine-American War.

Finally, the peasant and labor movement at this time was young and, unlike Bryan's Southern constituency, did not develop a critique of gold. Labor's primary objective during this period was to raise wages. Strikes organized by the newly founded Union Obrera Democratica de Filipinas (UOD, or Democratic Labor Union of the Philippines) led to wage increases, at least in Manila. During the UOD's first year in 1902, respondents of the American Federation of Labor estimated that the wages of around fifty thousand laborers increased by as much as 25 percent.[98] This form of industrial action was more critical than discussions of currency. Moreover, the UOD would not have been attached to the cause of silver, since the rising cost of living outpaced any increase in real wages that could have resulted from silver depreciation in the 1890s.[99] As we shall see, the rise in the cost of living was more a function of war than currency depreciation. Still, the general inflationary conditions precluded labor from developing a critique of a deflationary currency system.

Colonial officials, therefore, took for granted the Filipino incapacity to understand the workings of gold, leading to Conant's earlier comment that most Filipinos would accept the gold standard. In Conant's and the Philippine Commission's view, any opposition to introducing gold resulted from a Filipino tendency to value names and traditions.[100] Unlike Southern populists, who had an economic stake in silver, Filipinos liked silver simply because they were used to it. Their purported ignorance would make them ideal for the civilizing power of gold. Without any real opposition, the Philippines would serve as the perfect laboratory for silver-to-gold alchemy.

## New Coins

President Theodore Roosevelt signed the Philippine Coinage Act on March 2, 1903.[101] The law outlined the basic contours of the new currency system but let the Philippine Commission work out the specifics. Its primary provision established the gold standard based on a theoretical gold peso equivalent to fifty US cents.[102] It was a theoretical gold peso because it would not be minted; instead, silver coins would circulate to represent their value. To prevent the coins from being melted and sold for their bullion value, the amount of silver used to make each coin cost less than fifty US cents (because the silver in the coins cost less than the actual price of the coin, there was no incentive to melt the coins and sell the silver).[103] The government also issued paper bills, which could be used to redeem silver coins. Of note was the US-Philippine ten-peso silver certificate, which bore the image of George Washington and would become the basis for the design of today's one-dollar bill.[104]

The idea to circulate silver coins, which represented gold, came from Taft and the Philippines Commission. According to Taft, the commission was "anxious not to disturb the values of oriental peoples, and the Filipinos, who do not differ from other oriental peoples in that respect, have a great regard for tradition and names."[105] Conant shared this belief, wishing to "depart as little as possible from the existing customs of the people and their estimate of values" while stabilizing the value of silver coins.[106]

The law also allowed the Philippine government to issue bonds worth ten million dollars to finance the purchase of silver and establish a gold reserve.[107] It left open the specific mechanisms of this reserve, and the Philippine Gold Standard Act, passed by the Philippine Commission in 1903, fleshed out the details of the reserve fund and currency conversion. First, the act established a Gold Standard Fund (GSF), held in Manila and New York, which would back the new pesos in circulation. Initial funds for the GSF came from bonds authorized by the Coinage Act and seigniorage from minting new coins. Second, it established the Division of Currency within the Bureau of the Insular Treasury.[108]

Because the GSF held US money and not gold, the result of these two laws was not a direct gold standard. Philippine currency was technically not backed by gold but by a gold-backed currency, the dollar. This indirect gold standard would become known as the gold exchange standard, with the Philippine currency system as its prototype.

The coins first arrived in the Philippines in June 1903.[109] In recognition of the system's architect, the first silver coins were informally called "Conants." Upon Conant's death in 1915, his portrait would be printed on the one-peso bill.[110] Although Conant devised the system, he would not implement it. After the signing of the Gold Standard Act, currency policy fell into the hands of a young Edwin Kemmerer, who became the chief of the Division of Currency under the Insular Treasury.

A more formidable figure, Kemmerer was not an autodidact like Conant. When he arrived in the Philippines, he had just graduated with a PhD in economics from Cornell. His interest in monetary policy began as a college student at Wesleyan, where he followed the economic debates between Bryan and McKinley. In the 1896 election, he canvassed for McKinley in New York's Chautauqua County, trying "to convert Bryanites to the gold standard."[111] In his senior year, Kemmerer wrote a term paper on the quantity theory of money, believing this research would help him understand the debate between Democrats and Republicans. He continued to write about this topic for his dissertation at Cornell, where he received his PhD in June 1903,[112] the same month the Conants first arrived in the Philippines.

Kemmerer held similar views to social Darwinist bullionists like Fisher, noting in a 1907 Cornell lecture that the United States could uplift Filipinos because "the progress of political evolution, as well as of biologic, can be greatly expedited and to a large extent directed by the creation of a favorable environment and by the mechanism of artificial selection."[113] Filipinos were not "pioneers in the field of popular self-government, as were our Germanic forefathers; they have the benefit of the world's experience and the guidance of a benevolent nation." This nation would, in turn, teach Filipinos "the lessons of political honesty, of thrift and of self-reliance" since "they have yet to learn that political office is a public trust."[114] Although this was a rare lecture about the Philippines in which Kemmerer did not discuss the gold standard, the "values" he hoped the US would teach Filipinos were the same ones increasingly associated with the monetary system he favored. Gold was honest because it ensured money in circulation corresponded with a "true" value. It encouraged thrift because it limited what a government could spend. And it was a system of self-reliance because it required nations to rely on what they had. As such, politicians who adhered to these values would not betray public trust. They would serve as a check to the profligate colonial.

Compared to Conant, Kemmerer had a clearer view of the winners and losers in the new currency system. He knew that the shift to gold-based currency was an explicit privileging of importers over exporters—something he justified by claiming that exporters were Chinese and European while the importers were American. Writing about his time in the Philippines, Kemmerer noted that the beneficiaries of gold-backed currency were "American and European importing houses" that "were suffering from a continually falling exchange." Stating plainly the interests of US businesses in the Philippines, he added, "The American merchants who had come to the Philippines to cater to the American trade were much more largely interested in the import trade than the export trade."[115] In opposition to these interests, those who benefited from cheap silver currency were primarily "Chinese exporters, who were mostly dealing with China" and "the large European export houses, mostly English, Spanish, German, and French, who were reaping extra profits by the downward movement of exchange, since they were receiving continually more local pesos for their gold bills, and did not have to pay proportionately more pesos for their hemp, tobacco, sugar, and copra."[116]

As for Filipinos, Kemmerer thought they had no opinion, since "the great masses of Filipinos rarely came into contact with gold prices and knew nothing about the currency situation." He added, "They sold local produce and they bought local produce, for the most part at fairly constant and customary prices."[117] The comment obscured that Filipinos were increasingly becoming part of the export trade because of increased partnerships between Europeans, Chinese, and the local elite, as we saw earlier. However, by coding exporters as foreign, Kemmerer could justify privileging American importers in the Philippines. The conservative Philippine Central Bank would replicate such a rhetorical strategy for excluding exporters from the national interest in the postwar period (chapter 3).

It would take Kemmerer time to rid the Philippines of silver. Despite the arrival of Conant's coins in June 1903, Mexican silver was far from banished. The Conants, for one, were no larger than the Mexican coins, and Filipinos could not understand why they were supposed to be more valuable despite being the same size. Most businesses also accepted these new coins as equivalent to Mexican silver. As a result, those who carried the new coins sold this theoretically more expensive money to money changers for a greater number of Mexican pesos. This effectively made them richer because they now had more coins (Mexican), and many businesses still treated Mexican pesos and Conants as equivalents. Meanwhile, the money changers and banks who received the Conants used these coins to buy US currency and settle payments outside the Philippines.[118] Outside Manila, provincial traders continued to trade in Mexican pesos, and poor farmers did not have time to exchange their old money within the required time frame. Despite pro-American local officials promoting the new money, the shift to this new currency regime was slow.[119]

As had happened under the Spanish, there was once again a threat of cheap Mexican money driving out a gold-based currency. A 1904 article from *The Manila Times* noted that, despite the formal introduction of Conants, there was still a need to "save the archipelago from the mongrel money of the old régime."[120] It added that the Philippine

Islands were "not appreciably nearer the gold standard than they were six months ago" because "the new currency when liberated disappears as fast as any other currency representing gold."[121] At the time, it was already conventional wisdom among economists that bad money (cheap) drives out good (expensive) money—then as now referred to as Gresham's law. For *The Manila Times*, however, bad money was not only cheap but also mixed—tied to markets outside the civilized ambit of American gold.

Kemmerer's first solution was to insist that all businesses print placards in English, Tagalog, and Spanish that stated which currencies their prices were fixed to and at what rates they accepted other currencies.[122] Not long after, most shops began to accept the new currency at the higher official bank rate. This acceptance, however, remained limited to Manila.[123] To protect the new gold-backed currency, the government had to increasingly resort to more drastic measures, from using town criers to urge the public to exchange their Mexican pesos, to the government discounting acceptance of old currency, to an order that required local governments to purchase silver-based coins at officially determined rates.[124] Finally, the government was forced to penalize the importation of silver-based currencies and imposed heavy taxes on transactions using older coins.[125]

This new policy ensured the Conants stayed within the colony. By the end of 1903, only an estimated 3,910,000 Conants' worth of this money was circulating. By March 1905, however, that number had risen to 27,045,000.[126] The old currency, explained Kemmerer, "had practically been eliminated, and the Islands were firmly established upon a gold basis."[127] With his first patient cured, the money doctor Edwin Kemmerer would go to Egypt as a special commissioner to study British colonial banking.[128] It was the beginning of his storied career as a "financial missionary to the world."[129]

Yet Kemmerer's account of a peaceful transition to gold was only partially accurate. In the Sulu Archipelago, which the US military continued to govern as part of Muslim Mindanao, there was significant opposition to the new currency, since the Tausug people of the archipelago did not have enough gold to pay for a poll tax. The US military brutally suppressed such opposition by engaging in raids and massacres that sometimes exceeded the violence of campaigns against Native Americans.[130] At the forefront of these campaigns was General Leonard Wood, who in the 1920s would become one of the gold standard's greatest defenders in Manila (see next chapter).

The historian Patricio Abinales has cogently argued that administrative reform in the Progressive Era, both in the Philippines and the mainland, had a patchwork quality, where a centralizing state had limited success in curbing the centrifugal tendencies of local politics.[131] This dynamic was not the case with currency. In 1944, Kemmerer looked back on his career in the Philippines and recalled that "the nearest approach to the simon-pure gold-exchange standard that the world has yet seen was the currency system of the Philippine Islands as it was administered from 1905 to about 1910 under the Philippine Gold Standard Act of 1903."[132] In currency policy, there was no patchwork governance but complete centralization, achieved through strong administration and violence. The institution of hard money was a success. And it would remain rooted in Philippine soil in the decades to come. Advocates of the gold exchange standard had cause to celebrate. The peso's value finally stabilized, and foreign transactions kept the Gold Standard Fund afloat.[133] But this stability had less to do with anything intrinsic to the new system than with specific political changes in the colony.

Under the new system, the Philippines needed dollar reserves to back the Conants. Significant drops in dollar reserves would reduce the money supply, leading to less spending and a slower economy. Such was the inherent threat of a deflationary, hard money system. Yet this weakness would be obscured by circumstance. Economic historian Frank Golay provides two reasons for the initial success of the gold exchange standard in the colony. First, the reduction of army spending in the Philippines at the end of the Philippine-American War reduced import expenditures, paving the way for an export surplus in dollars. Second, the colonial government used a congressional relief fund to pay the remaining troops, who spent most of their salary in the colony and contributed to its dollar supply.[134] As for the export-depressing tendency of replacing a weak currency with a stronger one, this was blunted as well. As we shall detail in the next chapter, preferential trade between the United States and the Philippines ensured a market for Philippine exports. For the first years of its implementation, favorable financial conditions obscured the weaknesses of the new currency system.

Broadly, the effects of the new system were and are difficult to assess since it was being implemented at a time of war. For example, it is unclear how it affected prices, production, or wages, since the revolution against Spain and the war against the Americans had fundamentally disrupted all aspects of the economy. In 1903, Edward D. Rosenberg, special commissioner of the American Federation of Labor, noted, "Industrial and agricultural conditions in the islands are at present very much depressed." Edwards added that cholera, rinderpest, peasant revolts against Spanish-era feudal systems, the death of water buffalos necessary for agricultural production, banditry in the countryside (which deterred farming), and the use of Chinese labor combined to make food prices high even as Filipino laborers remained underpaid.[135] It was thus very difficult to assess the effects of currency policy on industrial relations and wages.

## Adulterated Gold

Though difficult to detect then, some of the new currency system's instabilities were already evident. Despite initial currency surpluses, revenue was necessary to build a colonial state, especially given the need to extend the infant bureaucracy outside Manila.[136] Moreover, largesse from the US mainland would be less forthcoming as successive colonial governments sought to make the Philippines fiscally independent. The prominent view at the time among Republican legislators like Henry Cabot Lodge was that the Philippines should become a hub for American trade while being fiscally independent from US taxpayers.[137] Measures were therefore needed to ensure the colony's fiscal viability, even as legislators sought to forge an empire on the cheap.

One such measure was the imposition of tariffs. Although one of the goals of US expansionism was to encourage free trade, the US Supreme Court ruled that Congress could determine tariff policy.[138] To prevent the Philippines from becoming a "fiscal nightmare," Congress allowed the new colonial government to impose customs duties on US imports until 1909.[139] Of course, debt was another recourse, and unlike the Spanish regime, the new American one allowed for long-term borrowing. Yet this regime was only fiscally expansive compared to its predecessor. All debt had to be authorized by the US Congress and subject to a debt ceiling, which, as we shall see in the next chapter, could turn Filipino politicians into supplicants during a crisis. Moreover, there was no countercyclical spending, and the money supply increased or decreased depending on the fluctuations of the world economy, as is consistent with the strictures of gold convertibility.[140]

It was in this context of fiscal restriction amid a growing colonial state that Kemmerer's "simon pure" standard required adulteration. In 1911, the colonial legislature passed the Gold Standard Fund law, which, according to then Governor-General W. Cameron Forbes, allowed the government to use a part of the fund that was "unnecessary for the proper protection of the currency" for government spending. This new fund let Forbes "use half of the fund for loans to provinces and municipalities for public works, and also in loans to railroads to expedite production."[141]

Establishing the GSF was an extraordinary step that would be much debated in the years to come (next chapter). Its logic, therefore, needs some clarification. Previous work by historian Allan Lumba views the GSF as part of a vaguely defined system of colonial "capital accumulation." For Lumba, Americans used the GSF to fund repressive "counter decolonization" projects,[142] leading him to conclude that the goal of US economic policy in the Philippines was the creation of liquidity for repression.[143] Strictly speaking, the money for repression came from military funding outside the Philippines, not domestic sources like the GSF. Beyond this technicality, however, Lumba fails to note that the GSF covered up the fact that the gold exchange standard had already drastically reduced liquidity. The economic logic of US imperialism was not to generate liquidity but, as we have noted, to forge an austere empire on the cheap. By the time Forbes was governor-general, extensive Band-Aids for the gold standard were necessary. The GSF was one such Band-Aid.

It was a helpful Band-Aid for colonial officials. "The money released by the operation," Forbes wrote in his diary, enabled him "to authorize the construction of a lot of public works right away, mostly roads, bridges, port works, and the new girls' dormitory for the Normal School."[144] The new law allowed the governor-general to transfer 2.7 million pesos to the general treasury fund and approximately 9 million pesos for loans to the public.[145] If Kemmerer described the period from 1905 to 1910 as the purest gold standard the world had ever seen, the new 1911 law was a move away from the platonic ideal.

As we shall see in the next chapter, the Gold Standard Fund would come under significant strain during the postwar deflation of 1920–1921, and American commentators would decry the drawing down of currency reserves by Filipinos, with Forbes arguing that the Philippine peso had become a fiat currency. Other Republican administrators would also conclude that the reserve shortage proved that the Philippine government should spend less. Forbes would thus become the champion of austerity.

But the injunction toward austerity is often selectively applied. Forbes's dirigiste tendencies as governor-general manifested in building a summer capital for American officials in the city of Baguio in the Cordillera mountains. Because of a widespread belief that white soldiers and officials mentally and physically deteriorated in a tropical climate, officials like Forbes felt the need to build a cool mountain retreat.[146] As commissioner of commerce and the police as well as governor-general, Forbes supported not just the city's construction—with its country and golf club—but also the road that allowed easy access to Baguio from Manila, known as the Benguet Road.[147] This road cost $1.5 million in 1905, three-quarters of what the US had paid Spain in the Treaty of Paris and significantly above the initial appropriation of $75,000. It was criticized as a money sink and a waste of taxpayer funds both in Filipino-run nationalist newspapers and the American-run *Manila Times*.[148]

Despite the criticism, Forbes would continue spending on Baguio with his two-million peso slush fund. "I have had a 'monkey and a parrot' of a time with the new Gold Standard Fund," he wrote in his diary at the end of the year.[149] It had "liberated" a lot of money "that I can use for loans and I can begin a lot of necessary public works." Baguio had been on his mind as he spent the money, noting that "it needs to be popularized among the Filipinos, who are inclined to think it is useful to and used by Americans only."[150] To encourage wealthy Filipinos to invest in the city, he set aside 170,000 pesos to construct private homes.[151]

By February of 1912, Forbes was in the summer capital, gratified upon "seeing the advance work on the railroad," noting that "the right-of-way through the town is quite a feature in the landscape." In an annotation later added to the journal, he ruefully pointed out that this spending would eventually be "blocked and thrown into the winds" by the Democrat Governor-General Francis Burton Harrison, who took over after the Democratic victory of Woodrow Wilson in 1913.[152] Indeed, by the time Harrison took over, Baguio already had a reputation, even among Americans, as a "white elephant," and Harrison saw Baguio as a symbol of Republican profligacy.[153] Upon assuming office, Harrison would publicize that the Republicans had amassed a budget deficit of seven million pesos.[154]

Accusations of profligacy provided fodder for Harrison's nationalist Filipino allies, who were also critical of Republicans because of their stance against Philippine independence. University of the Philippines political science professor Maximo Kalaw complained that the deficit was "seven million pesos in excess of our income!" This excess spending "had never been openly communicated to the people or their representatives." Kalaw concluded that, under Forbes, "there was an unpardonable lack of systematized plan [*sic*] in our previous financial system."[155] Then, as now, accusing one's political opponents of blowing up the budget deficit was a potent tool. As we shall see in the next chapter, Forbes would eventually get even.

In the meantime, the policy of "Filipinization" under the Democrats transferred crucial positions to Filipinos, serving as an opportunity for Filipinos to claim the mantle of austerity and dispel the image of a profligate colonial. The Philippine Commission, now with a Filipino majority, produced a report recommending the privatization of an auto line to Baguio, the reduction of funds for the budding summer capital, and, most importantly, the abandonment of Forbes's Benguet Road.[156] Because the road was already there, however, it was not quickly abandoned (it remains a convenient way to get to Baguio).[157] In the Philippine Assembly, then the colonial equivalent of the House of Representatives, Filipino politicians cut the annual budget—mainly still drafted by Forbes—by a million pesos.[158] Early in the Harrison administration, sustained cuts and increased taxes reduced the budget deficit from 7.5 million pesos in 1913 to 2.9 million in 1914, with the government posting a surplus of 1.1 million in 1915.[159] Austerity was victorious, but its champions were now Filipinos. It was a brief glimpse into a nationalized austerity discourse of postcolonial respectability that would become mainstream in the 1950s (see chapter 3). But this triumphal moment of nationalist austerity would not last long, as Filipinos would eventually need to spend once taking over parts of the government.

## All of Austerity's Defenders

The Taft era in the Philippines was a period of Band-Aids for austerity's shortcomings. The establishment of a gold standard often results in a restriction of the money supply. Still, congressional appropriations during the first years of colonial occupation ensured that money flowed into the colony. Eventually, playing loose with the gold exchange standard allowed for government spending despite limits on debt and Washington's insistence on the colony's self-sufficiency. In terms of trade, the export-depressing effects of an expensive currency were offset by free trade with the United States, as we shall detail in the following chapters. The booming export trade to gold standard countries, notably Britain, had been reoriented, and the trading horizons of the colony narrowed because of its new imperial master. But opening the US to

Philippine exports would create new markets for Philippine goods. This new trading regime would serve as the ultimate Band-Aid for Philippine export growth until the full expiration of preferential trade benefits in the 1970s. To say that it created a pattern of dependency would be an understatement.

Because of the "success" of the gold exchange standard, austerity had an excellent reputation in the Taft era, and competing factions in colonial governance vied to be its defenders. For money doctors like Kemmerer and the Republicans in the US legislature, the austerity of the gold standard was the ultimate way to discipline the profligate colonial. However, when the colonizer proved to be profligate, the colonized would embrace austerity and articulate it with nationalism. As the Taft era ended, Filipinos and their Democratic allies cut budgets and complained about Forbes's spending.

Such a dynamic could not last. Like the Republicans who first oversaw the colony, Democrats and Filipino elites would also realize that it was expensive to build a state. It was in this context that Filipino dirigisme emerged. But this effort at state-directed growth would crumble amid a major global economic crisis, leading to its failure. It was not, however, the crisis that would take the blame, but the profligate colonial. It is to this brief but significant episode that we now turn.

# CHAPTER 2

# Austerity Defended

*The Tragedy of the Philippine National Bank? 1916–1921*

In March 1921, the newly elected Republican president, Warren G. Harding, sent a fact-finding mission to the Philippines. Led by former governor-general of the Philippines William Cameron Forbes and former governor of the Moro Province Leonard Wood, the mission sought to determine the viability of Philippine independence. When the mission released its findings in November, it concluded that the Philippines was not ready for self-governance, citing economic mismanagement as a significant concern.

One of the "darkest pages in Philippine history," the report claimed, was the "story of the Philippine National Bank" (PNB). Because of speculative and bad-faith loans to the sugar and coconut industry, the bank was estimated to have lost $22.5 million. Even as Forbes and Wood wrote their report, criminal charges were being filed against the PNB's Filipino president, Venacio Concepcion—a former general of the Philippine Republic during the Philippine-American War—for issuing illegal loans to his wife's company.[1] Concepcion was convicted shortly after by a local court of first instance—a conviction upheld by the Philippine Supreme Court the following year.[2] When Wood became the new governor-general in 1922, he upped the ante and claimed that the PNB's losses had amounted to $38.5 million.[3] During Wood's term, an alleged "orgy" of Filipino "mismanagement" of the bank would become one of the key elements of his rhetoric against Filipino nationalism.[4]

There were financial, political, and even moral lessons to be learned. For Republicans like Wood and Forbes, it was that Filipinos and the Democrats who gave them disproportionate control over governance could not be trusted to spend wisely and preserve the integrity of their currency. For the money doctor Edwin Kemmerer, it was the need for a stricter adherence to the gold exchange standard. If the PNB had not tapped into its Gold Standard Fund to issue loans, he believed, there would have been no confusion in the monetary system.

What these accounts occlude is that the "crisis" of the PNB occurred amid a general postwar deflation that ravaged Philippine exports, making it difficult for exporters to pay their debts to the PNB. These accounts also neglect that almost the entire world struggled with gold convertibility after the Great War. Much of the occlusion was intentional. Instead of the story of the PNB being viewed as part of capitalism's boom-bust cycles, it has become a morality tale against spending and monetary inflation. It is largely a false tale.

This chapter investigates the rise of colonial developmentalism in the Philippines during the First World War and its subsequent repudiation during the postwar deflation. The Great War witnessed multiple challenges to austerity. In Europe, according to Clara Mattei, this was evident in "reconstructionist" and worker-driven strategies that eschewed the free market in favor of state management of the war economy.[5] This chapter will show that something similar happened in Southeast Asia, as notions of "ethical" colonialism dovetailed with developmental economic policy. In the Philippines, the end of the Taft era led to the first period of Democratic rule over the colony. The combination of wartime demand and a Democratic Party that gave local politicians leeway allowed for the emergence of a developmental colonialism akin to what was happening in other colonies in the region. This effort crumbled amid the crisis of 1920–1921.

With austerity on the rise, the profligate colonial once again became a central figure, and wastefulness became associated with the corruption of local officials. While telling the story of the PNB's collapse, I also begin my challenge to the good-governance discourse about Filipino development. As we shall see, the orthodox explanation for Philippine underdevelopment centers on its lack of good governance, as evidenced by rent-seeking and crony capitalism. The PNB crisis was among the first to be explained using these categories. This explanation was not only incorrect (as will be seen below), but it was also rooted in racist assumptions. As Allan Lumba argues, contemporary historiography on the PNB crisis "eerily echoes with racial assumptions" of colonial officials, "which assumed that Philippine racial habits of caciquism and affective bonds would trump any ethical republicanism or technocratic efficient state practices."[6]

More than its racialized origins, however, good-governance discourse in the Philippines has historically served as an adjunct to austerity. Within this rhetoric, a strong state and its strong institutions are defined by their capacity to withstand pressures to spend. There is, as such, no politics of money apart from keeping said money out of politics. Discussions of how to organize the monetary system ultimately become irrelevant amid demands to reduce corruption and rent-seeking. In the Philippines, this depoliticization of money is largely a colonial legacy produced during periods of economic crisis. The crisis of 1920–1921 is the most misunderstood and forgotten of these.

Empirically, this chapter challenges the two dominant interpretations of the PNB crisis, articulated by commentators from the time and rearticulated by recent academic work. The first is the simplistic idea—from officials like Wood and Forbes—that corrupt Filipinos spent and stole their way to near financial ruin. Under this exceptionalist logic—a logic we will see again in chapter 4—there were no global financial crises in the Philippines, only examples of large-scale corruption. This has been the explanation favored by scholars who reduce Philippine political economy to issues of rent-seeking, patronage, and oligarchic democracy. The second related explanation—traceable to Edwin Kemmerer—relates to the adulteration of the gold exchange standard. For Kemmerer, the original sin was using money from the Gold Standard Fund (see previous chapter) to engage in developmental spending through the PNB. In contemporary economic debates, the idea that a restrictive gold standard prevents economic crises is now considered extreme, reserved for libertarian "gold bugs" in the Republican Party and cryptocurrency zealots nostalgic over a halcyon era of "stable" money. It is, therefore, surprising that the most recent and complete account of the PNB crisis rehashes this view.[7]

Though these explanations differ in approach and sophistication, both implicitly justify austerity. If Filipinos are too corrupt to spend, they should not spend. If spending leads to an adulteration of a monetary standard and one's priority is monetary stability, balancing the budget is vital.

Against these views, I propose the most obvious explanation: the PNB crisis occurred amid a global financial crisis. Its troubles were not unique but shared by the world. This explanation is simple enough, but it is more interesting to see why commentators from the time and even today miss this conclusion. The answer relates to how austerity's logic hides in plain sight.

## The Many-Faced Bank

Founded in 1916, the Philippine National Bank had multiple functions. Which of these functions one sought to emphasize served as a Rorschach test for one's priorities. Prosaically, the PNB was a retail bank that accepted deposits. It was also a developmental bank because it loaned money to Filipino businesses, particularly the agricultural exporters. Finally, it was a state bank—the official depository of government funds and the issuer of currency notes. For example, a five-peso note in 1916 was labeled "Philippine National Bank Circulating Money" and bore the image of William McKinley. As we saw in the previous chapter, the ten-peso note was the basis for the present US dollar and bore the image of George Washington.

For a bank whose notes bore the faces of US presidents, however, it was ironically treated as foreign and deliberately placed outside the Federal Reserve System, reflecting a widespread belief among US officials that the Philippines should not be a financial burden to the mainland. Like the ambiguous legal relationship of the Philippines to the US as an "unincorporated territory"—neither fully part of the US nor entirely foreign—the PNB had an insider-outsider relationship with the Fed.[8] Though outside the Fed's official ambit, it was the Fed's "foreign representative" in the Philippines,[9] and its first president, H. Parker Willis, was simultaneously secretary of the Federal Reserve Board (he took a leave of absence from Washington to work in Manila).[10] As we shall see, Filipino nationalists came to emphasize the bank's developmental function. At the same time, American hard money advocates would discuss the PNB almost like a currency board whose sole duty was to ensure currency convertibility.

Like a currency board, the PNB, along with the Bureau of Insular Affairs, functioned to regulate the reserve funds of the Philippine colonial government. There were two such funds. The first, as we saw in the previous chapter, was the Gold Standard Fund, which maintained the value of Conants relative to the theoretical gold peso. The second was the Silver Certificate Reserve, which backed currency notes in circulation. This fund initially only included silver, but it became a mix of silver and US gold coins in 1906. The circulating "silver certificates" thus effectively became "coin certificates" (since they were no longer exclusively backed by silver), and, in 1916, they were officially designated "treasury certificates."[11] Simply put, these treasury certificates were the paper bills used for daily transactions.

This second fund initially regulated parity between the certificates and the Conants.[12] By 1918, however, the two funds would be merged into a Currency Reserve Fund, making it the reserve fund for all currency in circulation. After the establishment of the PNB, most of these reserve funds were deposited with the bank's agents in New York.[13] With the PNB working in Manila and the US, adjustments were simple: one could deposit money in the Currency Reserve Fund in the US and claim pesos in the Philippines, and one could also deposit funds in the Manila part of the fund to claim this money in the mainland. This system would, ideally, correct itself, but the PNB's enmeshment with colonial state-building precluded it from being a self-regulating currency board. As we saw in the previous chapter, Forbes had begun to use some of the Gold Standard Fund, and this pattern would continue under the PNB, which used reserve currency funds to help finance its various loans.

Forbes's investment strategies were desultory, to say the least, given his penchant for projects like building a summer capital for American officials. Investment policies would, however, shift with the election of Woodrow Wilson to the presidency in 1912, occasioning the end of the Republican Taft era in the Philippines.

## Developmental Colonialism

Wilson appointed the Tammany Hall politician Francis Burton Harrison to serve as governor-general of the Philippines. Harrison's central mission was to implement a policy of "Filipinization." Since the Democrats hoped to expedite Philippine independence, Filipinization entailed transferring the state apparatus to Filipinos. Under Harrison, authority over Muslim Mindanao and Luzon's highland provinces was transferred from the US military to civilian Filipinos. Harrison also permanently altered the composition of the bureaucracy. From 1913 to 1919, American officials in the colonial state dropped from 26 to 6 percent, with those in high office dropping from 14 percent to 5 percent.[14]

Beyond preparing the Philippines politically, Filipinization also entailed economic development, with Harrison's government encouraging the creation of national companies. There were two critical national companies: the National Development Corporation (NDC), which financed public coal and cement companies, and the PNB, which financed agricultural businesses.[15] Filipino politicians, particularly Speaker of the House Sergio Osmeña, sought to control this pattern of state-led economic development. Under Harrison, Osmeña established the Board of Control, which functioned as a "super board of directors" that oversaw the day-to-day affairs of government corporations.[16]

The legal historian Leia Castañeda Anastacio refers to this process as "Filipinizing developmental colonialism," arguing that it was a product of two different but complementary impulses. On the one hand, Osmeña, who earned himself the moniker "Father of Economic Nationalism," wanted to challenge what he saw as foreign dominance of the Philippine economy. On the other hand, Harrison was motivated by the aversion among American Progressives toward big business and the concentration of capital. Both impulses were "equally served by the policy preferring public/Filipino-led economic development."[17]

These shifts in economic policy were not exclusive to the Philippines. As Mattei argues, the First World War fundamentally altered capitalism, with states financing the war effort and supporting local industries. In Europe, several private industries became public, and governments began to function "as both buyers and sellers in economies that were designed to meet basic needs at home and drive the war effort abroad."[18] This was also the case for certain parts of Southeast Asia. In the Netherlands East Indies under Governor-General Paul van Limburg Strium, the Dutch notion of "ethical" colonialism allowed for "rapid increases in government expenditures" in "welfare education, and government services" during the war years.[19] In French Indochina, the republican Governor-General Albert Sarraut thought similarly, seeing colonial development as a necessary strategy to ward off communism.[20]

Mattei contends that modern austerity was "invented" amid an interwar repudiation of the economic experiments done during the First World War. She is correct in noting that modern conceptions of austerity took shape during this period, but this ossification did not happen in Europe alone. The story of the PNB shows how Americans used the postwar deflation to entrench colonial austerity in Asia.

## The Rise of the PNB and the Great Deflation

Like his Filipino colleagues in the colonial government, Governor-General Harrison took an expansive view of the PNB's mandate. For him, apart from facilitating currency exchange, the bank's signal accomplishments were helping to "break up the British monopoly of our foreign trade" and lowering interest rates.[21]

In its developmental capacity, the PNB was initially successful. Export surpluses surged during the war years because of its financing and favorable demand.[22] Figures 2.1 and 2.2 illustrate the effects of this war boom, aided by the PNB's developmental efforts: From the beginning of the war in 1914 until the crash at the turn of the decade, there was a steady increase in exports and the balance of trade. Figure 2, specifically, shows that the colony had been experiencing a balance-of-payments problem from 1910 to 1913 that would only resolve itself during the war (1914–1918) and the period of PNB support (1917 onward).

The PNB was instrumental in expanding the export base, which ended the years of trade deficits. By 1919, the bank had financed eighteen modern sugar mills that increased production without adding hectarage. These mills also allowed the sugar industry to transition from selling near-raw sugar that it could only sell domestically to refined sugar that could be sold abroad.[23] Figure 1 shows that exports peaked in 1920 at 302.2 million pesos. Of that amount, 89.2 million pesos came from the sugar industry.[24] The PNB also successfully stimulated the coconut oil industry,

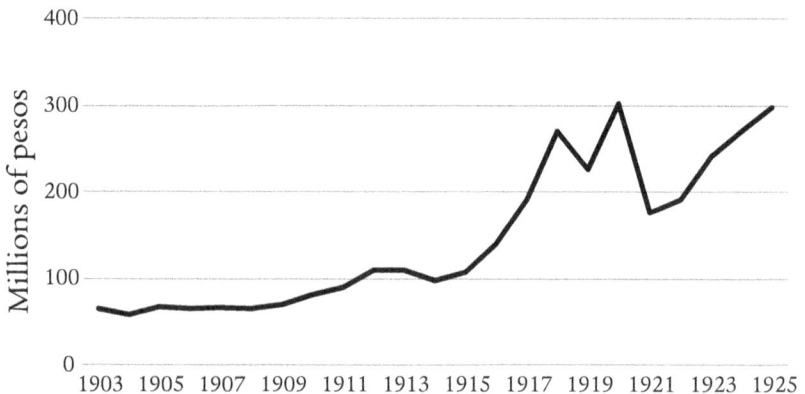

FIGURE 2.1.    Exports in millions of pesos, 1903–1925

Source: *The Philippines 1950: A Handbook of Trade and Economic Facts and Figures* (Manila: Department of Commerce and Industry, 1950), 22.

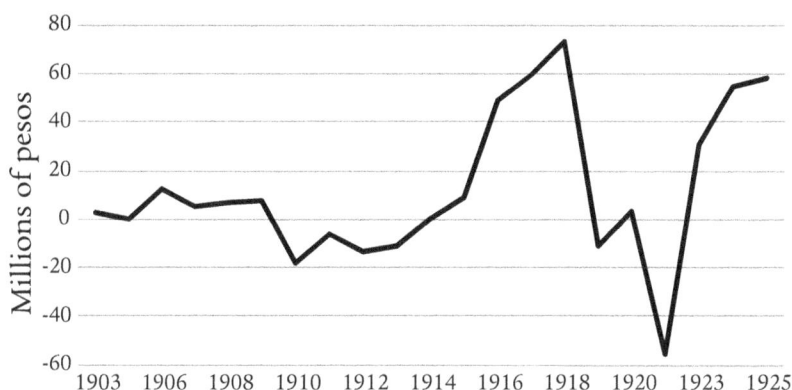

**FIGURE 2.2.**   Balance of trade in millions of pesos
Source: *The Philippines 1950: A Handbook of Trade and Economic Facts and Figures*, 22.

financing the construction of forty-one coconut oil mills by 1919. Not only was coconut oil an entirely new export that had yet to be traded before PNB investments, but its byproducts, like copra meal and cake, were also exportable.[25] The economic historian O. D. Corpuz notes that these two PNB investments—in sugar and coconut oil processing—allowed Filipino corporations "for the first time to venture into fields of processing and semi-manufacturing that had heretofore been exclusively under foreign capital."[26] Surveying the growth of industrial companies from 1909 to 1969, economist Yoshihara Kunio notes that Philippine industrialization began in earnest during this war and early interwar period.[27]

The historian Jim Richardson notes that this period of growth was also beneficial for the labor movement. He notes that 1917 to 1920 "witnessed an unprecedented economic boom" and that "business prosperity, a greater demand for labor, and price inflation produced a favorable climate for trade union organization and action." Unionization expanded as a result, especially for workers in trade and transportation (most of these unions would survive the economic crisis). As a result, industrial disputes increased from 49 from 1913 to 1916 to 269 from 1917 to 1920. Comparing the same periods, the number of workers involved in disputes also jumped from 9,094 to 37,420. Richardson adds that, in general, "the wage increases awarded during this time were more than sufficient to keep abreast of rising prices."[28] Fiscal expansion was leading to industrial expansion.

Osmeña's vision of a national economy, run by Filipinos, was ascendant. And the PNB was a symbol of national development. Because it was boom times, it was difficult to predict the gravity of the crisis that was to follow. The "great deflation" of 1920, as Adam Tooze explains, is "probably the most underrated event in twentieth-century world history,"[29] an observation more than apt for the Philippines. The event was destructive, and its effects were primarily centered on the United States and Asia, economic spheres in which the Philippines was entangled. Fearing a global gold shortage after the Great War, the US Fed engaged in deflationary policy (monetary austerity) as wartime demand dropped, causing an immediate decrease in prices.[30] Christina Romer computes the extent of the ensuing deflation in US agricultural prices by examining the ratio between the US wholesale prices of agricultural products relative to that of general goods, which was 1.14 in 1919 and 0.91 in 1921.[31] It was a movement more significant than other prewar recessions in 1894, 1908, and 1914, and a price movement this significant would not occur again until the Great Depression.[32] Within the context of the colonial relationship between the US and the Philippines, this had been the worst deflationary crisis the Philippines had encountered. And it would severely impact the fates of Filipino exporters who made less as prices in the US fell.

Other factors contributed to the recession. Apart from explicit deflationary policy, returning troops from the war created severe pressures on employment. With increased labor supply, employers could cut salaries and save on production costs, contributing further to the deflation. On top of this, the Spanish flu raged again in the United States.

Economic contagion quickly spread to Asia, with Japan being its center. Japan had been sufficiently linked to the US market at this period and was, like the Philippines, committed to the prewar gold standard. Any sudden drop in the US market would have had an immediate effect. The Bank of Japan's governor-general Junnosuke Inoue described the wartime boom and subsequent crash as a long climb followed by a sudden descent, like falling from the heights of Mount Fuji to the bottom of Lake Biwa.[33] In response to the news of deflation in the United States, the Tokyo Stock Exchange plummeted by 60 percent, there were 169 bank runs, and the Yokohama Silk Exchange collapsed.[34]

Like the collapse of the Yokohama silk trade and the bankruptcy of the textile business in Kansai,[35] export industries in the Philippines also suffered. The prices of all major crops exported by the Philippines to the mainland dropped in 1921: Abaca (Manila hemp) was down by 68 percent, sugar by 82 percent, and copra by 67 percent. Moreover, the value of total exports fell by 42 percent between 1920 and 1921.[36]

Figure 2.2 shows the aggregate effects of these changes on the balance of trade, illustrating that 1914 to 1921 constituted an ascent to Mount Mayon's heights followed by a drop to the depths of Lake Taal. There was, for instance, a 175 percent drop from 1918 to 1921.

The deflation naturally affected wages. Wage statistics from this period are varied in their reliability and consistency. Still, Richardson notes that "it is safe to conclude that the postwar slump resulted in significant wage reductions virtually across the board." Seamstresses who used to make from 0.80 to 3 pesos daily in 1920 were making 0.63–1.17 in 1923; chauffeurs during the same period saw their wages decline from 2.43 to 1.94, and carpenters, who made 5 pesos a day during the boom years, saw that number cut in half.[37]

Despite the gravity of the crisis and the inherent vagaries of developmental policy, the profligate colonial would take the blame for economic woes. In response to the tightening of credit and the need to replenish reserves, the US Congress raised the debt ceiling of the colony from $15 million to $30 million in July of 1921.[38] Increasing indebtedness was, of course, a response to the great deflation. Yet US officials and media framed it as an issue of mismanagement. Speaking to *The New York Times*, Leonard Wood noted, "The Philippine Bank is practically insolvent, through bad investments, bad management and inefficiency of its former officers."[39] In Wood's mind, mismanagement and debt were two sides of the same coin. The United States was, therefore, paying for Filipino sins when it raised the debt ceiling.[40]

Accounts in the US media of rising indebtedness in the Philippines also revealed the civilizational rhetoric through which Americans saw Philippine fiscal policy. New York's *Morning Telegraph* claimed, "The Philippines have asked for a bigger debt limit, probably just to demonstrate their advanced status as a civilized people." The profligate colonial was also again gendered, and accounts portrayed the colonial relationship as a dysfunctional marriage between a responsible husband and a spendthrift wife. The *El Paso Times*, for instance, asked, "The Philippines ask freedom and $15,000,000. Where will this divorce and crazy alimony stop?" Similarly, *The Sacramento Star* quipped, "In their divorce suit against Uncle Sam, the Philippines can't claim non-support."[41]

The need for extra credit turned Filipino politicians into supplicants. As the US Congress discussed raising the debt ceiling, Senate President Manuel Quezon voiced a need for "financial guidance" from "United States experts," admitting that Filipinos had "made a mess of national finance and need help."[42] It was an unusual statement from a politician known more for his nationalist bravado than his humility. It was also an early manifestation of a Filipino admitting his profligacy as a colonial.

## A Corrupt Bank?

Scholarly accounts of the PNB have dismissed the bank as a hive of corruption or focused on its role in cementing elite control over the Philippines.[43] For example, political scientist Paul Hutchcroft notes that the PNB was "the richest source of booty for the emerging national government" and that "the newly empowered landed oligarchs had plundered the bank so thoroughly that not only the bank but also the government and its currency were threatened by 'utter breakdown.'"[44] For John Sidel, the corruption of the PNB proves that Filipinization merely enabled the predation of an elite liberal class with roots among the anticolonial revolutionaries and intellectuals of the nineteenth century. With aid from the PNB, this class could "entrench itself in power, with easy and early access to the colonial state enabling the accumulation of vast concentrations of land, wealth, and political influence unimaginable under Spanish rule."[45] Alfred McCoy portrays the PNB's developmental strategy as a "clear example of crony capitalism," directly comparing the crisis of the 1920s and Marcos's crisis of the 1980s—a crisis we will turn to in chapter 4.[46] Finally, Joe Studwell's work, which documents the rise of corrupt "Asian Godfathers," says that, because of what happened to the PNB, the Philippines became "the pace setter in bank mismanagement" in Asia. He explains that "the PNB loan book grew on the basis of political favours extracted by powerful agricultural families." As a result, the "local godfathers had not only reduced the Philippine National Bank to insolvency, they had undermined the currency and left the central government on the edge of bankruptcy."[47]

These accounts view the PNB as a symbol of elite predation and the bankruptcy of Filipino nationalism in the early twentieth century, neglecting that the growth supported by the PNB did not just benefit the elites. In Studwell's case, his account is part of an orientalist vision of Asia, where conniving elites (mostly Chinese) conspire to get ahead, thus undermining economic growth. Tracing the chain of citations in these scholarly accounts, we arrive at one common source: the Wood–Forbes report of 1921. Accounts like Hutchcroft's, McCoy's, and Studwell's have taken arguments from Wood and Forbes at face value despite the report's clear partisan skew.

The view that corruption and mismanagement caused the collapse of the Philippine National Bank is so axiomatic that the PNB crisis is often held up as a prime example of the rapaciousness of the Philippine oligarchy—modern-day arguments against the profligate colonial. Effectively, these accounts of the PNB crisis replicate the assumptions of the Wood–Forbes report and ignore the challenges it received from the Filipino press. The credulity with which the Wood–Forbes report has been treated is startling. These two imperialists were hardly reliable sources; they suppressed information that could challenge imperial boosterism. Wood, in particular, was behind possibly the worst massacre in US military history (the Bud Dajo massacre in Sulu of 1906), and he covered up evidence of the deliberate killing of women and children.[48] And Forbes, as we saw, was no credible critic of wastefulness, given his spending priorities as governor-general. Yet the fairy tale of these two imperialists has been replicated more than the obvious macroeconomic story of boom and bust.

The great deflation occurred amid a US election that would significantly shift Philippine policy in the United States. Warden G. Harding's victory in the election of 1920 signaled an end to the Wilsonian promise of quick self-determination for the colony. The idea for a mission to assess the viability of Philippine independence came from a January 1921 meeting between President-elect Harding and Forbes.[49] In this meeting, Forbes suggested initiating a "system of inspection" run by American officials who "could assist the Filipino chiefs."[50] He also recommended the immediate removal of Governor-General Harrison.[51] Harding accepted Forbes's advice, and the former Democratic senator of Missouri Charles E. Yeater sailed for Manila to serve as Harrison's replacement as acting governor-general.[52] The Wood–Forbes mission would begin shortly after.

The Wood–Forbes mission had two functions. The first was the official goal of assessing the governance of the colony. Undergirding this aim, however, was a Republican attempt to criticize Filipinization under the Democrats. During his stint in the colony, Forbes was never asked about his political loyalties, nor did he volunteer them. However, he considered himself "in accord with the tenets of the Republican party" and was willing to "call myself out as a Republican if it seemed worthwhile."[53] As for Wood, his partisan position was no secret, being a prominent member of Teddy Roosevelt's "rough riders" in the Cuban-American War. Indeed, the partisan skew of the Wood–Forbes report was an open secret. As the medical historian Warwick Anderson has shown, the report reflected a widespread bias against Filipinization among critics of the Democratic Party, with the theme of Democratic and Filipino "mismanagement" also being pronounced in assessments of the medical system. During this time, Filipinos and the Democrats were not only being blamed for economic collapse but also for the rise in diseases like the flu.[54]

It was open season on all things Filipinization. The Republican-leaning *New-York Tribune* condemned Harrison for reducing American teachers from eight hundred to three hundred and allowing the courts "to have fallen under the domination of native politicians." It also criticized Osmeña and other pro-independence leaders for a supposedly traitorous visit to Japan and accused them of "opposing the spread of the English language and encouraging Spanish."[55]

However, the spheres of health and finance were most relevant to Wood and Forbes. Wood was a medical doctor, while Forbes was a banker, and the latter's views were typical of a hard money banker from the East. Like Edwin Kemmerer and the other money doctors who created the Philippine monetary system, he believed that the gold standard was a civilizing system that would move Filipinos away from the "medieval methods" of the Spaniards. Until the vestiges of the Spanish system had been banished, he argued, "the Filipino must have no voice in the government which would enable him to veto progressive movement." As governor-general, he was aghast when businessmen, particularly Filipinos, asked that older currency be redeemable with the new gold-based peso. Forbes saw the profligate colonial in infantilized terms, noting that Filipinos who wanted more credit were "exactly like some rather small child, who has been refused candy by his parents, crying out "Iwant [*sic*] that, I want that!"[56]

The Republican establishment had placed great stock in the results of the Wood–Forbes mission. Before the mission's departure, Wood wrote to former US president and former governor-general of the Philippines William Howard Taft to ask for advice on the mission's conduct. In his reply, Taft advised Wood to focus on Harrison's policy of driving away American civil servants, whom he considered "exceptional" officials who "set the pace" for a stable bureaucracy. Getting rid of these individuals, Taft continued, sowed "the seeds of inefficiency, inconstancy and graft" and led to a government of "machine-made Filipino politicians."[57] Taft ended his letter by urging Wood to present a critical account of Harrison's term: "How frank you ought to be about Harrison's shortcomings personal and otherwise, is also a question. He has been a disgrace to us by his domestic and personal indecencies and has seriously affected our standing among the Filipino people. Certainly the President is entitled to know this, even if it not be published."[58]

This special mission arrived in Manila on May 4, 1921, and stayed in the colony for four months.[59] By this time, Venacio Concepcion had already been replaced, and the PNB was not only under audit but had also become a vital focus of the Wood–Forbes mission.

The report's focus on Concepcion's corruption and the PNB likely came at the suggestion of former colonial administrator Dean Conant Worcester. Worcester was previously secretary of the interior under Forbes's government, and during the Harrison administration he had become an influential businessman and landowner in the colony. He was also one of the most despised imperialists of the Taft era. In 1908, the Spanish-Tagalog newspaper *El Renacimiento* published a column called *Aves de Rapiña* (birds of prey) that accused a certain colonial official of using his anthropological research to find gold deposits and tap unknown natural resources. Feeling alluded to, Worcester sued the newspaper, leading to its eventual demise.[60] Here was a man with an ax to grind with Filipino nationalists. And here was a man who had an interest in diverting accusations of corruption away from American officials.

Two months after arriving in the Philippines, Wood wrote Worcester to query "the most prominent business man of the Islands" concerning his thoughts on the colony's administration at a time when Filipinos "enjoyed practical autonomy."[61] Worcester set a low bar in his reply, noting that "in an oriental country an unjust government might be reasonably stable." Economic independence, however, was a prerequisite for "a separate and independent national existence." On this account, Filipino officials were a failure since financial administration had "become both incompetent and rotten." An investigation into the PNB, Worcester continued, would "conclusively demonstrate the very great present unfitness of the Filipinos to take charge of the financial administration of their country." He bemoaned Concepcion's appointment as president of the bank, claiming that even Harrison thought Concepcion was unqualified and only succumbed to pressure from Speaker Osmeña. For Worcester, Concepcion "was about as competent for the position as my chauffeur." The loans under Concepcion, moreover, "would embody some of the most surprising episodes ever unearthed in connection with such an institution." Because of the PNB, the Philippines was "on the road toward financial ruin," reversing the progress of previous administrations.[62]

As Wood and Forbes toured the Philippines, things were indeed getting worse at the bank, but not because of Filipino corruption. The increased scrutiny of the PNB had immediate effects, leading it to cut back on investments during a deflationary spiral. This pro-cyclical policy made the pain of the crisis more acute. For example, the lack of PNB support decimated the hemp industry in Mindanao, particularly in the Davao region. In the second half of 1921, a newspaper report estimated that the number of Japanese residents in Davao, which controlled the hemp trade, was reduced by around half. Since Japanese and Filipino planters were predominantly small landholders who relied on credit when hemp was not in production, the lack of credit meant they had to leave.[63]

Despite pressure from even American businessmen, the PNB refused to accept extensive clearings and hemp plantings as assets. According to an American correspondent, "All semblance of credit has been withdrawn, and the bank will not advance the planters a third of the value of the finished product in order to give them an advantage of an outside market."[64] The PNB, as an engine of economic development, had stalled. And its reputation would continue to be damaged by attacks from Leonard Wood.

When he became governor-general in October 1921, Wood continued to remind the public about the so-called mismanagement of the PNB. Beyond reiterating claims about the corruption of Filipinos and Democrats, he also began to make increasingly sensationalist claims. A report from the *Philippines Free Press* on July 1, 1922, read, "What are we to say now! Governor General Wood comes out and announces that the loss of the Philippine National bank, instead of the 57 million pesos stated in the Wood–Forbes report, is finally proved to be worse than that—the staggering sum of about 77 million pesos!"[65]

Apart from the 77 million peso loss, the *Free Press* reported that over 37 million pesos had been issued as fiat money, "Bolshevik money!—for which the government, if you please, stands guarantor." Naturally, the blame for this state of affairs was pinned on the previous administration, "the glorious administration of Governor General Harrison!"[66]

Wood's actions blindsided Filipinos in government. Before making public statements about the PNB, Wood had not spoken with Filipino leaders like Senate President Quezon or Speaker of the House Manuel Roxas. Wood also failed to consult the PNB's board of directors before publicizing information from internal, confidential reports. After an inquiry of Filipino officials into Wood's actions, Secretary of Commerce

Salvador Laguda pointedly accused the governor-general of undermining the bank's interests. "If the Governor were a functionary of the bank who can be subjected to an action of the board of directions, we will [sic] not hesitate to adopt energetic measures that he may be prosecuted and that the proper penalty may be imposed."[67]

While Wood was already unpopular among Filipinos, his handling of the PNB crisis further enraged nationalists. Camilo Osias, an increasingly famous young politician and educator, attacked Wood for calling his critics traitors and accused the governor-general of violating the colony's laws. "Governor Wood, the Filipinos will cooperate with you when you are right," Osias declared in a speech before the American Chamber of Commerce, "but they will not only not cooperate with you but will lawfully and firmly fight you when you are wrong. Those who violate our laws and statutes here, especially if high officials, are those who come under the class of traitors, because being trusted, they have betrayed their trust."[68]

Many Filipino responses to Wood and Forbes were printed in the nationalist and increasingly left-wing Spanish-language newspapers like *El Debate*,[69] while English-language newspapers like the *Philippines Free Press* only covered Wood's accusations. *El Debate*, for example, reported that Senate President Quezon accused Wood of obscuring facts and documents favorable to the bank. It also noted that the Philippine legislature had demanded that Wood provide documentation to prove his allegations.[70]

Government officials often seek to shore up confidence at times of potential market crisis. As early as June of 1921, the assistant secretary of commerce and interim PNB president Miguel Unson braced the public for a prolonged adjustment, telling the Spanish-language newspaper *El Ideal* that the effects of the deflationary crisis would last until 1923. He noted that sugar farmers had increased their yields, assuming continued increases in demand, and that it would take time for production to readjust to new market conditions. He also explained that, per his estimates, the PNB was not bankrupt, given its roughly $12 million worth of liberty bonds. Any improvements to the economy, however, would be palliative, and a full recovery could only occur once markets could absorb Philippine hemp and sugar exports.[71] Unson acknowledged the crisis but saw the potential for a steady recovery—a reasonable position for a bank official.

Unlike Filipino officials, however, Wood had no interest in allaying fears of a market collapse. Concerned that Wood's statements would trigger a crisis of confidence, the Philippine legislature suppressed the publication of his congressional report, but its contents were eventually published in the Spanish-language newspaper *La Vanguardia* and, eventually, *The New York Times*.[72] An anonymous lawmaker (who *the Times* assumed was Quezon) explained the legislature's actions by noting, "This agitation involves, not the political liberties already attained, but the economic life of the country, which is exposed to imminent danger of death by the concerted action evidently designed to destroy the credit of the Philippine National Bank."[73] For this lawmaker, the weakness of the PNB was becoming a self-fulfilling prophecy amid sustained criticism from the colony's chief executive.

Even American bankers feared the flames of panic that Wood continued to fan. At the time of the *Free Press* report, progress was, in fact, already being made in the restructuring of loans and the rehabilitation of businesses in which the PNB had a stake. In the same month that Wood was decrying the "losses" of the PNB, its recently appointed general manager, E. W. Wilson, declared that the bank's interests were safe, even though, because of foreclosures, it had effective control over numerous businesses. According to Wilson, around 34 million pesos were tied up in sugar businesses, while another 24 million were connected to coconut oil mills—54 million pesos in nonliquid assets. Discussions within the PNB, Wilson explained, revolved around how to rehabilitate these businesses to secure repayment of loans.[74] While it is true that the economic crisis prevented many of these loans from being paid on time, and many businesses were in arrears, the stabilization of demand as the United States entered the "roaring twenties" allowed the PNB to start collecting its debts. And there was increasing optimism about the bank's capacity to recover. Export earnings were close to their pre-crisis peak by 1925 (figure 1), and trade with the United States allowed the Philippines to dig itself out of its trade deficit as early as 1922. Unson's earlier predictions about the crisis ending in 1923 were proving prescient.

Under Wilson, the PNB initiated the foreclosure of coconut oil mills to recoup its losses. In September that year, the bank's attorney, Ramon Lacson, foreclosed the Santa Ana Oil Mills in Manila to protect the 308,746.67 pesos it had loaned to the corporation. Wilson was confident that taking over businesses such as Santa Ana were stopgap measures and that renewed foreign capital would allow for rehabilitation, noting that "the great trouble has been that the companies lacked capital. Nevertheless there is, I am sure, a great future for the oil industry here and the growing of copra and the milling of oil are bound to reach paramount place in the Philippine business."[75]

However, whatever recovery the bank made was attributed not to shifting economic conditions but to the strict austerity implemented by "experienced" Americans. *The Washington Times*, for example, celebrated the "reorganization, curtailment of expense, reduced cost of operation and of manufacture, efficiency instead of careless methods and waste that 'got by' during the war and the post-armistice boom." This new discipline was achieved because Governor-General Wood had "re-organized the directorate of the bank, which is now in experienced American hands."[76]

Filipino commentators disagreed. One month after Wood took office, *El Ideal* reported on the state of the "de-Filipinized" PNB, with Senate Majority Leader Pedro Guevara accusing Wilson's bank of lending 6 million pesos to the Commercial Bank of the Philippine Islands instead of aiding farmers. Guevera also pointed out that "the worst of the affair is that two million and a half of these six millions have been granted without any security, for the entry is made in the bank's books as current account from bank to bank."[77] The years of the PNB providing credit for Filipino exporters were over.

## Violating the Sacred Standard

Concomitant to ideas about irresponsible lending and graft of local politicos was a more sophisticated account that American economists were developing. These accounts were less sensational and not widely discussed in the press, but they were also defenses of austerity. They slowly trickled into policy circles, ultimately leading to a full restoration of hard money policy.

Increasingly, the crisis of the PNB was serving to justify the warnings of money doctors about the profligate colonial. In the previous chapter, we noted how money doctors like Edwin W. Kemmerer and Charles Conant argued that the gold exchange standard was necessary to rein in the spending of uncivilized Filipinos. It would not take long for the PNB to be a case in point. The period from the mid-1920s to the 1930s was the high point of the gold standard mentalité when economists desperately sought to restore the prewar gold standard. During this period, Eichengreen and Temin note, "the ability of governments to maintain this discipline [gold convertibility] was taken as a marker of the extent of the civilised world. The struggling countries of Latin America and eastern Europe kept trying and failing to adopt the gold standard, making adherence a hallmark of a developed economy."[78] Cautionary tales were useful for those who upheld this vision of the world, especially since the US was fighting for the global reestablishment of a gold-based system, which was taking a beating amid wartime spending, global deflation, and the initial rumblings of the Great Depression. Indeed, after the Great War, the US became a creditor nation to Europe, and the gold-backed dollar became the world's leading reserve currency. The sanctity of this gold-based system needed to be protected at its seams.

In 1934, George F. Luthringer, Kemmerer's doctoral student at Princeton, published a book on the gold standard in the Philippines. Luthringer, who would occupy various senior positions in the International Monetary Fund, would, like his mentor, begin his career studying the Philippines—further testament to how old Philippine hands served to shape the global financial order in the twentieth century. In his book, Luthringer argued that the PNB's spending had caused a crisis, noting that the bank had "dissipated the bulk of currency reserves" by using these as investments.[79] "*Any* investment of these pesos" (emphasis in original), regardless of whether or not they were for wise or unwise investments, violated the "corrective action" inherent in the gold exchange standard.[80] Under Kemmerer's "simon pure" gold standard (see previous chapter), pesos in circulation had to be redeemable through dollars deposited in the Gold Standard Fund.

To inflate reserves, Luthringer argued, officials engaged in what he considered monetary chicanery, noting that the PNB combined its silver and gold funds into one reserve fund from 1919 to 1922. This move evidenced an "unbelievable recklessness" on the bank officials' part. The effects of these actions "were disastrous," causing a "badly inflated monetary and credit structure" and leaving the colony with "a hopelessly inadequate dollar balance in the currency reserves." This situation was detrimental from "the standpoint of maintenance of parity"—an unquestioned good in Luthringer's eyes.[81] Apart from violating the parity of currency in reserve and currency in circulation, Luthringer complained, the spending of the reserves "promoted further price increases" in 1919.[82] Eighteen pages later, however, he notes in passing that this inflation was less severe than what happened in the mainland of the United States.[83]

Luthringer's study was not only supervised by Kemmerer but also based on the latter's notes from the period (Kemmerer also wrote the introduction). More importantly, it defends Kemmerer's advice to the

US War Department's Bureau of Insular Affairs (BIA) in 1918 to strictly implement the gold exchange standard. It is also explicit in its narrow standard for the economic good, namely "the standpoint of the maintenance of parity."

Unfortunately, Luthringer's work—a relic of conservative imperialist economics—influences present-day scholarship. Economic historian Yoshiko Nagano's monograph on the PNB crisis, the most comprehensive account to date, uncritically draws from Luthringer and Kemmerer to argue that because the BIA and the PNB "deviated from the fundamental principle of the gold exchange standard system," they "brought confusion to currency and exchange in the Philippines, and evolved into the grave financial crisis of 1919-1922."[84] Like Luthringer, Nagano notes that the PNB, with the approval of the BIA, used the Gold Standard Fund to invest in the booming export market. From 1912 until 1918, loans and investments from the fund increased by the year, reaching 80 percent by 1916-1917.[85]

More importantly, Nagano's standard for what constitutes a crisis is, as with Luthringer, parity, and thus "confusion" was in and of itself detrimental. Finally, Luthringer and Nagano view the PNB crisis as a problem of lending and spending. Had the bank not lent money to Filipino agriculture, it would not have drawn down its reserves and not have violated the gold exchange standard. Between the mismanagement and corruption narrative of the Wood–Forbes report and the pro-gold narrative of Luthringer, we have two American explanations for the PNB crisis.

## Through the Eyes of a Cacique Criminal

Any account of the PNB crisis will inevitably reproduce the ideas of tainted sources. On the one hand, scholars who forward the two versions above—the narrative about corruption and machine politics and the one about the violation of the gold exchange standard—reproduce the ideas of violent and racist imperialists. On the other hand, scholars who defend the PNB's developmental strategy duplicate the accounts of corrupt Filipino nationalists. We must therefore assess these accounts based on their empirical merit.

In this present account, we challenge the various narratives about the PNB's near collapse by taking a very impeachable source seriously. One of the earliest sustained rebuttals to the Wood–Forbes report and the Kemmerer account was that of disgraced PNB president Venacio

Concepcion. Concepcion was the first Filipino president of the PNB, replacing H. Parker Willis, who needed to return to the Federal Reserve.[86] Unlike Willis, a professor of economics and Fed secretary, Concepcion, a revolutionary general, was unqualified for the job. Even the pro-Filipino Harrison balked at Concepcion's appointment, yielding only because of pressure from Speaker Osmeña.[87] Concepcion was a crony of one of the colony's leading nationalist politicians. And he was undoubtedly a criminal (though not a mass murderer like Wood). But his account is more persuasive than the imperialist one.

In 1927, Concepcion self-published *"La Tragedia" del Banco Nacional Filipino*, which, from its title alone, questioned the extent of the bank's misfortunes. While it is easy to assume that the work is a relitigation of Concepcion's criminal case, only the last chapter of this ten-chapter book discusses it. In any case, it is the least convincing chapter of the book, where Concepcion admits that he had a stake in a company the PNB lent money to but that he was "not the only official of the Board of Directors who had an interest in companies that dealt with the Bank."[88] The other chapters, however, give us an idea of an alternative vision of the fiscal relationship between colonizer and colonized.

Concepcion begins by reminding readers that the PNB was founded because no institutions could "provide the aid necessary in cash or credit for the major expansion" of the country's businesses, particularly those in agriculture. Without such an institution, he contended, Filipino industry would rely on "foreign bankers" who only helped when their clients advised them to invest liberally. Such unpredictability would stall growth, for businesses would be denied "that potent fertilizer that in the field of economics we call credit."[89] Concepcion, therefore, foregrounded not just the need for a local source of stimulus but one unmoored from the uncertainties of the market and the caprices of foreign lenders. As we saw above, this stimulus was initially successful, creating the foundations for Philippine industrialization.

Concepcion's vision of banking was neither new nor foreign. In the United States, he explained, businesses received "all the stimulus, all the help they need to augment production and to increase the already significant traffic of merchandise." In the United States, moreover, "insignificant factories of kitchen utensils transform into great production sites for arms and munitions or agricultural implements." And in the country of so-called "scientific credit," funding would not stop until "the last horticulturist became a very important producer in the brief time it takes the hour hand to make four or eight turns around the clock" and "abandoned mills magically transformed into important textile factories."[90] If Concepcion aspired toward government support for industry, it was only because he was observing the developmental path of the metropole.

Behind Concepcion's purple Castilian was an understanding of what Fred Block calls the "hidden developmental state" in the United States.[91] The colonizer had never been a platonic market economy. Since its foundation, a potent Hamiltonian strain among policymakers has emphasized the need for government credit and the protection of "infant industries"—a developmental metaphor coined by Alexander Hamilton himself.[92] For Concepcion, denying the Philippines a line of credit was an act of hypocrisy. Or, in the words of developmental economist Ha-Joon Chang, it reflected a pattern of developed nations "kicking away the ladder" of economic growth for others.[93] As we shall see, this hidden developmentalism was already embedded in the US banking system under the Federal Reserve system, but the same largesse extended to US banks was unavailable to a colonial bank like the PNB.

Concepcion was no doubt corrupt. Sugar planters, particularly on Negros Island in the Visayas, overdeclared areas for cultivation to receive higher loans, and they also converted business loans into personal ones. At the same time, Concepcion's PNB looked the other way.[94] The historian Filomeno V. Aguilar has noted that Concepcion's incipient developmentalism constituted a form of "state gambling" that paid off when sugar prices were high but risked huge losses during downturns. In this regard, Aguilar compares Concepcion's PNB to the administration of Ferdinand Marcos, which likewise invoked nationalism to pour money into a network of corrupt businesses.[95]

Aguilar's comparison is apt. As we shall see here and in chapter 4, attempts at developmental policy and corruption are not mutually exclusive. In both the cases of the PNB and Marcosian developmentalism, corrupt politicians could foreground national development goals even as they enriched themselves, their friends, and their families. Indeed, as Patricio N. Abinales and Donna Amoroso have persuasively shown, a defining trait of Filipino state builders was a remarkable combination of "corruption and competence," and these leaders displayed an "achievement-oriented professionalism" even as they helped themselves to the spoils of the system.[96] Concepcion was one example of this kind of politician.

Corrupt as he was, however, Concepcion and others like him did not cause the crisis of the early 1920s. There was undoubtedly corruption in the PNB, but this corruption was not significant enough to prevent it from achieving its goal of stimulating Philippine exports. Moreover, a reduction in corruption would not have prevented the crash, since nations with more mature institutions like the United States, Japan, and, as we shall see, the United Kingdom also suffered during this period. If the corruption of the PNB was so debilitating, what explains the initial success of the PNB, and why does the 175 percent crash in the balance of trade (see figure 2.2) coincide with one of world history's greatest deflationary crises? Clearly, the deflationary crisis led to the erosion of the balance of trade, and Filipinos did not steal their way into a crisis. Reduced corruption would have made the crisis less acute, but it would have been a crisis nonetheless.

Filipino politicians and nationalist newspapers at the time did not have access to the files of the Wood–Forbes mission, and they could only engage in partial rebuttals. Moreover, the lack of economic training among Filipino politicians meant that, despite a strong gut feeling that there was something awry about the Wood–Forbes report, they could not refute the banking jargon that backed the report's argument. Examining the PNB files and notes from the Wood–Forbes report, however, allows us to refute many of the report's claims and affirm Concepcion's position.

Let us take the issue of the extent of the PNB's losses. We are unsure where Wood got the figure of 77 million pesos, but the number roughly corresponds with the total of uncollected loans of the PNB in 1919, which, according to the bank's records, was at 77,302,194.35 pesos as of July 31, 1919.[97] It is likely, therefore, that Wood based his figure on this record. If this number were the basis of Wood's claim, this 77 million would scarcely qualify as a loss. Naturally, unpaid loans are not losses, and Wood should have at least accounted for the fact that this 77 million was collateralized (how individual loans were collateralized was detailed in the PNB's records). The total loss was difficult to quantify then, especially amid Wilson's foreclosures and the restructuring of multiple debt arrangements. But claiming a 77 million loss after the Wood-Forbes report's initial claim of about half this number conjured an image of an escalating crisis and rising panic.

Wood's later allegations were exaggerated, making the earlier Wood–Forbes report look circumspect by comparison. And yet that report, too, left out significant facets of the crisis that would exonerate Filipinos from the charge of mismanagement. The papers of W. Cameron Forbes at Harvard's Houghton Library include scattered, unauthored, and untitled notes that appear to be either early drafts or extended commentary/correspondence related to the report.[98] These notes show that the corruption in the PNB was not limited to Filipinos and that an American had committed the most egregious act of bribery.

In his public pronouncements, Wood often referred to the questionable loans handed out by the PNB's Shanghai branch. The notes from Forbes's papers, however, explain that an American postal clerk received seven thousand pesos in gifts to hand out faulty loans that led to losses amounting to four to six million dollars. More strikingly, Forbes notes that losses in PNB's Shanghai Bank resulted not from Filipino but American corruption. Forbes wrote, "The bank decided to open a branch in Shanghai and an American postal clerk named Miller was detailed to go there. He sold silver and failed to cover it. The net loss is estimated to run somewhere between four and six million dollars, U.S. currency. The broker who conducted most of these negotiations made considerable cash presents to Miller: he admits having received some seven thousand pesos in this way. The Filipino people foot the bill."[99]

In another one of these scattered documents, Forbes (perhaps this time writing with Wood, given the use of "we") laments the fact that banks in China, Japan, and North Borneo "have instructions from their managers to dishonor notes of the Philippine Government and drafts of the Philippine National Bank." This was because an "untrained employee—an American, we regret to say—speculated in exchange with the direct loss of in between eleven and twelve million pesos."[100] None of these cases of American corruption made it to the final report. Nor are they mentioned in the Bureau of Insular Affairs' documents and newspaper clippings on the PNB.

Besides Forbes's scattered notes, the only mention of these cases I could find was in Concepcion's account. These cases of mismanagement and corruption were, arguably, worse than those of Concepcion, who only lent money to relatives and was acquitted of taking bribes. Yet Concepcion notes that Miller was merely suspended for his actions and that, despite promises from Wood that Miller would be tried, the case had been "relegated to oblivion."[101] Concepcion, meanwhile, ended up in jail.

In the middle of his book, Concepcion notes that he had also been singled out for exhausting the gold standard fund.[102] As early as 1927, therefore, Concepcion was already aware of Kemmerer and Luthringer's accusations regarding the PNB's violation of parity under the gold exchange standard. On this matter, Concepcion is blasé, insisting that because the PNB benefited from a "large volume of bills of exchange, from the exports of abaca oil and sugar," its gold funds were always "at a high level."[103] Concepcion's assessment was Panglossian, premised on the assumption that a continued export rise would replenish the colony's reserves. But, as we have noted, crises on the scale of 1920–1921 are difficult to predict, and boom times tend to make investors bullish. More importantly, the developmentally oriented Concepcion cannot be blamed for not making parity the end-all of his economic calculations. Luthringer and Kemmerer's standard of parity was not the only standard a developing economy needed to be concerned with. For Conception, the priority was investing in an export economy that would provide stable reserves in the long run. What was so objectionable about this priority?

Concepcion used terms like "general crisis" and "great depreciations" to describe his predicament. He consistently referenced deflation in the US as the proximate cause of the PNB's troubles.[104] In other words, he did not view the crisis as a local phenomenon. For Kemmerer, Luthringer, and Nagano, however, these years reflected a "confusion" specific to the Philippines when the currency standard was under strain. But what was happening globally during the years of "confusion" from 1919 to 1922? For polities worldwide, the pattern was similar: At the height of the war, they spent lavishly (either on munitions or the support of export industries), placing pressure on their currency reserves. And global deflation at the war's end triggered crises, especially in colonies that tied their export profits to demand in their colonial metropoles. The puzzle, therefore, is not why the Philippines struggled to maintain convertibility but why it did not give up on it like most of the world.

In a list of fifty-four polities compiled by Eichengreen, only five were able to remain on the gold standard from 1919 to 1922: Cuba, Nicaragua, Panama, the Philippines, and the United States—places that were under the gold exchange standard promoted by American money doctors, or the US itself.[105] One could argue, as Kemmerer and Luthringer did, that the Philippines was effectively off the gold standard at the time, given the collapse of reserves. But there was no need to formally abandon the system, given the expectation of the ultimate restoration of reserves. In any case, as we shall see, there was no doubt about convertibility by 1921. In contrast, Japan returned to convertibility in 1922, the Dutch East Indies in 1925, and Siam in 1928.[106] The postwar economic crisis was, in fact, so prolonged in Siam that it became a cause for the bloodless revolution that culminated in the end of the absolutist monarchy in 1932.[107] Thus, even if we grant that the Philippines had lost convertibility, this period was short compared to its neighbors.

In contrast to the Philippines, colonies attached to powers that had abandoned the gold standard during the war years were off convertibility. For example, since the pound sterling had become a fiat currency,[108] the Straits dollar of British Malaya, redeemable in sterling,[109] was also off the gold standard. The same can be said for the guilder and the Dutch East Indies.[110] Most tellingly, the pattern of credit increase in colonial Malaya during the war and the contraction after it was almost identical to that in the Philippines, despite the Malayan currency board being unable to invest any of its reserve currency (unlike the PNB) in the market.[111] This comparison shows that there was likely to have been credit inflation in the Philippines regardless of what the PNB had done, especially since both colonies were similarly structured by the dominance of Anglo-Chinese capital.[112]

The end of the global gold standard was, naturally, scandalous for money doctors. But not for those who sought radical new visions for economic policy. In Europe, the collapse of the gold standard placed austerity on the defensive, with loan-financed investments and expansionary credit becoming standard policy.[113] For those who sought alternatives to the cross of gold, its collapse was a moment to democratize economic management—an opportunity denied to the Philippines. Within this global backdrop, the Philippines, an American colony that doggedly tried to maintain parity, was exceptional. That it maintained some semblance of convertibility makes the Philippine case curious and speaks to the US commitment to preserving the gold standard at its seams. For although US media hysterically reported about the credit extended to the Philippines, there was no way the colonial government would have allowed the peso to turn fiat.

Unfortunately, accounts of Filipino profligacy portray the drawing down of the Gold Reserve Fund as uniquely reckless. We saw, for instance, that Wood and Forbes were scandalized at the possibility of the peso becoming a fiat currency, with the pro-Wood media eventually claiming that the peso had become "Bolshevik money." Yet this period's most prominent fiat currency was not Bolshevik but British. And the British only returned to gold convertibility because Benjamin Strong of the Federal Reserve Bank of New York kept interest rates low from 1924 to 1925.

If such a perceived paragon of responsible spending like Britain could spend down its reserves for munitions, why couldn't the Philippines do the same to boost exports? Moreover, was there even a risk of the peso becoming a fiat currency? As we saw in the previous chapter, the Philippine system became the basis for the US government to promote the gold exchange standard. Washington would not have let this system fail. Contrary to the free-market beliefs of its advocates, the prewar gold standard was never a system of automatic regulation. As Eichengreen has famously argued, the gold standard worked through "cooperative management," with the United States and European countries actively defending the reserves of the Bank of England.[114] A colonial gold exchange standard was likewise reliant on this cooperative management. The United States was the guarantor of the system, and no fiat currency would obtain unless the metropole withdrew its backing.

More broadly, the legitimacy of the burgeoning US-led global financial system would not be served if its greatest gold experiment, the Philippines, went into financial ruin. Even the pro-Republican press knew that the PNB crisis was temporary. For example, the *New-York Tribune* condemned the Harrison regime for allowing "Filipino demagogues and adventurers who urge independence for their own selfish purposes" to rise to power. It likewise complained that "the fiscal affairs of the islands have been thrown into chaotic shape, and things have gone backward instead of forward." Yet, buried within its complaints was the concession that, since the bank was a government institution, it was "in no sense in danger."[115]

In private, Forbes was aware of the regulated nature of the gold exchange standard and the ability of a state-regulated banking system to backstop crises. Writing to the secretary of war, he recommended "that the Philippine National Bank be made an integral part of the Federal Reserve system" and "that it serve the same purpose towards the commercial and private banks of the Philippine Islands that the Federal Reserve banks do towards the banks in the United States."[116]

Forbes's recommendation did not make it to the public report, and unlike buried stories of American corruption, it does not hint at anything sordid. But it is a more crucial slippage, as it notes a structural problem that plagued the PNB as a colonial bank. The PNB was not necessarily more profligate during the boom years than mainland banks. From 1920 onward, the Federal Reserve Bank of New York rediscounted to other member banks of the Federal Reserve System, creating a free-rider problem that allowed these banks to loan to favored clients in the manner of Venacio Concepcion.[117] This meant that US banks on the mainland could afford to be profligate without compromising their reserves. It also meant that US banks could more easily ride out a deflationary policy from the Fed.

As a colonial bank, the PNB did not have the same privileges. Fundamentally, however, all US banks—and in this category we must include the PNB—evinced some moral hazard, safe in the knowledge that convertibility had a guarantor in the US government. The banking crisis of 1920-1921 was not proof of the Philippine banking system's exceptional profligacy. Instead, it elucidated what can and cannot fail in colonial capitalism. Banks in the United States, then as today, were too big to fail. The PNB, on the other hand, was small and colonial enough to be denied credit. Maybe it ultimately was not allowed to fail, but US officials let it sputter—to prove a point about the profligate colonial.

The accounts of Wood, Forbes, Kemmerer, Luthringer, and academics that replicate their views portray the PNB crisis as exceptional and, therefore, distinctly Filipino. They are, as such, fundamentally similar explanations of the crisis. Rightfully critical of the corruption narrative of the Wood-Forbes account, Nagano offers the Kemmerer-Luthringer account as an alternative to what she views as imperialist discourse. She neglects, however, that the two accounts are anchored on the same assumptions about the profligate colonial. Like the Republican partisans, the money doctors also blamed the expansion of credit: Wood and Forbes disliked loans because they led to corruption. Kemmerer and Luthringer disliked loans because they led to the violation of the gold standard. Both were defenses of austerity.

The problem with austerity, however, is that its solution to a crisis of economic growth is to reduce economic growth. Put another way, austerity's perverse logic is that a crisis cannot destroy anything if nothing is created to begin with. If the PNB had adhered to the gold standard, the mills and refineries may, indeed, not have struggled during the deflation. But how many of them would have even been built? And in the absence of these industries, how much foreign reserves could the Philippines have built up after the war-torn years of the Philippine Revolution and the Philippine-American War? These are, naturally, counterfactuals that can never be answered. Yet they hint at the dangers of a prophylactic application of austerity.

## "Discipline" Restored

Ensconced in the authoritarian office of the governor-general and having discredited the Filipino and Democratic opposition, Leonard

Wood facilitated a swift reassertion of economic "discipline." Under his regime, there would be no return to the days of developmental spending, despite renewed efforts from politicians like Osmeña and Quezon. Wood bristled at attempts to restart developmental spending, comparing Filipino nationalists to "a boy who had been started in business by his father and had made a complete fiasco of it" yet "without attempting to clear away the wreck and show some signs of organizing power and the wisdom which he had acquired from experience, was demanding, without any explanation, money for another start."[118] One of Wood's first actions as governor-general was to slash the government budget by 28 percent.[119]

To re-secure austerity, Wood presided over the restoration of convertibility. With the Philippines no longer being run by Democrats and their colonial allies, the US Congress authorized a further increase of the debt ceiling to $45 million, allowing the Wood administration to replenish reserves.[120] In late 1922, Wood signed a revision of the currency law, which, according to Luthringer, was drafted to "protect the reserve fund from the foolish exploitation which was chiefly responsible for the collapse of 1919."[121] Under this new law, which was implemented the following year, the Gold Standard Fund was reconstituted, with the requirement that it contain reserves equivalent to 15 percent of currency in circulation. The new GSF, however, would become less important, as there had been a steady growth in the use of treasury certificates instead of coins. From 1922 to 1929, the value of coins was only 2 million pesos, while the value of treasury certificates was 47 million pesos.[122] Amid this increase in treasury certificates, the more important reserve fund became the Treasury Certificate Fund, which required a 100 percent dollar reserve for all currency in circulation, including the coins that the GSF already backed. This regulation was such an extreme overcorrection that by the end of 1932, government reserves amounted to 173 percent of currency in circulation.[123] Luthringer praised the new law as a reconstitution of the sacred standard and a departure from the "foolish" spending of the 1910s. But typical of his style of introducing inconvenient facts twenty or so pages after, he had to concede that "the present Philippine currency reserves are excessive."[124]

This extreme restoration of convertibility was essential to austerity's rise. It was evident in Europe. But it was also pronounced in Southeast Asia. In the 1920s, the French parliament turned down Governor-General Sarraut's various spending measures in Indochina amid the great deflation, the impending reparations crisis with Germany, and the devaluation of the franc. And in the Depression years, the legislature gutted the Ministry of Colonies' development budget.[125] A more striking parallel to the Philippines was the Dutch East Indies, where the new conservative Governor-General Dirk Fock took over in 1921. Fock became governor-general the same year as Wood, and historian Ruth McVey's description of the former's term is equally applicable to the latter: Taking office "at the onset of an international recession, which severely hurt the colony's export economy," Fock "introduced a series of draconian financial measures, cutting public expenditures to the bone."[126] If developmental spending in the Dutch East Indies had been done at the prodding of native Indonesians and not Dutch advocates of "ethical" colonialism, one could imagine Fock blaming corrupt nationalists as well.

The difference between the Philippines and its neighbors was that natives had implemented developmental colonialism. Therefore, this developmentalism's repudiation in the Philippines was racialized. The crisis challenged Sarraut's colonial republicanism in Indochina, and in the Dutch East Indies it challenged the Ethical Policy. In the Philippines, the crisis was certainly a challenge to Wilsonian "Filipinization." But it was, more fundamentally, a challenge to the notion that the colonized could spend.

## "Lessons" Learned

The Wood–Forbes report was categorical about its disdain for fiat currency. And if the report was not clear enough about this point, Edwin Kemmerer and his student George Luthringer certainly reinforced it when they blamed the crisis on the colony's incapacity to implement the gold exchange standard—a system Kemmerer had designed and promoted. What was necessary to protect this system? Austerity, naturally.

In Forbes's notes, he ties the insolvency of the bank and the Gold Standard Fund to the government going "extensively into business, which ought to be private," blaming the colonial state for investing in industries like coal and cordage and for investing in the railroad.[127] A few Filipinos, like University of the Philippines professor Maximo Kalaw, argued that this system was "socialistic" and beneficial for national development. However, for Forbes, this socialism was precisely the system's weakness. "Professor Kalaw," he argued, "is evidently an apologist rather than a critic."[128]

Leonard Wood made a similar point. At the height of his fanning the flames of hysteria about the bank, he noted that its losses were "the price the government has had to pay" for its "entering the field of business."[129] As governor-general, Wood attempted to impose his vision of private/public dichotomy by proposing to privatize major government-controlled corporations like the PNB and the Manila railroad company—attempts that Quezon and his allies successfully stymied through political cunning (deploying techniques such as mass resignation from the cabinet).[130] Despite successfully preventing large-scale privatization, Quezon's defense of existing government corporations showed that developmentalism was on the defensive.

Views about the nature of government banks have been replicated in contemporary historiography, as with many ideas from the Wood-Forbes report. Historian Peter W. Stanley decries how "Filipino political leaders" used the PNB "less as a bank than as a political and developmental tool of the government and the majority party."[131] Implicit in Forbes's, Wood's, and Stanley's accounts is a distinction between a "proper" bank that does not play a role in development (abetting crony capitalism in the process) and one that does. Yet when have national banks—from Hamilton's First National Bank to the present Federal Reserve—not been involved in propping up businesses or bailing them out? There was nothing atypical about PNB policy in the Philippines. It is easy to play a game of spot the theft. But what about questions of broader economic trends, priorities, and trade-offs?

True enough, developmental projects court corruption. But to what extent should acts of corruption prevent the state from taking an active role in economic development? And is it possible to view corruption as something that can be overcome by development and not a hindrance to it? Chang argues that the institutions of good governance that commentators from the Global North insist are prerequisites for development "were actually in large part the outcome, rather than the cause, of economic development in the now-developed countries."[132] He notes that the United States was a hotbed of cronyism and corruption after the Civil War, and it was not until the twentieth century that it professionalized its bureaucracy.[133] This slow professionalization occurred partly because, before achieving a certain level of economic growth, it was costly to invest in a professional bureaucracy.[134] The discourse surrounding the PNB crisis delegitimized an incipient industrial policy. It made state intervention in the economy synonymous with bad governance, thus precluding a model of development that countries like the United States had used to make themselves wealthy enough to clean up their systems.

The PNB crisis was undoubtedly a real economic crisis; credit contracted, firms were in arrears, and the bank required foreclosures to recoup losses. And we cannot deny that elite politicians like Concepcion used the levers of state power to extend corrupt loans to other segments of the elite. Yet it was not, as Nagano contends, "the most scandalous and sensational fiscal issue the Philippine government experienced under colonial rule."[135] As the economic historian Frank Hindman Golay—in one of the few sober academic accounts of the episode—explains, the changes in the reserve currency structure "occurred through transactions that were normal in the lending operations of the bank," and the 1920–1921 crisis was "short-lived," as the insular treasury quickly shored up its dollar accounts.[136]

It is disingenuous to portray the PNB crisis as a major domestic crisis, let alone the collapse of a single, corrupt bank. Such a version of events replicates American exceptionalism in its colony. In the early 1920s, the Philippines was already sufficiently tied to the economy of the mainland, and it was subject to the boom-bust cycles of the mainland's economy, not to mention the world. The PNB crisis was not a unique, isolated crisis triggered by the corrupt practices of backward politicos, and it was not triggered by gross violations of the gold standard; it was a product of a deflationary spiral—induced mainly by the metropole—that affected the colony and the rest of the world. The PNB, like any other US bank at the time, suffered. However, unlike other US banks, it could not be bailed out as easily. Put another way, after the war, the Fed engaged in an explicitly deflationary policy (monetary austerity in the metropole), and an American colonial bank went into crisis because of it, but it did not receive any support.

This would not be the first time in Philippine economic history that a broader economic crisis would be read exclusively in local terms. As we shall see in chapter 4, the 1980 global debt crisis was eventually interpreted as a local political crisis—a result, once more, of crony capitalism and the collapse of political order. Missing from both the accounts of the 1920s and 1980s is a linking of local events to international contractions.

Stripped of the global context, the PNB crisis became a morality tale, wrought as a warning for profligate colonials and those who abetted them. The lessons of this tale were threefold. First, profligate colonials could not be trusted to manage their finances, since this would lead to "socialistic" violations of the free market. Developmental policy would not be countenanced, especially if implemented by Filipinos. Second, Filipino profligate tendencies went hand in hand with the corruption of politicos. Hence, a managed economy in the hands of Filipinos was inherently corrupt. Third, an austere monetary policy regulated by gold would prevent developmental spending and the attendant corruption.

These lessons continued to shape economic policy even during Philippine independence. In the second half of this book, we examine how these lessons were nationalized during the postcolonial era.

# Interlude
## From Poor Little Rich Country to Model Postcolony

We now close the section of this book that covers the period of formal imperialism. However, the story of American imperialism and austerity does not end after the recognition of Philippine independence on July 4, 1946. Readers who picked up this book to learn more about US history and care less for the independent history of the Philippines should keep reading. After all, imperialism is most sophisticated when formally absent but discursively present.[1]

In the 1930s and 1940s, the Philippines, like most of the world, experienced a depression and a World War. It then had to build itself up from the rubble. Such rending events change the way people think about the world. Filipino policymakers were no exception; they, too, thought differently. But in a surprising way. The unique impact of the Depression on the Philippines obscured the constraints of dear money. More importantly, the profligacy of a vilified Japanese army that printed its way to inflationary oblivion hardened already hardening attitudes around hard money.

When the Philippines emerged as an independent nation after the war, it was ready to out-austere its colonial master. From the 1930s onward, Filipinos began to advocate for even harder money and more financial restraint than American policymakers. They would prove to be American austerity's most loyal and dedicated students. Many anticolonial and postcolonial nation-builders have sought to use the proverbial "master's tools" to dismantle his house. Postwar Filipinos believed they could master the master's tools more than the master and, in doing so, build a more robust house.

Oddly, the rhetoric of the Philippine state mirrored that of many Filipino immigrants to the United States, who wished to position themselves as a model minority.[2] In the same way that Filipinos in the US refused to become burdens to the state like more profligate minorities, the Philippine state refused to be a burden to the IMF and the World Bank, unlike more profligate postcolonies. In this way, postwar Philippines emerged as a model postcolony.

The following chapters discuss the economics of the postcolony. In the postcolony, there is formal sovereignty, but the question of what to do with that sovereignty is vexed. This sovereignty is also constrained. Sometimes, constraints are formal restrictions, as in the case of unfair treaties. Other constraints relate to the imagination, for the discourse of austerity would limit what policies Filipino economists and politicians could conceive of. Although neocolonial foreign policy continued to impose austere policy after 1946, our primary concern in these chapters is how Filipinos embraced austerity. In the 1940s and 1950s, it would be embraced by elite politicians. And in the 1970s and 1980s, even the left would champion some of its tenets.

After the great deflation of the 1920s, hard money would prove unassailable. Recall that after the crisis, the Wood administration created an even more restrictive currency system than the original gold exchange standard. While the Great Depression of the 1930s could have been an opportunity to rethink hard money, its effects were too mild to cause a reassessment.

The Depression, while destructive for the mainland, did little to alter the trajectory of economic growth in the Philippines. Literature on the 1930s rarely discusses the Depression as contributing to changes in production, employment, and the development of new industries.[3] While widespread unemployment and underemployment existed, these trends started in the 1920s during the great deflation. Although the country's major trading partner was the United States, the decline in American consumption did not significantly harm Philippines exports. Growth and export rates slumped from 1929 to 1931, but the downturn was not as pronounced as in the early 1920s, leading government officials to conclude that things could have been much worse. The decline was far from what the colony experienced in the great deflation of the early

1920s and mild compared to what the Philippines' neighbors experienced. For example, from 1931 to 1936, exports were only down 24 percent of their annual average value in 1926–1928, compared with Java, whose exports declined by 72 percent.[4]

Two reasons explain the buoyancy of exports. First, there was an increase in gold production. Second, and more importantly, sugar mills increased their production in anticipation of the US imposing a quota on duty-free imports from the Philippines.[5] Because Philippine exports remained robust, there was no balance-of-payments crisis during the 1930s. The government's tax reserves exceeded the legal minimum[6]—despite the stringency of the monetary system that Wood imposed after the great deflation. Thus, Philippine officials could finally brag about their currency's strength. During the great deflation, officials like Wood and Forbes and economists like Kemmerer and Luthringer looked down on Filipinos for the weakness of their currency system. During the Depression, Filipinos would trumpet a currency system that was "stronger" than that of the US.

In 1934, the United States devalued the dollar against gold in response to the economic downturn. Officials initially considered this shift good for the Philippines, since it held gold deposits in the United States. This gold could theoretically be sold to the United States to buy dollars at the newly devalued rate, but the United States refused to pay this "devaluation profit."[7] After it became clear that this profit would be difficult to obtain, Filipino officials began to worry about the inflationary effects of the peso being tied to a weakened dollar. Early proposals for an independent central bank included recommendations for the Philippines to place itself on an independent gold standard, bereft of the "defects" of America's new monetary system.[8] This was the first instance of Filipinos tying the idea of political independence to the concept of hard money. And it was evidence that Filipinos had internalized the imperialist logic of hard money.

Debates about a new currency system, however, would have to wait. In 1935, the Philippines began ten years of transitional administration as a prelude to complete independence after Manuel Quezon successfully negotiated the Tydings–McDuffie Act. With Quezon as its first president, the new Philippine Commonwealth's most urgent economic concern was the negotiation of trade agreements with the United States. A significant motivation for the US to grant independence to the Philippines was the desire of the domestic US agricultural lobby to end the preferential tariff system with the Philippines. Though outwardly confident about the fate of an independent Philippines, Common-wealth officials privately considered delaying independence, fearing the end of preferential trade.[9] The trade negotiations would be fraught and continue until the end of the Second World War.

The war and the Japanese occupation would prove disastrous. Like most of Southeast Asia, the Philippines saw its GDP per capita fall close to what it was in 1870, erasing almost eighty years of growth.[10] Manila's postwar devastation was second only to that in Warsaw, with at least four-fifths of the once-great city destroyed. The country's vaunted transportation system had also been destroyed, and there were almost no operable mines or factories.[11]

The Japanese also undermined monetary stability by introducing a very volatile fiat currency. The Japanese printed domestic currency in the Philippines to finance their war effort. The result was an exsanguination of Philippine riches to Japan and domestic hyperinflation. This dynamic was the case for all Japanese-occupied Southeast Asia, but the situation was slightly worse in the Philippines. From 1942 to 1945, the quantity of currency in the Philippines rose by 9 percent a month, and prices rose by 18 percent a month—a higher increase in money supply and prices than in Burma, Malaya, Thailand, and southern Indochina (there is little equivalent data for the north).[12] Moreover, the Philippines' experience of hyperinflation was more protracted than its neighbors. While most of Southeast Asia went into hyperinflation only in 1945, hyperinflation in the Philippines started as early as 1943.[13] Currency was so devalued under the Japanese that Filipinos called Japanese bills "Mickey Mouse" money. At the height of the hyperinflation, one had to carry small sacks of this money to buy a few quarts of rice.[14] By August 1945, the cost of living was 800 percent higher than before the war.[15] The literature on the hyperinflation of the Japanese occupation of Southeast Asia does not explain why it was slightly worse and more sustained in the Philippines. One reason could be the wide acceptance of Mickey Mouse money in the country, where there were few alternative currencies in circulation, unlike in the Dutch East Indies. Moreover, Philippine exporters, wholly cut off from their traditional markets in the United States, were forced to trade with Japan and use its currency.[16]

The restoration of American administration in 1945 necessitated the restoration of Filipino-American money. And as we saw in the previous chapter, prewar laws effectively stipulated a 100 percent reserve requirement for the Philippines. But regardless of how dire the postwar crisis was, Filipino representatives had faith in the quick return of hard money. For example, in 1943, during the lead-up to the Bretton Woods negotiations, the exiled falangist Philippine minister of finance, Andres Soriano, bragged to US officials that the Philippines would not likely require financial assistance given the peso's strength.[17]

Soriano was optimistic. Emergency disbursements from US taxes were necessary to shore up reserves, and through these, the country reverted to a fully backed currency. As with the period after World War I, this quick return to convertibility was remarkable since few other countries prioritized strong currencies after the war. This strange situation—a country with low tax collection and poor use of limited funds but a strong currency—led former UN economist Shirley Jenkins to call the Philippines the "poor little rich country" of Asia.[18]

However, this poor little rich country needed to be rebuilt despite its strong currency. Unlike Europe, however, the Philippines did not benefit from American largesse, and there would be no Marshall Plan for the former colony. Although war damages were estimated at $1.6 billion,[19] US rehabilitation packages only amounted to $390 million, which a survey mission judged sufficient to prompt some reconstruction.[20] To add insult to injury, the US made this rehabilitation contingent on signing the Philippine Trade Act of 1946, popularly known as the Bell Trade Act.[21]

Nationalists have pilloried the Bell Trade Act for its "parity rights" provisions that gave American citizens the right to own land and exploit natural resources in the Philippines. Less discussed, however, is the act's provision that obligated the Philippines to maintain the peso at the colonial-era rate of two pesos to one dollar. Under the agreement, the Philippines could not change the peso's par value without the White House's consent. It was one of the many "obnoxious infringements on Philippine sovereignty" in the treaty.[22] And it was explicitly written to benefit American investors in the Philippines. The act's namesake, US Representative Jasper Bell, inserted this provision to ensure American investors in the Philippines earned more when remitting to the United States.[23] As US Representative Wilbur D. Mills explained, the US implemented fixed parity to ensure that "when capital decides to revert to the United States, it may come to the United States without depreciation."[24]

One benefit of the Bell Trade Act was an eight-year extension of free-trade relations followed by gradual tariff imposition over twenty years. However, this concession was insufficient to jump-start the battered Philippine economy. Trade deficits plagued the country after the implementation of the Bell Trade Act, placing pressure on foreign reserves. The need for rehabilitation ensured high consumer demand, but because there was not enough domestic production, local products could not satisfy that demand. As a result, importation rose—a trend further enabled by the expensive currency, which made this importation cheap. The situation did not bode well for the economy, which had slowed down to a point where unemployment was at 15 percent.[25] Still, it was a "bonanza" for importers in the Philippines, 90 percent of whom were American. The import bonanza led to a balance-of-payments crisis. In 1949 alone, reserves dropped from an already low $260 million to $185 million.[26]

Trade deficits would be the defining feature of the economy in the immediate postwar period, becoming an urgent problem that most policymakers sought to address. The easy solution would have been the repudiation of dear money. But this action was impossible, initially for legal reasons. Then it would be impossible for ideological ones.

The economic priorities of the postcolonial Philippines would not be so different from those of colonial Philippines.

# CHAPTER 3

# Austerity Nationalized

*The Politics of "Independent" Central Banking in Independent Philippines, 1949–1960*

On January 17, 1958, the Philippines celebrated its first national "Austerity Day." Under the Department of Education, schools across the country promoted thrift and industry through the practical arts, food production campaigns, and other "vocational" activities. The day was part of newly elected President Carlos P. Garcia's austerity campaign, which had two related goals. On the one hand, Garcia encouraged Filipinos to tighten their belts. On the other, he urged them to "achieve maximum production" by "flexing the muscles." His policies would "boil down to a new way of life for all of us—a life of frugality, self-discipline, and industry."[1] The president wanted Filipinos to earn more, spend less, and save more. But he also wanted them to toil more.

Garcia's campaign vindicated the policy direction advocated by the Central Bank of the Philippines, established in 1949. Specifically, it vindicated the bank's governor, Miguel Cuaderno Sr., who had led the institution since its inception. For nearly a decade, Cuaderno had advocated maintaining the dollar-to-peso rate at 2 to 1 and restricting spending. An article from the *Philippines Free Press* best summarized his reputation: "When the president got funny ideas on how to spend government money extravagantly for political purposes, Cuaderno put his foot down. When the politicians . . . bloated the national budget, Cuaderno . . . wielded the axe and cut the budget down to size. The Central Bank in Cuaderno's time imposed monetary and fiscal discipline on the government."[2] The head of the central bank was the adult in the room who communicated the "hard truths" about the country's finances.

Cuaderno, too, would deliver a public speech on Austerity Day. And like other monetary hawks, he justified austerity as a form of inflation fighting. In a speech before university students in Manila, he displayed a theological zeal when he declared that inflation was "an economic evil" that "not only retards economic progress but also multiplies its basic problems."[3] "In adopting austerity as an instrument of economic policy," he continued, "the Government wants to avoid a spiraling of inflation which will work more hardships to the people than what they will have to bear under austerity, and which will likely defeat the very aims of our developmental efforts." "Austerity," he concluded, "is too small a price to pay to achieve these objectives."[4]

Officials like Garcia and Cuaderno were not profligate colonials. Unlike the Nacionalistas and the PNB officials of the 1920s, no one could accuse them of playing loose with monetary and fiscal policy. If the newly independent nation-state sought respectability, and the name of the economic respectability game was austerity, the Philippines passed the test. No longer could Filipino politicians be accused of financial recklessness. Under Cuaderno, the country had an "independent" central bank that, in restraining the spending of its state and people, symbolized state strength. Until today, the seminal textbook in Philippine history looks back at Cuaderno's central bank as an "island of state strength" amid a morass of corruption and rent-seeking.[5] Like Leonard Wood or W. Cameron Forbes, Cuaderno deployed austerity to supposedly rein in the corrupt tendencies of the Philippines oligarchy. Cuaderno symbolizes the good-governance discourse discussed in the previous chapter.

Cuaderno was the first Filipino to promote what Adam Tooze calls the "central bank myth," where the central bank as a "countermajoritarian institution" stands in the way of government spending, thereby assuring investors that their desire for low inflation will be prioritized over increasing employment or providing social services.[6] Like other advocates of austerity, Cuaderno pushed for, per Mattei, a "depoliticization of the economic" through the unchecked governance of a technocracy.[7] Adhering to this central bank myth reassured investors and garnered international respectability.

But Cuaderno's central bank myth was distinct from that promoted by his developed-world counterparts because he voiced it amid processes of decolonization. His skill lay in combining this politics of respectability with the language of nationalism. For the first half of the twentieth century, austerity was the economic language of imperialism. But by the 1950s, bureaucrats were reconciling it with nationalist state-building. With the developmentalism of an earlier generation of politicians delegitimized through accusations of corruption and the recent trauma of Japanese profligacy during the war, the postwar Filipino statesman would style himself as a symbol of financial rectitude.

Austerity became a show of national pride, proving that the new nation-state could stand on its two feet and earn the world's respect. As the decade progressed, austerity even took on a pro–Third World sheen because, according to Cuaderno, poor countries could not afford expansive social programs. By the 1970s, advocates of austerity would style themselves as anticolonial, with defenders of a strong currency claiming (mistakenly) to be opponents of imperialism. The shift from austerity being the economic rhetoric of colonialism to a symbol of nationalist pride is one of Philippine history's most remarkable yet understudied volte-faces. That this shift has gone unnoticed again underscores austerity's history of hiding in plain sight.

This chapter narrates how Philippine austerity was reconciled with Filipino nationalism. It focuses on the career of the central bank's Cuaderno, who should be considered the father of Filipino austerity. It looks at how he weaponized the nation's fear of inflation to maintain the neo-imperial imposition of hard money while reining in spending and bolstering his image as a disinterested bureaucrat and ardent nationalist. In this way, Cuaderno brought the logic of hard money from the colonial period into the period of independence and state-building.

## A Central Banker Emerges

In 1969, a major volume on Southeast Asian economic nationalism noted that Miguel Cuaderno "exercised greater influence over postwar economic policy than did any other person."[8] More than the towering figure of monetary policy, however, Cuaderno served as a bridge between the economic ideas of the American period and the postwar state.

After graduating from law school and placing second in the bar, Cuaderno worked as a secretary to the pro-Filipino Governor-General Francis Burton Harrison. He then left the Philippines briefly to audit courses in economics and banking at the London School of Economics (still, as with most Filipino economic thinkers of his time, Cuaderno was largely self-taught). In the early 1930s, he worked in various capacities at the Philippine National Bank (PNB), where he served as its acting president at one point. After twenty years, he left government service and became the first president of a private Philippine Bank of Commerce in 1939. Upon the conclusion of the war and the complete transition to independence, he returned to government work, serving as secretary of finance from 1946 until 1949. He spent the rest of his career as central bank governor from 1949 until his retirement in 1960.[9]

As someone who worked with Harrison and the PNB, Cuaderno had a front-row seat to the rise and decline of colonial developmentalism discussed in the previous chapter. We do not know how the events of this period shaped him, but his career was a departure from the policies of this earlier era. No one could accuse Cuaderno of being a spendthrift like Osmeña, Harrison, or a predecessor at the PNB, Venacio Concepcion.

At least not with public spending. In terms of personal consumption, however, Cuaderno was indebted to Harrison's mentorship. According to his son-in-law and personal secretary, Cuaderno developed a lifelong taste for luxury because of the American governor-general's influence. In his time at the central bank, Cuaderno always flew first class, stayed in the best hotels, and eschewed buses in favor of chauffeured cars. He dined in New York's most expensive restaurants, had suits regularly made by tailors on Saville Row (Brooks Brothers for when, presumably, he was being austere), bought his shirts and ties from Sulka's Paris store (haberdashery to royalty), smoked Turkish cigars, and changed his sports car every two years.[10] In public, Cuaderno believed that "investment for production" needed to take "precedence over pure consumption," often rehearsing austerity's adage to produce more and consume less.[11] It was not an injunction that applied to himself.

As an economic thinker, Cuaderno was aware of the interweaving implications of austere policy. He had been obsessed with a strong peso since the 1930s,[12] and it was through the lens of "monetary stability" and the risks of inflation that he saw all issues. If his critics argued that the peso needed to be devalued, he would retort that a weaker peso would make imports more expensive and lead to inflation. If his critics argued that the government needed to spend more money or lower interest rates, he would reply that these policies would increase demand, which could lead to more inflation. It could also lead to more importation, reducing foreign reserves and making it more difficult to maintain the currency peg. These ideas were consistent throughout Cuaderno's career, and he would implement them from day one at the bank.

## Continuity Through Controls

In June 1948, President Elpidio Quirino signed the Central Bank Act into law. In January of the following year, the bank was formally inaugurated, with Cuaderno as its first governor. The bank's immediate goal was to address the postwar exchange crisis described in the interlude.

On paper, the new body had tools to address the crisis. Under the new act, the Philippines was no longer required to have 100 percent foreign reserve backing for all its circulating currency. Cuaderno could, therefore, boast that "the abandonment of the exchange standard in favor of a managed currency system" reflected "the burning desire, long maturing in our people and leaders, to manage our destiny."[13] But abandoning one of the world's most restrictive currency regimes—one that was stricter than the original gold exchange standard (recall that even the pro-gold George Luthringer called the system excessive)—was a low bar for monetary independence.

Because the Bell Trade Act mandated that the Philippines maintain the ratio of two pesos to one dollar, the central bank had to use its reserves to stabilize the currency. If the price of the peso decreased because its supply increased, the bank would have to sell its dollars in the open market to arrest depreciation. This arrangement, like the colonial gold exchange standard, limited fiscal expansion, since increasing government spending would have necessitated expanding the supply of pesos in the market, weakening the currency in the process. Increased government spending could have also led to an increased demand for imports (more money circulating meant more money could be used to buy imported goods), which would have strained foreign reserves, since imported goods require payment in reserve currencies. This system was less restrictive than the 100 percent reserve requirement, but not by much.

A recent history of Cuaderno's central bank argues that this period signaled a "departure from the colonial economy."[14] Yet the renewal of dear money policy—the maintenance of the same rate imposed by colonialism—was a sign of continuity. This was evident to commentators from the time, with Shirley Jenkins remarking that postwar monetary policy "did not differ in any substantial way from that existing when the Philippines was under American sovereignty." Jenkins knew this situation was a product of colonialism, adding, "As a result of its former ties with the United States, the Philippine Republic had a 'hard' currency, one of the few in the postwar world."[15] The central bank's policies did not depart from colonial patterns. Instead, the new bank served as a postcolonial legitimization of the economic priorities of the American colonial period—another way to mask the neocolonial nature of the Philippine economy in nationalist garb.

Within this context, the Philippine government had to address the dwindling of foreign reserves. One way to do this was to depreciate the peso, making imports more expensive, lessen the need to use foreign reserves to stabilize the currency, and create export incentives. Such a move, however, required the US president's approval and was still opposed by Representative Bell.[16] More importantly, Cuaderno would not countenance such a measure.

Instead of dispensing with dear money, Cuaderno designed a system of exchange controls under which the central bank would limit importation by limiting access to dollars. Under the plan, the central bank restricted the foreign exchange (dollars) allocated to businesses. This system was primarily Cuaderno's brainchild, but it was a policy recommendation already made in 1947 by a joint Philippine-American commission headed by Thomas Hibben of the US Department of Commerce.[17]

An Import Control Commission, under the executive branch, initially determined which businesses received dollars, labeling imports essential or nonessential based on reconstruction and developmental criteria. However, these powers passed to the central bank in 1953 because of perceived corruption in the commission.[18] While this administrative change reduced the executive's power over the granting of import licenses, it did not prevent coordination between the central bank and the president, since most of the bank's monetary board still consisted of presidential appointees.

Because this strategy of exchange controls entailed active intervention in the economy and was ostensibly geared toward industrialization, the nationalist left has romanticized these controls as part of a halcyon era of economic nationalism.[19] Scholarship that focuses on the corruption of the banking system, however, has noted that these controls opened opportunities for rent-seeking, creating a new avenue for the state to dispense "booty" to allies.[20] This observation, as we shall see, is no doubt accurate. But what has yet to be remarked upon is how Cuaderno used these controls to forestall any fundamental reform to the restrictive, colonial-era monetary system. Indeed, Cuaderno conceived of exchange controls as a system to prevent currency depreciation. In this regard, he had help from an old friend of Filipino monetary conservatism.

To review and approve Cuaderno's policies, the IMF sent a mission headed by George F. Luthringer, who, decades before, had written a dissertation defending the gold exchange standard in the Philippines under the supervision of Edwin Kemmerer (see previous chapter). According to Cuaderno, Luthringer advised against devaluation and endorsed exchange controls as an alternative. These measures were then supported by the US treasury secretary John Snyder and finally approved by President Harry Truman.[21] This solution would again be endorsed by a US economic survey mission the following year that included American and IMF economists.[22] The vaunted controls of nationalist lore were, thus, instituted amid the full support of the IMF and the US government.

Because of these arcane policy moves, the new decade would begin with a commitment to two forms of "control." The first control was the dollar peg, which kept the peso expensive. The second was the limiting of dollar allocations. Cuaderno often spoke of these "controls" in the same breadth, viewing them as a package. However, we should note that both controls encouraged different outcomes. The first form of control, by keeping the peso expensive, encouraged importation from the US. The second form of control, by ensuring that only a few importers had access to dollars, limited importation. Rather than a package, it is better to think of the second form of control as a bandage for the bleeding caused by the first form of control.

## A Rivalry Is Born

As the central figure in the creation of the postwar economic system, few figures were more revered than Cuaderno. And since his policies received the support of the IMF and the US, it was easy for powerful politicians to endorse his views. Throughout the 1950s, however, one figure emerged as Cuaderno's main rival. Salvador Araneta was an industrialist and lawyer from one of the Philippines' oldest elite families. A Jesuit-educated advocate of Christian Democracy with immense noblesse oblige, he was attracted to the ideas of John Maynard Keynes and the fiscal expansiveness of Franklin Delano Roosevelt's New Deal. With deep ties to the exporting sugar-planting elite, he had also grown to disdain the expensive peso.[23]

Unfortunately, Araneta's wealth has led critics of elite democracy in the Philippines to dismiss him as a mere representative of a rent-seeking class without examining his ideas or policy positions.[24] It was a problem that Araneta had to deal with even then. Frank Golay explains that it was easy to sympathize with Cuaderno since his opponents were wealthy, and their "luxurious consumption habits" had "been paraded before the Philippines in the columns of newspapers for many years." The economist Emmanuel de Dios also notes that because Cuaderno's critics consisted of the planter elite, debates in the 1950s were hamstrung by "a dilemma in political correctness that hardly encouraged the objective assessment of the soundness of policy."[25]

For Cuaderno's term as governor, he and Araneta engaged in what the media called a "Great Debate" of economic policy.[26] Against Cuaderno's austere policies, Araneta pushed for bold spending, peso depreciation, and full employment.[27] In this debate, Cuaderno's camp was known in government circles and the media as the "hard manly school"—tying austerity once again to masculine virility—while Araneta and company were known as the "Keynesians" or the "freewheelers."[28]

The Great Debate began during the administration of Elpidio Quirino (president from 1948 to 1953) when Araneta first spoke against the central bank's deflationary policy and called for a "New Deal for the Philippines."[29] With Araneta having been appointed Quirino's secretary of economic coordination in 1950, there was some optimism in the media that he could "put money to work." But Araneta's querulous and independent streak led to his resignation after one year.[30]

In any case, Quirino himself was an economic conservative who was more ideologically inclined to support Cuaderno. Hence Cuaderno mostly had his way from 1950 to 1953. As Araneta noted, during the Quirino administration, very few "dared to question the wisdom of the monetary, gold, and foreign exchange policies of the Central Bank," and "the dictums enunciated by Governor Cuaderno of the Central Bank were accepted with reverence, almost acts of faith."[31] Similarly, Cuaderno recalled, "It was not difficult for the Monetary Board and me to act as we thought best, because Quirino recognized the importance of a central bank that was as free from extraneous interference as possible."[32] Things would change, however, with the election of the Philippines's first populist president.

### The Technocrat and the Populist

Elpidio Quirino was not reelected in 1953. The president had been accused of electoral fraud and violence against the opposition, leading commentators to warn of a potential dictatorship.[33] For his entire presidency, the media also buzzed with corruption allegations, from the blackmailing of Chinese refugees to the corrupt disposal of wartime surplus. More important for our purposes, the president's allies were accused of profiting from dollar allocations under the central bank's controls.[34] The Senate's finance committee investigation showed that the Import Control Commission had granted multiple million peso licenses to unknown businessmen and insignificant corporations, including one implicated in an immigration quota scandal. The head of the commission refused to testify in Congress, claiming President Quirino had barred him from appearing.[35]

Those who received dollars under the control system were doubly lucky, since they bought dollars at an effectively discounted rate. If a business were allocated dollars, that business could buy a dollar at the official rate of two pesos. However, because the demand for dollars was high, this same business could sell these dollars on the black market for as much as 2.8 pesos and profit.[36] The two types of controls—the limited dollar allocation and the currency peg—therefore worked together to create a profiteering opportunity for government allies.

Quirino lost the election to his former defense secretary, Ramon Magsaysay, who styled himself as a man of the people and claimed to come from humble origins (he was middle class). With the help of the US Central Intelligence Agency, the Catholic Church, and the educated upper class, Magsaysay won with 70 percent of the vote.[37] Magsaysay was a different president from Quirino; he was a charismatic leader who was impatient with bureaucrats and directly appealed to the people. His populist instincts also made him eager to accelerate the pace of development.

Unsurprisingly, Cuaderno would find such a figure frustrating. In his view, Magsaysay had a "propensity to act on the spur of the moment" and, toward the end of his term, became increasingly "irritable" because of the many demands on his time and attention.[38] Worse for Cuaderno, Magsaysay allowed advocates of "easy money" into his administration. The governor was particularly frustrated that Magsaysay appointed Araneta to serve as secretary of agriculture and natural resources—a sign that "Dr. Araneta and a few of those who shared his ideas influenced a few of President Magsaysay's decisions on economic matters."[39]

Magsaysay, who approached economic issues with common sense, vacillated between the freewheelers and the manly camp. On the one hand, he saw himself as a man of action and was fascinated by the Araneta group's ideas about active economic intervention. The president was also sympathetic to Araneta's criticism of the Quirino administration as passive. This sentiment was pronounced early in his term when he tried to distinguish himself from his predecessor.[40] On the other hand, his concern for the common *tao* (person) made him sensitive to inflation fearmongering. Even if previous years had been deflationary, any price increase was, from the perspective of Magsaysay's common sense, harmful to the average Filipino. These concerns became more urgent as he approached the election year of 1957.

Magsaysay's indecision did not please anyone. Though he was consistently popular and almost guaranteed reelection, critics accused him of not having a coherent economic plan. And both Araneta and Cuaderno complained when the other got his way. The situation was, however, more frustrating for Cuaderno, who was used to Quirino's unconditional support.

The relationship between the presidential palace and the central bank was tense. Cuaderno acknowledged that Magsaysay's desire to boost spending came from "a sincere feeling for the masses."[41] But he was alarmed by how quickly Magsaysay's social policies increased the money supply, which grew by 42 percent from December 1954 to December 1958.[42] He was more frustrated when, in 1955, the executive earmarked two billion pesos over four years "to accelerate the pace of economic development."[43] During the Magsaysay years (1954 to 1957), the money supply increased by an average of 9.2 percent yearly.[44]

Cuaderno's exasperation with the growing money supply reflected his broader frustrations with democratic demands for development. "The difficulties of programming in the Philippines, as in many underdeveloped countries," he wrote in 1960 as he recalled his time under Magsaysay, "are compounded by constant pressures brought to bear upon the monetary and political authorities to speed up the pace of development."[45] These pressures, of course, were democratic ones that clashed with Cuaderno's view of the economic technocrat's power. He had made a more explicit version of this antidemocratic argument in a speech to the IMF in 1950 when he noted that "in determining the objects of public expenditures and in assigning priorities among competing objects, the politics of a democracy is often preponderantly guided by short-run objectives rather than long run benefits."[46]

Against Cuaderno's technocratic authoritarianism, Magsaysay was imposing his democratic mandate on the central bank. And he did so through a personalistic style that irked Cuaderno even more. On at least two occasions, Cuaderno was subject to Magsaysay's infamous temper, with the president publicly berating the governor over minor policy disagreements (like the rules over the importation of soft drinks), occasions that led Cuaderno, who was used to more deferential treatment, to walk out of the presidential palace.[47]

Magsaysay was also known to visit the central bank premises, violating the sovereignty of what was increasingly known as the "Republic of Aduana" (the central bank was located on Aduana Street in downtown Manila). Because of pressures to investigate irregularities in the distribution of import licenses, the president went to Aduana twice to pressure the monetary board to make improvements.[48] For Cuaderno and other believers in the central bank myth, this behavior violated the central bank's independence; democratically elected politicians should not interfere in the undemocratic sphere of economic expertise. Cuaderno blamed Magsaysay for his "frequent attempts to interfere in the operations of the Central Bank," which made it difficult for its officials "to discharge its responsibilities well."[49] For Cuaderno, the executive had no right to criticize the bank; it just had to support it, noting that the bank should "receive the unrestrained backing of the President of the Philippines in the event of a controversy on monetary measures between the Administration and the Central Bank." Such backing, he added, was most important "during periods when the Central Bank deems it necessary to pursue policies of monetary restraint."[50]

Cuaderno took pride in repudiating the president. Yet he could be selective in this repudiation. For example, in 1957, Magsaysay sought to help a political ally, former representative Jose Cojuangco, purchase over six thousand hectares of the sugar plantation Hacienda Luisita from the Tabacalera company—the last major Spanish investor in the Philippines. Since Tabacalera wished to exit the Philippine market, it demanded payment in dollars, forcing Cojuangco to apply for a loan and dollar allocations from the central bank. Using dollar allocations this way was exceptional, as these dollars were earmarked for essential imports. The central bank, however, authorized the dollar allocation and the loan, aiding a Magsaysay ally in the process. In this instance, however, Cojuangco was a Cuaderno ally as well. In the 1940s, Cuaderno was president of the Cojuangco-owned Philippine Bank of Commerce and, as central bank governor, remained a close friend of the powerful businessman.[51]

The Luisita example reflected how Cuaderno treated the executive in practice: The central bank would only insist on its independence when the governor wanted to get his way. However, at other times, the firewall between elected officials and the bank was less rigid. This was particularly true for fiscal policy. Cuaderno insisted that elected politicians should have no say over monetary policy—the traditional turf of the central bank. But, on fiscal issues—the turf of elected politicians—Cuaderno did not believe the central bank could be sidelined. Since the central bank's "primary responsibility" was "monetary stability," he argued for "the closest coordination between the investment policy of the Government, its fiscal policy and monetary policy in general."[52]

The climax of the Great Debate between the freewheelers and the manly camp occurred in the second half of Magsaysay's term, and it centered on fiscal policy. Because Magsaysay had been accused of lacking a coherent economic vision, he sought to "revitalize" the National Economic Council (NEC).[53] Created by President Quezon in 1935, the NEC was supposedly responsible for advising presidents on economic matters and formulating a national economic plan. For most of its history, however, it had provided only piecemeal advice to presidents and failed to write and implement national plans.[54] Magsaysay asked Congress to pass a law that enhanced the powers of the NEC.[55] Under the new law, the NEC chair would serve as the economic arm of the president.[56] To reflect a broad array of opinions and to give it a democratic mandate, the council would be composed of eight government officials: four nominated by the Senate and the House and three members from the private sector.[57]

On paper, the revitalized NEC had vast powers: It could draft the government's overall economic plan, review all programs related to economic development, assess ways to finance public projects, inventory government resources, establish goals for public and private investments, define criteria for tax exemptions, and coordinate the statistical activities of the government. Its most significant power, however, lay in its mandate to determine fiscal policy priorities and prescribe allocations of foreign reserves that, with the president's approval, would be binding on the central bank.[58] Not only could this body of democratically elected officials and their appointees limit the central bank's power, but it was also beginning to promote a vision distinct from Cuaderno's (though he sat as one of the council's ex officio members). Through the NEC, Araneta and his allies would promote their ideas about credit.

One gets a sense of the NEC's vision in a policy framework published in January 1956, when Araneta's group had already gained dominance over the council. It stated that fiscal policy was a way of "stimulating the level of, and the pace of growth in production, income, and employment," and noted "the Philippine budget has been in near balance" and that "the long-run price trend has been downward." Meanwhile, it complained that production had "not been adequate to absorb even the annual addition to our labor force, much less to raise the income of those already employed."[59] As we shall see, these observations were mostly correct.

Cuaderno disdained the NEC, bristling at what he saw as executive encroachment on dollar allocation. And he was also wary of the Magsaysay government potentially excluding him from fiscal policy. That Cuaderno would insist on being a critical voice in fiscal policy was surprising for a central banker. Then, as now, central banks often determined monetary policy, while fiscal policy was handled by Congress and the president—in other words, by elected officials. Cuaderno knew and understood this delineation, but he believed that such a neat division of labor was ill-advised in developing countries, where democratic pressures for development were more pronounced.

When Cuaderno spoke abroad about the differences between central banking in the developed and the developing world, he emphasized that monetary authorities in the developing world required more power than their developed-world counterparts to arrest inflation. In a speech to the IMF in September 1955, amid rising tensions with the NEC at home, he complained that authorities in the developing world were often "under pressure from all sides to accede to economic gadgeteering."[60] He reminded developed-world economists that, in the developing world, one could not "rely solely on such measures as manipulating the bank rate or engaging in open market operations to counter undesirable economic trends." Such "classical methods" were not enough.[61] Abroad, Cuaderno was vague about what other methods developing-world central bankers needed to resort to, but his actions back home were unambiguous.

By the time the NEC published its new vision, Cuaderno was already reasserting his influence on the Magsaysay government and had started to undermine the NEC. The previous year, Cuaderno lobbied Magsaysay to "appoint a top-level fiscal committee," called the Fiscal Policy Council (FPC), to set a ceiling on government borrowing.[62] Cuaderno conceded that the proposed FPC effectively duplicated the tasks of the NEC, saying that "the functions of the Fiscal Policy Council could very well be performed by the National Economic Council." The NEC, however, was prone to policy recommendations that were "highly inflationary in nature" and ignored Cuaderno's proposals to place limits on issuing bonds.[63] Despite being an ex officio member of the NEC, Cuaderno was often a minority voice in the body, and he could not do much but dissent during meetings.[64]

Magsaysay initially rejected Cuaderno's proposal for an FPC.[65] But the tide slowly turned in the governor's favor amid pressures on the president. In 1955, Magsaysay's alleged profligacy was already being ridiculed in the press, which must have irked a president known to be sensitive about his public image. One editorial cartoon, for instance, featured a drawing of then-Secretary Araneta printing money and handing it to the president.[66]

Pressure was building both internally and abroad for Magsaysay to abandon the freewheelers. As early as July 1954, he had created a central bank survey mission, headed by a former Supreme Court justice, to assess the validity of criticisms against the central bank, especially amid alleged favoritism in the allocation of foreign exchange.[67] Cuaderno appeared before the commission, fearing that failure to justify his policies could lead to Congress curbing the central bank's powers.[68] The commission's report had yet to be finalized in early 1956, but Magsaysay was already aware it had sided with Cuaderno. What turned the tide, however, was not this commission but the US. According to Magsaysay's biographer, the president had quietly asked the US State Department to commission a study of Cuaderno's policies. The report endorsed the views of the manly camp and finally convinced Magsaysay to take sides.[69] Once again, the US was the guarantor of Cuaderno's hard money policies.

On February 7, 1956, the president submitted his budget report to Congress. In it, he echoed Cuaderno's talking points, noting that "the most significant feature of the current economic status has been our success in maintaining monetary stability in the face of public borrowings for development and extensions of liberal credit for private enterprise." He then thanked the IMF for supporting the fiscal conservatism of the government and warned of the "potential dangers of over-expansion."[70] Cuaderno had finally won over the president.

Araneta resigned from the NEC shortly after (he would never again occupy a government position), accusing Cuaderno of being subservient "to a clique in official circles in Washington which is being upheld by the president."[71] Meanwhile, Magsaysay's most prominent critic implicitly sided with Araneta and the "freewheelers." Lamenting the growing unemployment, the anti-American senator Claro M. Recto demanded that local currency be used for "internal financing," even conceding that "a mild inflation is sometimes permissible" in pursuit of development goals.[72]

The public criticism hardened Magsaysay's resolve to implement austerity. In private, he contrasted "the wonderful economic theories" of the freewheelers with his "common sense" plan anchored on the wisdom of a sari-sari store (general store).[73] Here was one of austerity's most potent metaphors: the comparison between the state and a household or a small business. The metaphor has always been imprecise; states, unlike households and businesses, can tax, issue bonds with different maturation dates, and must promote the common good. But the metaphor's simplicity continues to appeal.

With the freewheelers out of government, Cuaderno began reasserting his dominance. In February of 1957, Magsaysay signed an executive order finally establishing Cuaderno's Fiscal Policy Council. Unlike the NEC, the FPC would be smaller, consisting only of the secretary of finance, the budget commissioner, the chairman of the NEC, the central bank governor, and the president as chair.[74] This new council immediately reduced the bond sales earmarked for development spending from 264 million pesos to 194 million.[75] More importantly, the central bank was now at the center of fiscal policy. Cuaderno effectively won the Great Debate against Araneta at the close of the Magsaysay presidency. He would become even more victorious in the next administration.

## High Cuadernoism

President Magsaysay died in a plane crash in March 1957 and was replaced by his vice president, Carlos P. Garcia. Garcia was elected to a full term in November of the same year and would become Cuaderno's most dependable patron.

After Garcia's election, the country again faced a crisis of dwindling foreign reserves. According to documents from the US National Security Council, the allocation of dollars to domestic allies went into overdrive during the election year. And because of lax regulation, importers and exporters also evaded exchange controls. The result was an increased circulation of dollars, increasing the demand for imports. In less than a year, foreign exchange reserves dropped from $210 million to $85 million.[76] This crisis resulted from Cuaderno's controls: The system inherently discouraged exporters since the peso was overpriced. And in an election year, the incumbent could weaponize the dollar-allocation scheme to reward friends and punish enemies, all while creating even more demand for imports.

Cuaderno, however, blamed the inflationary pressures created during the Magsaysay administration. For Cuaderno, excess liquidity under Magsaysay raised consumption and prices and ate into foreign reserves by increasing import demands.[77] Having turned the crisis into one of liquidity and inflation—instead of one created by his system's loopholes—Cuaderno could now propose a solution that, once again, avoided tinkering with controls. Rather than decontrol, Cuaderno and Garcia imposed cuts and limited credit.

The president's austerity program would not be mere talk. On the month of the austerity "celebrations," the government slashed the 264 million pesos allocated for social and development to 145 million.[78] In 1959, the central bank also engaged in various "credit restraint measures," such as raising bank reserve requirements; the net result was "to sterilize" 134.7 million pesos that year. That same year, "more powerful" limitations on demand were registered in fiscal policy, with the disbursement of monies from bond sales being slashed from 147 million to 84 million pesos.[79] Most significantly, Cuaderno was emboldened to raise interest rates. Even before Magsaysay, the central bank maintained relatively low rates, with the rediscount rate—the minimum rate the bank set for lending to other banks, which in turn influenced the aggregate rate—hovering at 1.5 to 2 percent.[80] In the first few months of the Garcia administration, however, Cuaderno raised the rate by 2 percentage points, to 4 percent.[81]

Apart from the usual suspects, there was little new opposition to Cuaderno's stabilization plan. The latest critic of Cuaderno's policies may have even enhanced the central bank's reputation. In 1959, administrators of the Philippine National Bank engaged the services of German banker Hjalmar Schacht, who visited the Philippines and concluded that it was not undergoing rampant inflation and could therefore spend more and depreciate its currency.[82] Schacht was then a private banker known for advising developing-world politicians. Earlier in the century, however, he had been Hitler's central banker and economics minister. Against such a figure, Cuaderno could finally style himself as a democrat. In an extemporaneous speech before the Rotary Club, where he referenced a meeting with Schacht, Cuaderno claimed he did not push for devaluation because "I could not be a Hitler. This could not be done in a democracy."[83]

With little credible opposition, Cuaderno repudiated all fiscal and monetary expansiveness. By raising interest rates, Cuaderno's stabilization program was even more radical than what he had done during the Quirino years. Yet it is unclear why the relative expansiveness of Magsaysay needed repudiation. Despite the rapid expansion of the money supply from 1954 to 1957, the wholesale price index only increased by an annual average of 1.6 percent. Moreover, real GNP increased by an average rate of 6.7 percent.[84] What was increasingly apparent when Garcia took office was that more Filipinos needed jobs.

In late 1956, as Cuaderno was reconsolidating his power, there was a widespread belief that unemployment was unacceptably high (as with most of Southeast Asia, there was unreliable unemployment data for the early 1950s), with the government being criticized by the press and the opposition party for its failure to create high-quality jobs. Central bank estimates pegged unemployment at close to 2 million people in a population of roughly 24 million. A prominent businessman estimated that of the 150,000 who became employable in a year, only 25,000 found jobs, and a United Nations expert advising the NEC predicted that one-third of the population could be out of a job in five years.[85]

These figures were likely exaggerated, but they reveal the economic anxieties and pressures of the time. Indeed, these figures were repeated regularly in the editorials and opinion pieces of the *Philippines Free Press*, the weekly paper of record. Reading the newspaper, one gets a sense of the volatile implications of a system that prioritized price stability over the welfare of workers. As a January 1956 editorial noted, "With unemployment outracing industrialization—mostly fake, to gain tax-exemption—the country is fulfilling the classic communist prediction of 'ever-increasing misery' for the masses, requiring the maintenance of a big army to keep the unemployed submissive and all hell from breaking loose."[86] Such quotes hinted that Cuaderno's regime could not be maintained indefinitely without the threat of government repression.

The frustration with economic policy and the economists that designed this policy was captured by Teodoro M. Locsin, perhaps the most widely read journalist of the time, who wrote that "unemployment is the primary problem," and because economists had failed to solve the problem, "they should all be fired" so "the government can start over again."[87]

By the end of 1957, Cuaderno himself had to admit that the country had an unemployment problem, noting that a recent household survey revealed the number of jobless had increased by 7 percent from 1948 to

1957. However, he quickly dismissed the problem by stating that there was "an increase of 31.7 per cent in the number of employed."[88] This was a remarkably callous and inane statement. Naturally, the absolute number of employed would have increased with a growing population and workforce. However, the fact that unemployment increased significantly as a percentage meant that more and more Filipinos were out of jobs.

Cuaderno's critics, like Araneta, believed that one solution to the unemployment problem was incentivizing exports, since more exporters could hire laborers. Another sad reality, evident by the mid-1950s, was that the Philippines was a lagging exporter. The country's export industry was not only weak; it lacked diversity, as it relied primarily on raw, agricultural goods. The immediate postwar period created a worldwide expansion of exports, such that, by 1957, world exports had reached 187 percent of prewar levels. In the Philippines, that growth was just 127 percent. It was a rate inferior to other countries with similar exportable commodities. It was also inferior to countries that, unlike the Philippines, had not overpriced their currencies.[89] Since the labor force was growing, exceeding growth in nonagricultural jobs, there was a need to encourage investments in new export industries to create jobs.[90]

The solution for Araneta and his allies was to depreciate the peso to make exports cheaper and more competitive. But Cuaderno dismissed such a reform, asserting, first, that world demand was too elastic, hence Filipino exports would not necessarily be more competitive. Second, that the production of export commodities, except for sugar, would stay the same. And third, that any Philippine currency depreciation would merely encourage retaliatory depreciations from other countries.[91]

All three arguments were specious. The first argument assumed that elasticity in the world market negated the effects of making exports more competitive. Yet even if, say, world prices dropped, relatively cheaper exports would still be relatively more competitive. The second argument dismissed the long-term impact of incentivizing export industries through cheaper currency. As for the third argument, large-scale retaliatory depreciations were difficult under the Bretton Woods system, where countries were required to obtain consent from the IMF before depreciating their currencies.

What Cuaderno wanted was the status quo—a status quo that ensured continued unemployment. That Cuaderno pushed an expensive

currency, high interest rates, and reduced spending amid an employment crisis shows how his monetary and fiscal austerity directly led to
industrial austerity. His entire tenure at the central bank was part of a
regime of working-class repression, and it fed into various other government efforts to create industrial "peace."

Previous accounts of working-class repression in the 1950s have
rightly focused on agrarian counterinsurgency campaigns amid growing peasant militancy. Yet another remarkable attribute of this period
was how the postcolonial state forestalled the growth of an urban labor
movement amid deteriorating wages and increased unemployment. In
the early 1950s, the government actively canceled union registrations on
charges of engaging in "subversive" activities. The secretary of labor, who
was simultaneously chair of the largest confederation of trade unions,
delisted as many as 391 unions in 1952 alone, including Catholic-led
anticommunist unions.[92] Despite the repression, deflationary trends in
agriculture by the end of the Korean War prompted a series of strikes
demanding higher wages. In 1952, there was a two-thousand-worker
strike in a Negros lumber mill and other acts of labor militancy in the
sugar, lumber, and banking sectors.[93]

A magna carta for labor was enacted in 1953, which limited the
capacity of the labor department to cancel union registration, expanding the number of registered unions and the number of strikes.[94] This
slight uptick in labor activity and organization occurred during the fiscal expansion of the Magsaysay years. But despite legislative victories,
broader economic conditions were not conducive to the growth of a
vibrant labor movement. By the end of the Garcia administration, most
unions were so-called "company unions," allied with employers. This
situation was unsurprising, given the unemployment problems of the
time. In 1960, one of the most respected labor analysts noted that the
inability of labor to maneuver was a function of labor's precarity amid
high unemployment and underemployment.[95] How, indeed, does labor
check the power of capital when jobs are scarce and protesting laborers
are easily retrenched and replaced?

Cuaderno's regime of austerity helped create these conditions. During the high-austerity years of the Garcia administration, unemployment was unchanged, and underemployment increased by 30 percent.[96]
And inequality, already high, continued to grow. Between 1956, the year
Cuaderno reasserted control, and 1961, shortly after he left office, the
disparity between the wealthiest 20 percent of Filipinos relative to the
poorest had worsened by 9 percent.[97]

This industrial austerity, naturally, cannot be blamed on one person, as the presidents of the time were aware of the immense unemployment problem. But Cuaderno's neglect of employment issues and refusal to countenance expansive monetary and fiscal policy precluded solutions. Betraying once again that he was aware of the problem, he noted that "in a country in which there was a pressing demand for more employment and better living conditions," it was difficult to argue against bold financing programs like those presented by Araneta.[98] Despite acknowledging the problem, he refused to provide solutions. As early as the Quirino administration, Araneta was already asking Cuaderno, "How can we solve the problem of unemployment as soon as possible without deficit financing?"[99] He never received an adequate reply.

Cuaderno could not deny that deficit financing had reduced unemployment, especially in the New Deal–era United States. However, he insisted on the inability of the Philippines to absorb demand. As early as 1951, he was arguing that, in the US, there were enough "unused plant facilities" such that the demand created by deficit spending would immediately harness back to production" the "reservoirs of unemployed resources."[100] Such a situation would not be inflationary, as it stimulates immediate production, thereby balancing increased demand with more supply. Nine years later, during the Garcia administration, he would make the same argument to the University of the Philippines Economics Club as part of a broader diatribe against the "naïve belief" that Keynesian spending could hasten economic growth.[101] The argument was incredibly facile, as the New Deal was inflationary. Moreover, the expectation of more inflation helped increase short-term spending (consumers buy more today if they expect goods to be more expensive in the future), further stimulating the economy.[102]

Cuaderno's statements, however, were more than ill-informed rhetoric. It revealed his thinly veiled commitment to industrial repression. Cuaderno talked about labor as one of many "resources" that needed to be "productive" to ensure that production kept pace with demand. The Philippines, he argued, had these "resources," but they could not be productive "without passing through a protracted period of conversion, construction, training and development." However, because of the "degree of immobility of these resources," they could not "add effectively to the total volume of commodities available for consumption during the period of conversion." Hence, utilizing them would merely give them "purchasing power," which would increase demand and "raise domestic prices all the more."[103]

This jargon-laden rhetoric dehumanized workers—reducing them to mere resources—and obfuscated the heartlessness of Cuaderno's views. But these views are easy enough to parse in plain language: Workers do not deserve to become consumers—to purchase their everyday needs—if they do not immediately produce more. Having rendered the employed worker a potentially dangerous source of inflationary demand, Cuaderno believed these people were better off remaining "reservoirs of unemployed resources." This statement was Cuaderno's extreme version of the austere adage to consume less and produce more: If you cannot produce immediately, you had better not consume at all.

The rhetoric of nationalism obscured the severity of Cuaderno and Garcia's austerity. Garcia not only gave Cuaderno administrative support but also rhetorical cover. In 1958, Garcia altered his rhetoric and emphasized economic nationalism instead of austerity. Garcia's nationalist thrust led to legislation prioritizing Filipino citizens in dollar allocations. There was, however, nothing new about this policy. Since implementing his "controls," Cuaderno had already argued that his selective allocation of dollars was geared toward supporting vital domestic players.

Not only was there nothing novel about Garcia's new thrust, but it was also a codification of broader racist efforts to discriminate against Chinese Filipino businessmen, who were routinely denied naturalization despite being born in the Philippines. Bereft of citizenship, they would not receive dollar allocations. This legal impediment against Chinese citizenship was, aptly enough, another policy legacy of Miguel Cuaderno, the primary advocate of abandoning birthright citizenship in the constitutional convention of 1934, of which he was a member. At the time, he raised fears of people "without a drop of Filipino blood" exploiting the country's natural resources, the ominous outsider adopting local citizenship yet "mentally reserving the citizenship of his blood, the citizenship of his parents."[104]

## Cuadernoism in Decline

Garcia's nationalist program, known as "Filipino First," has been romanticized in nationalist historiography as part of building an anticolonial consciousness after years of American "mis-education."[105] In reality, it was just a new way to market Cuaderno's policies, which prioritized the inefficient and uncompetitive industries of a national industrial class at the expense of urban wage growth.[106] It was also informed by an explicitly racist, anti-Chinese logic. And finally, it was an economic program that fused the power of the Garcia administration with that of the "independent" central bank. It was a racist rebranding of the administration's austerity program.

By 1959, the line separating Garcia and Cuaderno had been blurred. That year, as another response to the balance-of-payments crisis, Garcia proposed a 40 percent tax on dollar purchases. This move was a soft devaluation that had few of its benefits. On the one hand, it made buying dollars for importation more expensive. On the other hand, exporters who brought dollars back to the country still lost out because they only received two pesos for every dollar earned. The proposal was unpopular even within Garcia's Nacionalista Party. Still, the president insisted on the measure and ordered his allies to convene a bicameral extraordinary congressional committee to discuss his proposal. As his representative, Garcia sent Cuaderno to lead the pro-taxation group.

Cuaderno's statement in Congress was a mishmash of his usual talking points. He argued that the country's most significant problem was inflation and that a tax would give the government fiscal space and prevent it from engaging in the inflationary policy of printing money—a red herring, since Cuaderno would never countenance printing money. Testifying against him was Alfredo Montelibano, a prominent sugar exporter and close ally of Araneta's at the NEC, who had been calling Cuaderno "mentally dishonest" in the media. Even before Montelibano walked into the Senate hall, observers had already noticed that Cuaderno was fondling what they suspected was a loaded pistol near his hip. At the beginning of the session, Cuaderno could also be heard murmuring, "I'll shoot that fellow." When Montelibano walked in, legislators had to physically step between the two adversaries, while Cuaderno dared Montelibano to "repeat what you said last night," to which Montelibano replied: "I'll gladly repeat it; you are mentally dishonest." When Montelibano removed his glasses and took a fighting stance, Cuaderno began to grope again at his hip. Once legislators had calmed Cuaderno down, the central bank governor requested a delay in his testimony as he feared he might kill Montelibano.[107]

The opposition Liberal Party quickly criticized the ties between the central bank and the government. Leading the charge was House minority floor leader Ferdinand E. Marcos. The representative from Ilocos accused Garcia and Cuaderno of proposing a tax that would be used as money to grease the Nacionalista machine. "It is now clear from the statements of Governor Cuaderno," he explained, that the money collected from the plan would be "utilized for what the proponents of the measure piously call 'rural and community development projects.'" This money, he added, would "become a huge contingent fund at the disposal of Nacionalista leaders." "Almost all serious and right-thinking men," Marcos concluded, "have expressed their objections to it, yet President Garcia and Governor Cuaderno insist on this dangerous experiment."[108] In his statements, Marcos challenged central bank policy and punctured the image of central bank independence that Cuaderno had carefully cultivated.

Unfortunately, the decline of Cuadernoism would not occur amid a systematic challenge to austerity. What would dent his regime was an unraveling of the governor's image of professionalism. His reputation for independence was slowly giving way to a new reputation as Garcia's pet economist. And even his vaunted controls could no longer command the respect they used to. For his entire career at the central bank, Cuaderno had insisted that, because of its independence, the bank had allocated dollar reserves rationally. Yet this was not how the public perceived its actions, for, by the late 1950s, corruption and controls had become synonymous. As Golay noted, "The windfall arising out of exchange and import controls was shared by various participants in importing activities including bona fide importers, 'ten percenters' [middlemen who received kickbacks], legislators, and bureaucrats implementing the controls."[109]

By that time, moreover, the black market that Cuaderno's dollar controls created had become a fact of life. A report from the *Philippines Free Press* described the blatant conduct of the city's "dollar agents": "On the sidewalks of Manila's Escolta [then the city's main shopping street]; on the porch of the Manila Post; and in the vicinity of the port area, numerous dollar agents may be found every day. An observer will conclude that their business is profitable: they sport nice clothes and high-priced shoes, wear sunglasses, and smoke imported cigarettes." The prices these agents paid for dollars were significantly north of the official two pesos; for instance, a large sum of dollars could be bought for a rate of as much as four to five pesos. According to one of the dollar agents, these dollars would then be smuggled to Hong Kong. "The illegal activities of these agents and their alien bosses," the *Free Press* noted, "are an open secret." And one had to "wonder why they are not apprehended by the authorities."[110]

Thus, the black market was highly profitable to those who received central bank dollars. By purchasing dollars from the central bank at the official rate and reselling this money to the black market, those favored by the bank could double their money without investing any of it. As a *Free Press* editorial argued, "import control, followed by exchange control produced graft and influence-peddling on a truly awesome scale" since selling dollars at the official rate "to those fortunate enough to get dollar allocations" gave them instant profits. "A man who got a million-dollar allocation made a million pesos at least on the spot," it added. It was thus that "exchange control and influence-peddling became inseparable."[111] The central bank, which implemented exchange control, and the presidential palace, which engaged in influence-peddling, were also becoming inseparable. Looking back at his presidency, even Garcia had to admit that, because of controls, it was "easy to make anybody a millionaire"; one merely had to "give him a license and it's done."[112]

With reports of the corruption and illegal activities generated by "controls" becoming a common feature of the news, Cuaderno's economic regime could not last. In allowing for the passage of Garcia's tax on imports, the anti-control block in Congress gained a significant concession. They passed the president's tax law but included a provision that ordered the central bank to abolish exchange controls.[113] Cuaderno grudgingly complied, designing a "gradual decontrol plan." His plan involved a dual-rate system, where essential imports could still be bought at the original rate of two pesos to one dollar, while a "free market rate" of 3.2 pesos to a dollar was introduced for nonessential imports. This was, however, not a free-market rate since the bank would still control this new rate. Cuaderno's plan involved more and more transactions shifting to the "free market" rate gradually, hence his term gradual decontrol.[114] The plan was so convoluted and its idea of "decontrol" so limited that certain congressmen considered it a ruse designed to make decontrol fail. Once legislators heard of the plan, half of the House and two-thirds of the Senate signed resolutions calling for immediate and complete decontrol.[115]

Typical of Cuaderno, he would not allow Congress to tinker with central bank policy. He recalled that "members of the Senate and the House of Representatives as well as businessmen complained that they were not informed previously of the details of the plan." Yet he insisted that given "the diverse interests" involved, "a public hearing on it would have rendered impossible the adoption of the plan."[116] Having completed his final task in the same spirit of technocratic authoritarianism that had informed his entire career, Cuaderno would resign and end his term in December 1960.

In his memoirs, Cuaderno downplayed Congress forcing his hand, writing that, by the end of 1959, "I was ready to recommend the adoption of a plan providing for the gradual lifting of exchange and import controls." It was only possible, he added, because his stabilization program under Garcia had put in place "strict fiscal and credit measures."[117] It was a late effort to save face; it was impossible to deny that economic policymaking was no longer going his way. The technocratic Republic of Aduana was giving way to the democratic Republic of the Philippines.

## Strange Afterlives

Despite praise for his integrity as a bureaucrat, his de rigueur celebration as the founder of the central bank, and his reputation as an economic nationalist, one is hard-pressed to find a reasonable defense of the *effects* of Cuaderno's policies. Indeed, those who have studied the results of Cuaderno's programs—as opposed to those who have merely examined his "strength" as a bureaucrat—routinely view them as failures. An economic history of the period notes that, because of an insistence on a strong peso, the Philippines "borrowed foreign technology, imported raw materials and capital goods mainly from the United States, and produced imitations of American goods."[118] This observation is shared by the leading expert on Philippine currency policy, Raul Fabella, who explains that because "assembly plants depended on artificially cheap imported inputs," industrialization of the Philippines "remained skin-deep and stunted." Hence, "Why the Philippines moved from top to bottom in the East Asia economic league table is not a mystery."[119] Similarly, David Timberman argues that the extended effects of foreign exchange controls and an overvalued peso "were disastrous relative to the performance of other countries in the region."[120] Perhaps the best summary of the 1950s comes from former planning secretary Cayetano Paderanga, who concludes his short postwar economic history of the Philippines by noting, "It is evident that during the first decade of independence, the Philippines was [sic] bent on maintaining a particular exchange rate it was willing to sacrifice growth." This pattern was evidenced by "very tight monetary and fiscal policies" that prioritized inflation fighting above all else.[121]

The numbers bear out such conclusions. The Phillips curve, which shows that low inflation corresponds with high unemployment and low growth (when people are unemployed, they consume less and contribute less to growth), largely applies to postwar Philippines.[122] Beyond this aggregate data, however, the story of the Cuaderno period becomes more apparent if we split the decade into two halves. Despite deflationary policy, the first half of the decade saw solid economic growth, partly because of the Korean War, which increased demand for Filipino products.[123] By the middle of the decade, however, copra prices were down, and the US Congress started to impose a quota on global sugar exports, reducing Philippine exports and slowing growth.[124] GDP growth would not return to its immediate postwar levels again until 1970.[125]

The results of Cuaderno's policies, especially on the balance of trade, were so disastrous that even an official history of the central bank is forced to criticize its founder's policies. According to this history, the opportunity to devalue the peso after the expiration of the Bell Trade Act in 1955 was a "missed opportunity" to shore up foreign exchange reserves,[126] noting that the current account balance deteriorated from $173 million in 1950 to $65 million in 1958.[127] Indeed, by the end of the 1950s, export earnings were below 10 percent of the country's income.[128]

Finally, despite the fearmongering, there was hardly any inflation during the 1950s. The average inflation rate for 1951–1959 was 0.1 percent. In fact, from 1952 to 1955, during the Great Debate, the Philippines was undergoing severe deflation.[129] The economy needed to be stimulated, but the central bank refused to be identified with the profligate colonial.

Cuaderno's policies were failures. But his story was not over. From the 1970s onward, it has slowly been rewritten. Part of this rewriting relates to his celebration by advocates of a strong bureaucracy, who, as we have seen, have mistakenly viewed him as an enemy of corrupt rent-seekers. Of greater interest, however, is Cuaderno's celebration among anti-imperialists on the left.

A contemporary account of Cuaderno's time presents his currency policy as part of a broader attempt at "economic decolonization" amid an "unyielding IMF." It also views him as the key figure among Filipino policymakers who "countered pressure from American businesses that attempted to impose neocolonial trade relations."[130] Finally, a recent op-ed portrays the Cuaderno years as halcyon days of import substitution before IMF-dictated "debt-driven governance."[131] These accounts are at variance with accounts about and by Cuaderno from the time. Cuaderno was one the most reliable allies of US business interests and the IMF in the Philippines.

Late into his tenure in 1957, Cuaderno was one of only two active Asian government officials to serve as a plenary speaker for the International Industrial Conference in San Francisco—a conference of businessmen and government officials that sought to promote international investment in the developing world. In that conference, Cuaderno shared the stage with such figures as World Bank President Eugene Black and US Vice President Richard Nixon. In his speech, Cuaderno affirmed that the US presence in the Philippines created "a happy and fruitful relationship" and that "during all those years of foreign tutelage our people enjoyed practically as much freedom as those ruling the country." Moreover, the Filipino-American relationship was "devoid of economic exploitation and domination."[132]

His attitude toward international financial institutions was no less ambiguous. In 1956, he was elected chairman of the joint board of governors for the IMF and the World Bank. And Cuaderno was clear about why he commanded such respect in these circles: He was "a constant supporter of the Fund's effort to make member countries, especially the underdeveloped ones, observe sound economic principles."[133] By Cuaderno's reckoning, his importance lay in his role as the Third World face of global austerity. Through his example, he could make other developing countries follow the dictates of the IMF. As he ended his career, Cuaderno insisted that everything he did had the IMF seal of approval, noting, "Every year since 1953, our economic position and economic policies have been examined by the technical staff of the International Monetary Fund. These foreign experts had invariably reported favorably on the policies of the Central Bank and had endorsed the position the Central Bank had consistently taken, namely, that economic development by inflationary means inevitably brought about balance of payment difficulties."[134]

How did this loyal servant of the IMF and austerity become a symbol of a lost Eden of economic nationalism?

By 1971, Filipino economic nationalism had found a new voice in Alejandro Lichauco, who had become the intellectual heir of the nationalist senator Claro M. Recto. Lichauco, like Cuaderno, was a lawyer, businessman, and a mostly self-taught economist (though he had an undergraduate degree in economics from Harvard). But unlike Cuaderno, he reveled in being an outsider and was known for challenging mainstream economists from the University of the Philippines. Lichauco is one of the more important characters in our story, as he is the central figure in deodorizing austerity's dear money tenet through the rhetoric of nationalist anti-imperialism.

In 1970, Lichauco was elected a member of a constitutional convention convened to rewrite the constitution of 1935. In that capacity, he wrote a report that supported his position of placing explicit anti-imperialist provisions in the constitution. The report was a frontal attack on the US and its Filipino "collaborators," particularly President Ferdinand Marcos and his technocrats. When Marcos declared martial law in September 1972, Lichauco was one of the first people arrested, and he would remain in prison until January 1973.[135] That year, the Marxist New York–based Monthly Review Press published his paper in book form as the Lichauco Paper. His subsequent writings would be based on the key themes of this paper.

Lichauco's work received a left-wing imprimatur through an introduction from Paul Sweeney, a titan of neo-Marxist economics, and Monthly Review editor Harry Magdoff. Though the duo saw Lichauco's approach as "left-bourgeois critique" because it did not analyze class struggle, they noted that Lichauco "may strike a responsive chord among many non-capitalist opponents of imperialism because of a long history of antagonism to, and interference with, industrialization in the Third World by the leading capitalist nations."[136]

Lichauco's ideas were riddled with contradictions. On the one hand, he admired the export-oriented developmental states of East Asia. On the other, he viewed his country's "export bloc" with suspicion and consistently opposed East Asian–style currency depreciation for the Philippines.[137] On the one hand, he saw the parity rights provision of the Bell Trade Act as a neo-imperial imposition. On the other, he defended the overpriced currency, which was an imposition of the Bell Trade Act.[138] On the one hand, he wrote a fawning introduction to Salvador Araneta's economic essays.[139] On the other, he would spend the 1970s and 1980s defending Miguel Cuaderno's repudiation of Araneta's proposals. On the one hand, he was a Communist sympathizer, becoming an active member of Maoist front organizations in the 1970s (see next chapter). On the other, he defended policies that protected domestic capitalists even as they grossly underpaid their employees.[140]

The historical record of the Cuaderno years transmogrified under Lichauco's confused pen. In his narrative, Garcia—the man who celebrated a National Austerity Day and allowed Cuaderno to cut budgets and raise interest rates—became a spender repudiated by the "monetary austerity" of President Diosdado Macapagal, who was "working in active collaboration" with the World Bank and the IMF. More crucially for our purposes, Lichauco viewed currency depreciation as part of the "money and credit conditions imposed by the IMF" in the 1950s and 1960s.[141] This view was false because the IMF of the Bretton Woods era was concerned with monetary stability and the prevention of competitive depreciations. Under Bretton Woods, devaluations could only occur in times of crisis.[142] And while the IMF was open to devaluations in the 1950s and 1960s, it was reluctant to insist on this solution when developing nations proposed other mechanisms to address balance-of-payments problems.[143]

It was Lichauco's "anti-imperialist" defense of dear money that led him to reinterpret the career of the father of Filipino austerity. In his account of the Luthringer-led IMF mission of 1949, Lichauco claimed Luthringer "was already insinuating" to Cuaderno "the use of devaluation in lieu of controls" and that Cuaderno "had the strength of character to resist that suggestion," proving that the governor "had the simple courage to talk back to the IMF and the U.S. government."[144] Given our knowledge of Luthringer—a Kemmerer student who was a consistent defender of dear money in the Philippines—it strains credulity to think that it required bravery to convince him of the value of an expensive peso. As for the US, we have already seen that its interest during this period was to encourage Philippine importation of US products, which led it to impose dear money under the Bell Trade Act.

Lichauco's own source—Cuaderno's memoir—belies his conclusion. In a paragraph that Lichauco block quotes, Cuaderno notes, "Dr. Luthringer discussed with me the question of whether or not a devaluation of the peso, in lieu of exchange controls, should be adopted by the Philippine Government." Luthringer merely discussed devaluation and did not insinuate anything. And as Cuaderno himself affirms, "The Fund representatives agreed with me that devaluation was not advisable."[145] Lichauco would again engage in semantic gymnastics to make it seem that the IMF in 1957—led by the hard money banker Per Jacobsson—was ideologically committed to devaluation.[146]

The IMF and the US government indeed refused to loan the Philippines money in 1957, noting that they favored devaluation over Cuaderno's stabilization plan.[147] The conclusion, however, should not be that Cuaderno emerged as a left-wing critic of the IMF and the US's imperialism. Instead, it should be that Cuaderno maintained his devotion to hard money at a time when US currency policy was shifting. Put simply, under Cuaderno, the Philippines had become more austere than its colonial master.

Unfortunately, the notion that Cuaderno challenged IMF representatives on the issue of devaluation is so well entrenched that accounts similar to Lichauco's are routinely rehearsed in academic literature.[148]

As a result, left-wing and nationalist analysis associate devaluation with neoliberalism and imperialism, effectively enshrining dear money as pro-Filipino.[149] In the 1950s, however, Salvador Araneta rightly viewed dear money as a relic of colonialism that contributed to economic dependence on the United States.[150]

Why was Lichauco constructing a left-wing nationalist defense of dear money in the 1970s? As Lichauco himself often affirmed, the context of his historical work was the budding Marcos dictatorship. And the goal of the Lichauco paper was to expose the president as a pawn of imperialism.

In a strange twist of history, Marcos's political dictatorship put the final nail in the coffin of Cuaderno's economic dictatorship. As Lichauco wrote his report, Marcos was overseeing the most significant depreciation of the peso since the nineteenth century, effectively ending the era of dear money that began with the introduction of the gold exchange standard. This shift was a victory for anti-austerity. But Marcos was a brutal kleptocratic dictator and would soon become the symbol for everything the left stood against. Our final chapter will examine how the Philippine left embraced austerity to oppose a dictator.

CHAPTER 4

# Austerity Democratized

*Dear Money, the Dictator, and the Miserly Left, 1970–1986*

Profligate is not the only antonym for austere. Extravagance is another. And few figures in the twentieth century embody extravagance more than Imelda Marcos. Casual observers know her for her three thousand shoes. However, as one half of a conjugal dictatorship, she was more than the Third World's most famous shopaholic. As minister of human settlements (1978–1986) and governor of Metropolitan Manila (1975–1986), she birthed a "third world city in first world drag," building monuments for the regime amid widespread poverty.[1] Her edifice complex is exemplified by the Cultural Center of the Philippines complex, an array of exposed brutalist concrete rising from Manila Bay.[2] Through her monuments, "Madame Meldy" wanted to create a Manila that could rival the world's great cities. But in doing so, she needed to hide or even destroy what she saw as ugly poverty.[3] During the IMF / World Bank conference of 1976, for example, the government erected fences around informal settlements to make them inconspicuous. Yet even with the fences, these testaments to urban blight remained unsavory and were ultimately demolished.[4]

When there is extravagance amid poverty, calls for austerity become resonant. And if we imagine the Marcos regime as exemplified by the excesses of its first lady, it becomes easy to decry wanton spending; Imelda Marcos is the platonic ideal of the profligate colonial. But in economics, the opposite of austerity is not always extravagance. Austerity is also often in tension with state developmentalism.

The Marcos regime exemplified two forms of anti-austerity: extravagance and theft on the one hand, and a strong interventionist state on the other. On paper, Ferdinand Marcos sought to build an export-driven developmental state like his country's East Asian neighbors. Like his neighbors, as well, Marcos believed this state developmentalism required the centralization of power.

A key element of Marcosian developmentalism was challenging dear money policy. This chapter examines Marcos's failed developmental project and pays close attention to the peso's devaluation in 1970. A key yet understudied event in Philippine history, it was the largest devaluation of the peso since the 1870s. It was also the end of the imperial hard money regime that had been in place since 1902. Significant as this change was, however, it did not create an export-oriented East Asian economy like that of Korea's or Taiwan's. While currency depreciation was a common strategy for these developmental states, and the Marcos regime had developmental pretensions, the depreciation of 1970 was not implemented as part of a purposeful reorientation of economic priorities. It was a reaction to a sharp decline in foreign reserves and the threat of an economic crisis. This policy context did not augur well for the reputation of a cheap peso.

More crucially, Marcos's devaluation strategy collapsed during the Third World debt crisis of the 1980s—a crisis that battered the Philippines more than its neighbors. This crisis, the largest downturn since the Japanese occupation, led to the dictatorship's fall and a repudiation of its economic policies, including depreciation. Export-oriented developmentalism was tainted by the dictatorship that attempted it. As Caroline Hau notes, "The failed attempt by Marcos to create a developmental state had intellectual repercussions for the concept of the developmental state itself."[5]

The key figures in this chapter include the two chief technocrats who envisioned an export-oriented state for the Philippines: finance minister Cesar Virata (b. 1930), and head of planning Gerardo Sicat (b. 1935). These two men represented a new generation of US-trained economists (unlike self-taught lawyers like Cuaderno and Araneta), and their economic vision was a departure from the hard money economics of the 1950s. But they oversaw an economy roiled by multiple crises—from dwindling reserves due to electoral spending, unprecedented typhoon seasons, and oil shocks, to a sudden rise in global interest rates. They also worked for a corrupt and violent dictator, and we cannot separate their legacies from the authoritarian government they propped up. As Teresa Tadem notes, they were "either oblivious to or simply ignored the political machinations of Marcos in perpetuating himself in power."[6] Perhaps they were also seduced by the dictator's power to remove policy roadblocks.[7]

Alongside these technocrats, this chapter also examines the left-wing opposition to Marcos and how it responded to the dictatorship's economic policies. Lifting from Eric Hobsbawm, I previously called the Marcos period a Philippine "age of extremes"—a period that distilled the fundamental tensions of the twentieth century.[8] On the one hand, Filipinos saw the rise of a militarist, authoritarian government. On the other, this period was also the high point of Filipino Maoism. The growth of the Maoist Communist Party was contingent on its opposition to the dictatorship. For reasons of principle and strategy, it had to oppose Marcos at every turn. It thus developed an economic critique that repudiated everything Marcos represented, including what they saw as Marcos's profligacy. If, as I have previously noted, the polarization of this Philippine age of extremes had the political effect of sidelining liberal centrism,[9] in this chapter I contend that this same polarization led to the enshrinement of austerity both on the left and the right.

I tread lightly in these pages, knowing that a sympathetic assessment of some of Marcos's policies may feed into present-day authoritarian nostalgia. In this respect, I am guided by Salvador Araneta's example, who believed that Marcos's forwarding of monetary reforms did "not justify his continuance in power as a dictator."[10]

## The Road to Devaluation

As we saw in the previous chapter, Miguel Cuaderno left the central bank with a plan of gradual devaluation—a policy program supported by his allies from President Garcia's Nacionalista Party. Garcia, however, lost his reelection bid to Vice President Diosdado Macapagal of the Liberal Party (vice presidents are elected separately in the Philippines). Consistent with the Liberal Party's view that import and exchange controls bred corruption, Macapagal acted swiftly to accelerate Cuaderno's timetable. The new president did not wait for Congress to revise Cuaderno's plan and ordered decontrol through executive fiat.[11] In 1962, Macapagal floated the peso. Exporters, however, were still required to surrender

20 percent of their receipts at the old ratio. By June of that year, the rate stabilized at 3.9 pesos to $1—a rate the central bank defended and eventually formalized in 1965.[12]

Despite this depreciation, the 1965 rate was still a protected rate. More importantly, the rhythms of Cuaderno-era economics still played out. The government would oscillate between periods of tightening the money supply to contain inflation and expanding this supply to address public demand for services—at all times being loath to increase taxes. Periods of monetary expansion drove up domestic demand for imports, which continued to place pressure on government reserves.[13] Whatever devaluation occurred, therefore, was not enough to fundamentally alter the postwar patterns of the Philippines economy.

The intellectual climate of the Macapagal presidency still mirrored that of the Cuaderno era. For Macapagal and his economic advisers, decontrol was part of an anticorruption campaign, not a repudiation of economic orthodoxy. Macapagal's most prominent economic technocrat, Sixto K. Roxas, who served as assistant executive secretary for economic affairs, explained in 2009 that he "had been advocating decontrol as the only way to cut corruption."[14] Roxas eventually developed a more thorough critique of an overpriced currency. However, during the Macapagal administration, he believed Cuaderno's "controls" were "effective" because "they stimulated investments and created a class of Filipino entrepreneurs."[15]

No postwar president had been reelected, and Macapagal was no exception. In 1965, he was defeated by Senator Ferdinand E. Marcos. Marcos had once been Macapagal's party mate and ally in the Liberal Party, and as we saw in the previous chapter, he was a leading critic of Garcia's and Cuaderno's policies in the 1950s. However, when Macapagal broke his promise not to seek a second term, Marcos switched parties and ran against the incumbent.

Marcos's first term began with a massive expansion in spending and credit. By July 1966, the credit the central bank made available to commercial banks was three times what it was in December 1965. The bank also lowered the basic rediscount rate from 6 percent to 4.75 percent, making borrowing cheap and credit abundant.[16] This increased spending climaxed toward the end of Marcos's first term. In 1969, the government's net deficit was ₱934 million, three times larger than the deficit in 1968 and roughly equal to the cumulative deficits from 1961 to 1968.[17] This spending led to the first major economic crisis of the Marcos regime.

The foreign exchange crisis of late 1969 to 1970 aptly represents the various economic tensions under Marcos. Primarily, the crisis was evidence of corruption sparked by electoral spending; 1969 was the year when Marcos successfully used the levers of state power to make himself the first Filipino president to win reelection. There was a 20 percent increase in the money supply in the last four months of the year.[18] And as much as $50 million went into Marcos's campaign, a significant portion of which was public money.[19] Yet there was more to the crisis than just corruption.

Although the proximate cause of the credit crunch was electioneering, developmental spending also placed pressure on the currency system. In real terms, government spending had already risen by 43 percent in the nonelection years of 1964 to 1968.[20] And annual average infrastructure spending from 1966 to 1969 was up by 70 percent compared with the previous four years. The results of this spending were impressive. In this period, the government built 1,388 kilometers of concrete roads (up from the 321 kilometers of the previous four years). Around 225,000 hectares of farmland received irrigation (up from the 90,000 hectares of the previous four years). The government also erected 40,000 prefabricated classrooms (up from the 5,002 of the previous four years).[21]

More than any other event, therefore, the crisis of 1970 reflects Hau's measured assessment that Marcos's policies were not only "naked instruments by which Marcos effected a power-grab for himself" but also "politically rational moves to simultaneously court voters while pursuing national development projects."[22]

Another cause of the crisis of 1970 was bad timing. Much of Marcos's pre-election spending was financed with short-term loans, which needed to be paid by 1970. That year was also a year when three major typhoons hit the Philippines. As Marcos told a business group in January of that year, "We have unfortunately financed the foreign exchange requirements of our development with credits of short maturities. I am told by my advisers that because of the increase in short-term debts, the total payment for interest and amortization this fiscal year ending June 1970 will take over half our export earnings."[23]

There was thus a need to depreciate once more. Dwindling exports and foreign exchange reserves require boosting exports; a devalued peso would have made Philippine exports cheaper and more competitive. Moreover, defending a currency puts pressure on foreign exchange reserves. When the supply of pesos increases because of relaxed fiscal and monetary policy, the price of the peso drops. To defend a currency's value, a government needs to buy its currency from the market using its foreign exchange reserves of dollars to decrease its currency's supply and raise its value relative to the dollar, putting pressure on foreign exchange reserves. Floating the peso was thus a clear way out of a foreign exchange crisis.

Of course, this process was always going to be painful, as it courted inflation and resistance from Filipino importers, who benefited from the expensive peso. A keen politician, Marcos knew that depreciating the peso would require him to expend significant political capital. In January of 1970, the IMF began to pressure the Philippine government to devalue. In his diary, Marcos wrote, "We cannot accept this."[24] The following day, he wrote that he had ordered the central bank governor Gregorio Licaros to write an aide-mémoire to the IMF stating that "we will not agree to a devaluation and will take any measures short of it."[25] By the 1970s, the terms of IMF conditionality had changed; unlike in the immediate postwar period, it pushed the Philippines to devalue. Marcos was chafing from the pressure.

Despite the change in the global policy climate, viewing devaluation as a policy imposed by the IMF is inadequate. As we saw in the previous chapter, the case for devaluation was first articulated by Salvador Araneta in the 1950s, long before international financial institutions insisted on it as a condition for loans. Moreover, even within the Marcos administration, there was already some advocacy for depreciation. Placido Mapa Jr., Marcos's director of the Program Implementation Agency (the technical staff for social and economic projects), had advocated a floating rate since the Macapagal years. Mapa, who had PhD in economics from Harvard, had formed a strong opinion about currency policy in his youth. A nephew of Araneta's, he was influenced by his uncle's ideas on currency policy.[26] In Marcos's first term, however, Mapa was a minority voice, and it would take the crisis of 1970 for advocates of depreciation to gain influence.

## The Old Guard Gives Way

Mapa's uncle, Araneta, was in fact still an active political figure in the early 1970s. But his and his rival Miguel Cuaderno's status as economists had declined. By then, they were no longer economic authorities but partisans in the country's war for democracy. The two would meet again in 1971. That year, President Marcos called for a convention to draft a new constitution, and the two aging rivals both became convention delegates. Having both been delegates to the previous convention of 1935, the two were grand old men of the Republic.

The convention came at a time of great turmoil. Inflation was high, student protests had turned violent, and Marcos was contemplating declaring martial law. These were, according to the time's leading chronicler, "days of disquiet, nights of rage."[27] On the convention floor, Cuaderno became a leading voice of the pro-Marcos camp, arguing against a provision that would have prevented Marcos from staying in power after his second term.[28] Meanwhile, Araneta, who tried in vain to weaken the presidency's powers in 1935,[29] warned against executive overreach and insisted that presidents be limited to two terms.[30] As in the 1950s, their exchanges were intense. At one point, Araneta fumed when Cuaderno called one of his proposals "crazy." And, in private, Araneta believed Cuaderno supported Marcos because the former central bank governor constantly needed to be close to power.[31]

But their disagreements would be inconsequential. Before the convention had finished work on a new constitution, Marcos declared martial law in September 1972 and immediately used the military to arrest opposition figures, including convention delegates. Fortunately for Araneta, he was visiting his daughter in San Francisco when the arrests started. He would be stuck in San Francisco and begin a life of exile from there.[32]

Despite his hatred for Marcos, Araneta was a fair man. In 1975, he was asked about Marcos's economic policies, specifically his devaluation of the peso in 1970. Araneta explained that Marcos was "implementing many of the economic theories I had advocated." The dictator did "not have a Cuaderno around him" and did not "care about the advice of the Americans." On economic matters, Araneta conceded, "he has guts."[33] After decades of bitter fights over the currency, Araneta finally got his wish. But he was no longer part of the conversation.

Cuaderno's disappearance into sycophantic obscurity and Araneta's exile represented not just the final gasp of the Great Debate. It also signified a passing of the economic guard, occasioning a shift in the critique of dear money policy. Araneta's pro-devaluation position was anchored on common sense and polemical prose. It was also framed in the language of social justice and Christian Democracy. During the Marcos period, however, technocrats who argued dispassionately with data sets institutionalized the critique of dear money. Depreciation would thus become part of the language of economic efficiency that buttressed authoritarianism.

The ascendance of a new finance secretary almost immediately shifted the Marcos government's position on the peso. Cesar Virata, who, as secretary of finance, would become Marcos's most influential technocrat, was a lifelong critic of dear money. He developed his pro-depreciation view as a college student in 1949, when he realized "the US lobby was strong to keep the exchange rate at 2:1."[34] This view would only harden as he gained professional experience. As a business consultant who had spent time in the budding developmental economies of Taiwan, Japan, and Korea, Virata observed that exports were not growing in the Philippines because businesses were hamstrung by the central bank's system of controls.[35]

Virata was a young Wharton graduate, not yet forty, and dean of the University of the Philippines' business school when Marcos appointed him. He joined the government in the middle of February 1970 as part of a major cabinet reshuffling that occurred amid the crisis. According to the confidential report of the British ambassador, "the Administration, beset by economic problems and deserted by its customary allies, was in a state of virtual paralysis." The entry of technocrats like Virata "gave the Administration a more progressive and businesslike image."[36] Virata would occupy various senior posts for the entirety of the Marcos dictatorship. When the regime fell in 1986, he was concurrently finance minister and prime minister.[37]

Almost immediately after his appointment, Virata would push for devaluation. Before his first monetary board meeting, Virata scheduled an emergency meeting with Marcos. He told the president that the board wished to float the peso but that he was unsure where the price of the peso would settle (it would eventually settle at 6.45 to the dollar the next day). "Can you take the consequences of this change?" he asked. Virata knew that further inflation would only fan the flames of student demonstrations against the Marcos regime. Marcos replied that the monetary board should proceed if Virata felt it was the right solution. With his marching orders, Virata returned to the monetary board and called for a total decontrol of the peso while nixing odious exemptions for jewelry and luxury goods importers.[38] Virata's loyalty to Marcos can be traced to this moment—the moment when he became convinced that Marcos would let economic managers make painful decisions while the president dealt with the political fallout. Given Marcos's political hesitancy to float the peso, we can be confident he knew these political risks. Yet, at least in 1970, he insulated the bureaucrats from these risks.

On Saturday, February 21, 1970, the central bank announced a free-market exchange rate for the peso. It euphemistically described this solution as an alternative to devaluation, but, as *The New York Times* reported, the move "was expected to have the same effect."[39] Virata was now in charge of the currency system he had envisioned for the Philippines as a college student.

Though Virata was young, Marcos assured the new finance secretary of his support.[40] And with the president's backing, Virata took a broad view of his duties. While his predecessors only sought to raise finances for the government's fiscal needs, Virata saw the department as a center of reforms for various parts of the government.[41] He also believed in the centrality of economic planning and, like Ramon Magsaysay in the 1950s, advocated for a strong National Economic Council (NEC). In July 1970, he asked Marcos to appoint economics professor Gerardo Sicat to chair the NEC. Virata knew that Sicat was the fastest-rising star in Philippine economics. As dean of the University of the Philippines College of Business, Virata oversaw the Department of Economics. He also helped the department become an independent School of Economics in 1965.[42] By this time, Sicat, already a full professor in his early thirties, was the school's most promising thinker.

Today there is little that distinguishes Sicat and Virata's bearing. Both are soft-spoken, urbane, formal, and evince the patrician qualities of men whose gifted minds have brought them close to immense power. Yet their present-day similarities belie their different backgrounds. While Virata grew up a member of the propertied class and was raised among professionals and public servants, Sicat's childhood was one of upward mobility. Neither of his parents went to college, and he worked his way through the public school system to the University of the Philippines and, through Fulbright and Rockefeller scholarships, to a PhD at MIT. Though academically more accomplished, Sicat has always looked up to Virata. In 2014, he published the eight-hundred-page biography *Cesar Virata: Life and Times; Through Four Decades of Philippine Economic History*—one of the few tomes that fuses a life history with a broad commentary on Philippine economic history. (Sicat's prose, unlike that of most of his fellow Filipino economists, is not leaden.)

Sicat himself looks back at his and Virata's entry as part of a broader professionalization of the government's economic agencies, noting that many of the managers before Virata's ascension were "public servants with some knowledge of finance and economics." Many of them, he adds, were "successful businessmen, who had limited theoretical training."[43]

Yet, even more than Virata, Sicat, with his PhD in economics, brought academic heft to Marcos's new economic team. At MIT, Sicat studied under some of the most eminent economists of the time, listing Charles P. Kindleberger, Paul Samuelson, Amartya Sen, Paul Rosenstein-Rodan, W. W. Rostow, Everett Hagen, and Albert Ando as some of his teachers.[44] With the possible exception of Rosenstein-Rodan, who was associated with the Austrian school, these economists were broadly sympathetic to the New Deal consensus of postwar American economics, and most were avowed Keynesians. Indeed, Sicat attended MIT because he wanted to work with Samuelson,[45] who had by then a reputation as a leading voice in neo-Keynesianism.

In 1970, while preparing to leave for a research fellowship at Yale, Virata told Sicat that Marcos had selected him, Sicat, to join the cabinet as chairman of the NEC.[46] At thirty-four, Sicat feared that he was "too young to head the national planning agency," yet he "felt humbled and honored to be given a chance to contribute directly toward nation-building."[47] Sicat's appointment came after a prolific period of research, during which he had written multiple articles about export-oriented growth, eventually published in 1972 by the University of the Philippines Press as *Economic Policy and Philippine Development*. The essays in the book formed the core of Sicat's economic vision, which he carried into his time in government. Upon their publication, Sicat noted that he had altered none of these views when he entered government and that many had even been strengthened.[48] Also, in the late 1960s, Sicat worked on an assessment of Philippine industrial policy with American economist John Power.[49] In these works, Emmanuel de Dios explains, Sicat outlined the effects of postwar import substitution "on the recurrence of balance of payments difficulties (hence macroeconomic instability), skewed income distribution, rural-urban migration, industrial concentration, the character of foreign investments, and uneven regional development, among others."[50] Thus, even before entering government, Sicat was already providing the theoretical and empirical grist for the pro-depreciation position.

Along with Power, Sicat took a long view in explaining the origins of the crisis of 1970, effectively tracing its roots to Miguel Cuaderno's policy errors. Without denying that campaign spending strained foreign reserves, the two argued that "the balance-of-payments problem in the Philippines is deeper and more persistent," tracing its origins to "the decision to defend in the 1950s the pre-war parity of the peso in the face of a price level far out of line as a result of wartime inflation."

They added that "deflationary policy plus import controls" were the main policy instruments that failed to address "a continuing underlying tendency towards deterioration of the trade balance that required increasingly stronger measures to offset it."[51] This position has been one of the most consistent in Sicat's long and prolific career. Amid a growing debt crisis in 1984, for example, he claimed that "the most serious economic policy error of our independence" was the insistence on a strong peso.[52] And in a 2018 column for *The Philippine Star*, he argued, "The desire to sustain the two-to-one exchange rate with the US dollar by Filipino leaders was a dream that had little basis in reality."[53]

Over the years, Sicat has, indeed, spoken of devaluation in terms of market efficiency, and he has not hidden his disdain for the titans of so-called left-wing nationalist economics like Claro M. Recto. Because of this reputation, academics have called him a "Right-wing (conservative)"[54] and even a representative of "forces with a belief in neoliberal economics" (that included the World Bank and the IMF).[55] These positions, however, dismiss how fundamental a departure devaluation was from the orthodoxies of the Philippine economy, many of which were informed by impulses more reactionary (imperialism and austerity) than whatever vague conception of "neoliberalism" his critics have forwarded. They also neglect that Sicat's critique of 1950s policy rested on the assumption that it was austere and deflationary. Finally, Sicat's ideas about depreciation were premised not on a blind subservience to the United States or global financial institutions.

In the late 1960s, he had his eyes trained on the developmental path of East Asia. Sicat's lectures from this period are replete with references to the export-oriented developmental states of Japan, South Korea, and Taiwan. In one lecture from 1967, for example, he lamented that the Philippines had stubbornly stuck to import substitution, even as the East Asian states began to focus on exports—a lost opportunity, since the Philippines had preferential access to the US market.[56] In another lecture from 1970, he pointed out that, also in the 1950s, East Asian states "began clicking once they had opted for realistic exchange rate policies and continued to retain them," once again unlike the Philippines.[57] That Sicat conceived of depreciation as part of an export-oriented strategy inspired by East Asian developmental states of the time should make us reconsider the trite assessment of Marcosian economics as neoliberal. For regardless of how one assesses the developmental state, Chalmers Johnson is correct in noting that the developmental state, in utilizing

both the power of the market and the state, challenges "Western preference for binary modes of thought."[58]

Sicat and Virata's ascendance mark two key shifts in economic policymaking. First, they represented an intellectual and generational shift
that resulted in a push for an export-driven economy like East Asian
economies. Second, the finance ministry's muscularity undercut the
central bank's power. If, in previous years, the central bank could be auto-
cratic, now it had to contend with the technocrats that served an auto-
crat. This was especially the case in the sphere of currency policy, where
Marcos gave Virata his full backing to depreciate the peso. Naturally,
the central bank remained influential, particularly in regulating banks
and managing foreign capital. In this regard, it did abet the growth of
crony industries under Marcos.[59] When considering the broader macroeconomic history of the twentieth century, however, the central bank
was less important in the 1970s than in the 1950s and 1960s.

## Effects of Decontrol

Many features of Marcosian economics were already evident in the
first term; it was, indeed, a time of largesse and corruption. But the
shift in currency policy and the rise of technocrats around Virata
after the crisis of 1970 reoriented the regime's priorities. After 1970,
Sicat's version of export-oriented industrialization not only became
"an entire scientific programme that could be further elaborated," it
also became "government orthodoxy (at least rhetorically)."[60] Technocrats like Sicat had immense input on policymaking from 1970 until
1979. Looking back on seven years of martial rule in 1979, the US
Embassy noted, "The policy influence of the economic technocrats
predates martial law, but their voice has clearly been strengthened in
the past nine years."[61] It described Virata, minister of trade and industry Vicente Paterno, Sicat, and budget minister Jaime Laya as "competent, hardworking" and mostly untainted by corruption, in contrast to
politicians close to the regime.[62]

An assessment of devaluation and export orientation, therefore,
requires that we focus on the 1970s, as this was the high point of the
technocracy and the first time since the imposition of the gold exchange
standard in 1902 (apart from the brief period of Japanese occupation)
when a theoretically coherent alternative to the dear money policy was
implemented. The period of 1971–1979 was not only the period of the
technocracy's influence but also the period before the Third World debt

crisis of the 1980s—an unprecedented event that will require a separate discussion below.[63]

The immediate effects of devaluing the peso were swift and went according to plan. The peso had fallen to 6.435 to a dollar by September and stabilized by the end of the year.[64] Its price would remain roughly the same for the entire decade. Writing to Marcos in January 1971, the central bank's governor, Gregorio Licaros, noted that the economy "responded favorably to the remedial measures" of the previous year. The new exchange rate had "substantially corrected certain critical imbalances in the country's external accounts and has laid the groundwork for the long-run development and growth of the economy." As a result, the balance of trade improved from a deficit of $67.6 million in 1969 to a surplus of $83.5 million. "The main contributor to this recovery," explained Licaros, "was the 21 per cent increase in export receipts to a level of $1.015 billion, the highest recorded in Philippine history." Meanwhile, international reserves increased from $125.9 in December 1969 to $236.6 million in December 1970.[65] The central bank was equally optimistic in 1973, noting that its international reserves had increased from $137 million in 1970 to $400 million.[66]

The central bank may have been too optimistic. While the 21 percent increase in exports after the depreciation was significant, it came after a major slump in the mid-1960s (see figure 4.1). And despite improvements

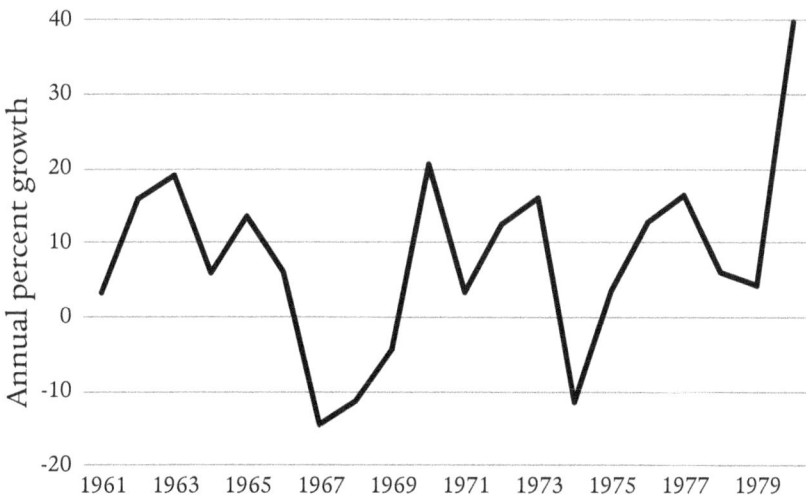

FIGURE 4.1.  Exports of goods and services (annual percent growth)
Source: World Bank.

in the balance of payments, the 1970s were an inflationary period for the Philippines. As early as 1970, the central bank had already noted that the new rate "exerted anticipated pressure on the level of consumer prices," which rose by 22 percent in 1970.[67]

Inflation did increase after the election of 1969 and the depreciation of 1970, as can be gleaned in figure 4.2. This inflation was made worse by the typhoon season of 1970, when the country was hit by three of the strongest typhoons in its history. But the currency price adjustment shock was temporary and began to wane by 1972. The Marcos technocrats, however, were unlucky, because the oil shock of 1973 hit just as inflation was going down. When OPEC countries declared an oil embargo after the Yom Kippur War, oil prices rose exponentially, contributing to the "great inflation" of the 1970s. Figure 4.2 shows the Philippines was affected by this global crisis of 1973 in a manner that tracked with its neighbors.

Despite the inflationary pressures, the 1970s were a relatively stable period of growth for the Philippines. Offering a measured assessment of the government's progress in 1979, the US Embassy noted, "The Philippine economy has been growing steadily if undramatically."[68] This steady, if undramatic, growth is best assessed comparatively using the real per capita GDP growth rate. Because this indicator corrects

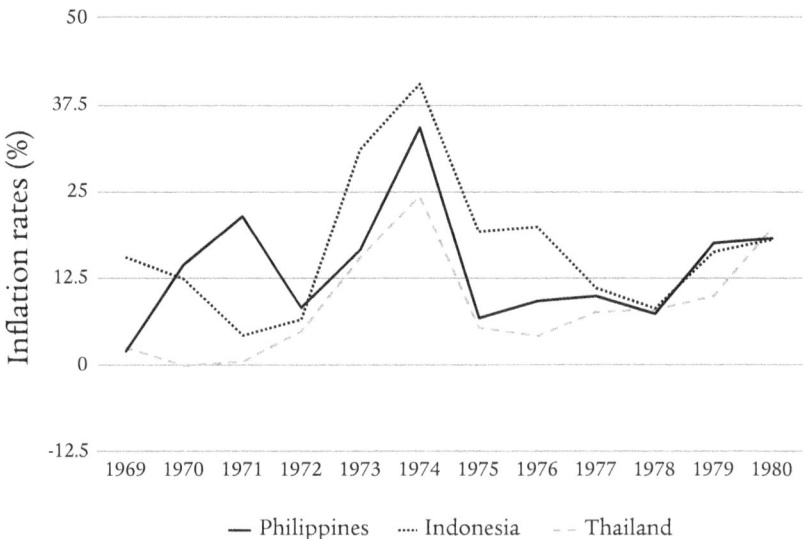

**FIGURE 4.2.**    Inflation (consumer price index)
Source: World Bank.

for population growth and inflation, it is a better measure of changes in quality of life than nominal GDP (table 4.1). At an average rate of 3.3 percent a year, growth in the Philippines was below the average of Southeast Asia, above the world average, and roughly at par with all of Asia and the developing world. There is no UNCTAD (UN Trade and Development) data for the 1960s, but a separate data set for real GDP per capita growth in the Philippines shows that it was 58 percent higher from 1971 to 1980 compared with 1961 to 1970.[69] To put things into greater perspective, based once again on UNCTAD data, the real per capita growth rate in the 1970s was slightly lower than that of the first decade of the 2000s (roughly 2.7 percent)—a period of relative economic stability.

For Sicat, fiscal expansion was the main engine for this growth. In 2011, he insisted that the Marcos regime's success should be measured by the extent of its spending, noting that public capital formation was 1 to 2 percent of GDP before Marcos and jumped to roughly 6 percent in the 1970s. For someone routinely labeled neoliberal, this was an interesting statement.[70] Sicat was using the expansiveness of the state to measure economic success.

As for exports, which Sicat envisioned as the prime driver of his economic plans, they grew at a rate that "placed the country in league with most rapidly growing Asian exporters" (see figure 4.1 for export growth rates, which averaged 7.6 percent). Like the reports from the US Embassy, confidential reports from the British Embassy indicate that it, too, was moderately optimistic about the Philippine economy, particularly the growth of its exports. By the late 1970s, these reports were noting that the Philippines was weathering slumps in global prices because of the increasing diversity of its exports. The annual report for 1979, for example, noted a 38 percent increase in nontraditional exports.[71] At the beginning of the decade, 76 percent of export earnings came from five traditional export commodities: coconut products, sugar, forest products, copper, and gold. At the end of the decade, that percentage was down to 46, as the Philippines manufactured more garments and electrical products.[72]

Export growth was undoubtedly a vindication of Sicat and Virata's vision. However, what they and other technocrats created fell short of an export-oriented developmental state. While the nominal exchange rate declined, it only moved from 6.44 pesos to a dollar in 1970 to 7.6 in 1980. More importantly, inflation at home vitiated most of the gains that exporters made from a nominally cheaper peso. The real exchange

Table 4.1  Real GDP growth rate percentage per capita (1971–1979)

| | TOTAL | 1971 | 1972 | 1973 | 1974 | 1975 | 1976 | 1977 | 1978 | 1979 | AVERAGE |
|---|---|---|---|---|---|---|---|---|---|---|---|
| Philippines | 29.43475 | 2.684019 | 2.780126 | 6.106613 | 0.94119 | 2.948527 | 6.076264 | 2.791524 | 2.340337 | 2.766148 | 3.270527 |
| World | 19.58808 | 2.307969 | 3.393617 | 4.365622 | 0.196098 | -1.07788 | 3.40354 | 2.315041 | 2.446286 | 2.237788 | 2.176454 |
| Asia | 29.82171 | 3.909189 | 5.539754 | 5.954877 | 0.146358 | 0.830805 | 4.208146 | 3.332541 | 2.532926 | 3.36711 | 3.313523 |
| Southeast Asia | 41.50319 | 4.825786 | 4.336427 | 6.460243 | 3.169687 | 1.932946 | 6.251858 | 5.551236 | 4.570847 | 4.404155 | 4.611465 |
| Developing economies | 30.00545 | 4.155318 | 4.266913 | 5.168275 | 3.722398 | 0.673212 | 4.71473 | 3.98768 | 1.249504 | 2.956336 | 3.333939 |

Source: uctad.uctadstat.org.

rate, which measures how many goods can be purchased domestically after export dollars are converted into pesos, became worse for exporters in the 1970s. This meant that the peso remained expensive in real terms, and businesses still had a greater incentive to prioritize the domestic market.[73]

In the Marcos administration's final years, Sicat acknowledged that export-driven growth in the 1970s was inadequate. He would, however, without naming him, blame Miguel Cuaderno for this failure. In 1984, as the economy was in a tailspin, he argued that the Marcos economic team tried to promote as much exportation to the US market as remaining preferential trading agreements allowed. These interventions, however, were "two decades too late," since by then, "our neighbors had already preempted a large ground in our potential markets" and "the climate of growth of international trade" which helped those neighbors "became altogether different and certainly more restrictive."[74] In the 1950s, the central bank had chosen a different course from Asian neighbors and "sentimentally" attached the peso to its prewar price.[75] The result, concluded Sicat, was that the Philippines missed out on the industrial growth experienced by Hong Kong, Taiwan, and South Korea in the 1960s.[76]

Such statements are easily read as excuses for the dictatorship's failures. Except that Sicat had been making the same argument even before joining the Marcos government. As we saw earlier, he was making the same points in the late 1960s. Sicat believed that changes in the 1950s allowed East Asian "tigers" like South Korea, Taiwan, Hong Kong, and Singapore to emerge—a mostly correct observation. Recent research on comparative takeoff points of economic growth between the Philippines and these economies has shown that, despite the Philippines starting at a better postwar position, these four economies had overtaken the Philippines in the 1960s, before the Marcos period.[77]

Sicat was also correct in noting that an overvalued currency played a part in this story. Taiwan, for example, depreciated from the late 1950s onward, leading to a 9 percent fall in the real effective exchange rate from 1956 to 1959.[78] The Philippines could have also devalued at this time, since this was the period after the expiration of the Bell Trade Act. This was also a better time to devalue than 1970, as the country could have exploited preferential trading options with the US to the fullest. Moreover, unlike the early 1970s, the late 1950s was not a period of high global inflation. This meant domestic inflation was less likely to eat into export earnings. Finally, the most effective depreciations are strategic and not reactive. While the Marcos regime was able to depreciate the peso in 1970, it did so not because of strategic deliberation but because of a balance-of-payments crisis.

## The Filipino Maoist's Inflationary Subject

Though the economy was stable in the long run, the economic changes of the early 1970s created enough shocks to engender opposition. The early 1970s were a period of economic change and political crisis. The first year of the new decade began with a string of student protests known as the First Quarter Storm. These protests occurred amid rising fears that Marcos was consolidating power to impose authoritarian rule.[79] In 1971, the protests would continue with students establishing barricades in various universities, most notably the University of the Philippines (UP), Diliman—the country's flagship state university.

Undergirding the effervescence of student activism was a renewed Communist movement. The old Moscow-oriented Partido Komunista ng Pilipinas (PKP, or Communist Party of the Philippines), ascendant in the 1950s, was sclerotic by the Marcos period and chose to collaborate with the dictatorship. However, breakaway youth leaders established the Maoist Communist Party of the Philippines (CPP) in 1968 with the aid of anti-Marcos politicians.[80] By the 1970s, the CPP's aboveground "National Democratic" organizations had outsize influence over student activism, particularly at UP Diliman. And because of its united front policy with the nationalist bourgeois, the CPP had brought into its orbit many elite fellow travelers who were raised on the economic nationalism of Senator Claro M. Recto

The first left-wing response to the devaluation was an op-ed by the CPP's youth wing, the Kabataang Makabayan (KM, or Nationalist Youth), published in the University of the Philippines student newspaper, the *Philippine Collegian*. The op-ed appeared in March 1970, a month after the central bank announced its "free market" rate. Situating the devaluation amid US and IMF-directed neocolonialism, it argued that "for the past 20 years, the IMF has 'advised' dozens of Latin American governments to implement tight money policies characterized by devaluation, restrictive credit and inflation—all to the benefit of imperialist countries, principally the US."[81] This argument was false. As we saw in the previous chapter, the IMF's developing-world policy in the 1950s and 1960s was characterized by an opposition to multiple exchange rates and a general preference for "sound money." More importantly, devaluation is the opposite of tight monetary policy, and restrictive credit policies do not lead to inflation but are often used to curtail inflation.

Similar misinterpretations of macroeconomic theory were voiced by other organizations affiliated with the CPP. The most vocal in this regard was the Movement for a Democratic Philippines (MDP), a Communist-affiliated umbrella organization for the protest movement that included non-Communist bourgeois fellow travelers like Alejandro Lichauco (see previous chapter for Lichauco's background). Given Lichauco's interest in economics, his importance within the MDP, and his public disdain for depreciation, the MDP's positions were largely shaped by his views.[82] In 1972, the MDP released a pamphlet that argued that "the colonial pattern of trade, strengthened by the peso and dollar devaluations, continues to drain the country of $50 million yearly. Precious capital continues to flow out as our top exports remain cheap agricultural raw materials, while our imports, expensive finished products." It also noted, without explaining how, that the "US-dictated peso devaluation" continued to destroy "our native industries."[83] Where the MDP got the figure of $50 million is not clear, nor is what this figure even represents. What the pamphlet seems to be implying, however, is that a trade surplus—"top exports" that "flow out" from the country—constitutes a "drain" on the economy. Viewing a trade surplus as exploitation is unorthodox, to say the least, even for thinkers averse to mercantilism.

Lichauco's own writings exhibit similar misunderstandings of devaluation as an economic strategy. In the famous Lichauco paper of 1972 (see, again, previous chapter), he argued that devaluation "makes it cheaper for foreign capital to buy into the economy of the devaluing country."[84] Such a position was consistent with long-standing rhetoric among nationalist elites that viewed protecting local capitalists from foreign competition as paramount. Lichauco, however, neglected that while a cheap currency may make foreign investment easier, it also encourages domestic exportation. While Lichauco portrayed himself as a defender of the Filipino industrial class, he was, in truth, defending the import-dependent segment of that class that had failed to innovate despite preferential treatment during the Cuaderno years.

Because he saw devaluation as a zero-sum game, Lichauco dismissed it as part of a "process of neocolonialization" that prevented countries "from utilizing exchange controls to rectify any imbalance in its international payments."[85] "Devaluation," therefore, "preserves the open character of the economy."[86] This was ostensibly a protectionist argument against free-market policies. It was also a celebration of the "protectionist" policies of Miguel Cuaderno in the 1950s, which Lichauco contrasted favorably against Marcos's central bank.

This idea of devaluation as a free-market policy would become a central theme in almost all of Lichauco's subsequent writings. In 1988, he wrote a textbook on "nationalist economics" in which he contrasted the "nationalism" of dear money advocates like Cuaderno and advocates of devaluation like Marcos (conveniently neglecting that Cuaderno was a Marcos supporter in 1971). In that work, Lichauco noted that after the devaluation of 1970, "pesos were converted to dollars, and dollars converted to pesos, at a rate established, not by the government, but supposedly by market forces."[87] The association of the unfettered free market with the cheap peso is now so ingrained within the left that Maoist-aligned groups continue to this day to view the cheap peso as a product of open market transactions, as we saw in the case of the IBON Foundation (see introduction).

The argument that the central bank sought a "market rate" for the peso lent credibility to Lichauco's views. Indeed, it did seem like Marcos's central bank had given up on managing the country's currency. Yet even the "market rate" of the peso was not a floating rate, for the central bank kept it stable at roughly 7 pesos to a dollar. More importantly, Lichauco failed to explain why state intervention must ensure an expensive currency. Is it not possible for states to intervene to keep their currencies cheap? And is this not equally, if not more, protectionist? As political economist David A. Steinberg puts it, "Keeping the exchange rate undervalued, i.e., at a highly competitive, below-market value is a form of protectionism that gives local industries an edge over their foreign competitors."[88]

Because of his tenuous analysis, Lichauco was able to reframe imperialism's relationship with hard money, noting that "in the years ahead, devaluation will play an increasingly important role in imperialist strategy in Asia. As the United States and Japan compete for control over the expanding Asia market, they will need, more than ever, sources of cheap raw material as well as cheap labor. . . . The Philippines is a traditional source of cheap labor, and this can be made progressively cheaper still, dollarwise, through the progressive devaluation of the peso."[89]

In incorrectly tying devaluation to the interests of imperialism, Lichauco and the Maoist left elided the history of the United States enforcing dear money on the Philippines for most of the century. In fact, Lichauco insinuated that devaluation had always been the policy of the Americans, noting that "for the greater part of this twentieth century, that is to say, except for the brief decade of the fifties when we regulated our economy, the Philippines has operated its economy on the basis of the principles I have just discussed."[90] Since the so-called imperial policy was devaluation, Lichauco effectively claimed that the Americans had always advocated for a cheaper peso. All the earlier chapters of this book belie this claim.

In making these points, Lichauco also elided the nationalist history of peso devaluation—a tradition represented by Lichauco's friend and client, Salvador Araneta.[91] Henceforth, the strong peso would no longer be the cause of economic conservatives like Miguel Cuaderno but of the nationalist left.

While the Maoist left, along with its allies, was developing new ways to support dear money, it was also exploiting the frustrations of the workers most affected by new inflationary pressures. For Lichauco, "devaluation wreaks havoc on the cost of living and the lives of people in the devaluing country."[92] As for the MDP, it claimed that the new rate made it harder for Filipinos who were "relying on import materials [kagamitan], spare parts, oil and gasoline."[93] This was undoubtedly true, but, as we saw, the increase in the price of imports did not necessarily mean a decline in living standards for most Filipinos. The inflation was most acute for those in the transport sector, who relied the most on foreign oil. However, this sector was not the CPP's natural constituency.

Austere, anti-inflation rhetoric requires focusing on victims of inflation, what we may term the inflationary subject. However, the primary victims of inflation—the rentier class that finds the value of its investments plummeting—are not sympathetic figures. Monetary hawks have therefore focused on the defenseless victims of declines in asset values. For example, in 1925, Winston Churchill's Conservative Party claimed that anti-inflationary hard money policy (a return to the gold standard) benefited poor widows who relied on pensions, displacing attention from the wealthier segment of the rentier class.[94] Instead of defending the assets of bankers and their investors, Churchill made it seem like he was protecting the widow's pension.

Naturally, Churchill's and the CPP's motivations were different. Churchill was defending hard money policy to benefit the rentier class. Meanwhile, the CPP and its allies were defending hard money to oppose a budding dictatorship while supporting the interests of an import-dependent bourgeois, which it viewed as necessary for a "national democratic revolution" that would lay the groundwork for socialism.[95]

Nevertheless, both groups were raising the specter of inflation for political ends.

Who would be the CPP's inflationary subject—its equivalent of the widow with a pension? Unfortunately for the party, its ideological constituency did not suffer because of inflation in the 1970s. As a Maoist organization, the CPP espoused/es a protracted revolution from the countryside. On paper, the primary group it seeks to organize is impoverished farmers. In its propaganda, the CPP, then as now, emphasizes the peasant as a symbol of the toiling masses. During inflationary times, however, farmers are not the ideal symbols of exploitation, because producers charge more. From 1970 to 1980, nominal farm wages increased yearly, and real farm wages held steady and even rose during the middle of the decade.[96]

While the inflation of the 1970s was mostly benign or beneficial for farmers, it had an outsize effect on a sector whose livelihood depended on cheap oil: jeepney drivers. The jeepney is both a symbol of nationalism and the urban class. Originally postwar US army jeeps repurposed as passenger vehicles, they eventually became the most common form of public transportation. Often painted with colorful images, they are symbols of the creativity and work ethic of the Filipino working class. In January 1971, jeepney drivers launched a strike that shut down transportation in Metro Manila, its neighboring provinces, and major cities like Cebu and Davao. According to historian Joseph Scalice, this strike was when the student movement was "wrenched into the wider world" of national politics.[97]

Ostensibly in support of the jeepney drivers, students set up barricades at various universities and led several marches. Beyond campaigning for the interests of the drivers, however, student radicals used the opportunity to chant radical slogans in support of "people's war" from the countryside. They also ratcheted up the tensions by cursing the police and moderates who refused to join the strike. Protests quickly turned violent, with over one hundred injured and four dead during one march.[98] By the end of the year, jeepney drivers had become disillusioned with the student radicals, now wary of being used as tools for revolutionary sloganeering. To signal that they continued to support jeepney drivers, CPP-affiliated organizers founded a federation of jeepney drivers. Most of its members, however, were students, and its office could be found in the student organization building of UP Diliman.[99]

The government was aware that student activists had found a powerful cause célèbre in the figure of the jeepney driver. A confidential military intelligence report from January 1971 noted that students used the price of oil to target the administration. It explained that Maoist-affiliated students, particularly members of the KM, went around Metro Manila, exhorting uncommitted jeepney drivers to join the strike. The KM's chairman was reported as "blaming the administration" for "conspiring with the American imperialists in raising the prices of gasoline and oil."[100]

The jeepney strike and the student agitation frustrated government officials. Writing to Marcos on January 12, 1971, the head of the Board of Investments Caesar Z. Lanuza said that the "strike of jeepney drivers is threatening to escalate to unmanageable proportions if there is continued violence and vandalism." Lanuza decried "the almost lack of any sober understanding among the striking drivers" and accused the media of "disseminating inaccurate, misleading and often times inflammatory publicity" that threatened to provoke violence. Lanuza was particularly frustrated that the public could not fathom the reasons for price increases. The sale of crude oil, he added, "is cartelized on a worldwide scale." "If the international oil companies represented locally choose to be difficult (and they can) I wonder whether even an oil commission could really be effective in dictating on their price policies." For Lanuza, the solution was to "incarcerate the mobsters and ring leaders who, from all indications, are acting in total ignorance of what this whole thing is about."[101] Lanuza's letter captures the authoritarian sentiment in government that would result in one-man rule.

The CPP's increased focus on inflation and the cost of living reflected its tacit view of the Filipino as a consumer who deserved cheaper prices rather than a producer who deserved higher wages. Unlike the labor movements of the 1920s (see chapter 2), which used strikes to negotiate higher pay, the CPP did not have an incentive to push for such changes. Since its goal was to recruit more combatants for its New People's Army, there was, in fact, a perverse incentive for the party to prevent strikes from being resolved favorably. Rather than laborers getting wage increases, the CPP preferred to make them vulnerable to state repression, driving them into armed struggle.[102]

The CPP also did not have the incentive to organize against the most sclerotic sector of the elite—the same import-dependent class cultivated by Miguel Cuaderno's policies—because its Stalinist strategy entailed close collaboration with this section of the nationalist bourgeois. Indeed, most of the strikes it organized targeted "foreign-owned" businesses of Chinese Filipinos, with the CPP's labor arm promoting racist sentiments against the "intsik" (a derogatory term for Chinese). It even explicitly blamed unscrupulous Chinese Filipino businesses for price increases.[103] These were the same businesses that had been deliberately excluded by the nationalist policies of the 1950s under Miguel Cuaderno (recall that Cuaderno and President Garcia both advocated anti-Chinese policies). Here was another through-line from the right of the 1950s into the "left" of the 1970s.

## The Volcker, Imelda, and Aquino Shocks

The new decade began with political and economic crises. But Marcos would survive and grow even stronger. To stay in power despite being term-limited, he imposed martial law in 1972 and ruled effectively as the head of a military junta.[104] Under the new regime, Marcos jailed political opponents, shut down Congress, censored media, and ruled by decree. The military regime killed, illegally detained, and tortured thousands.

Despite the regime's brutality, however, much of the public initially responded with quiescence. After the protests and political machinations that began the decade, the rich and middle class were open to a state that promoted "discipline." On paper, Marcos crafted an ideologically coherent message to justify military rule. In his "New Society," the government would wage a "democratic revolution from the center," combating Communists on the left and oligarchic politicians on the right. This rhetoric not only appealed to the elite but also provided the United States with an ideological cover to support the regime.

Marcos also hid the worst of the regime's brutality by targeting political others who were out of sight for the middle class and elite. On the one hand, the regime killed, imprisoned, and tortured Communists who had started to organize in the countryside. On the other, it waged a brutal war against Muslim independence fighters in the southern island of Mindanao. These military operations were bloody, but the bien-pensant were mostly insulated from their horrors.

The regime also achieved stability through economic growth. As we saw above, the growth rates in the 1970s were stable—significantly improved from the 1960s. After the balance-of-payments crisis at the start of the decade, unprecedented storm seasons, and two oil shocks, technocrats could hold their heads high in 1979. "Few of the problems that the Philippines would face in the 1980s were evident in 1979," explain economists Robert Dohner and Ponciano Intal.[105] Indeed, figure 4.1 shows that exports peaked at the end of the decade—a brief moment when the dream of an export-oriented economy seemed possible. However, the second oil shock of 1979 would prove costlier, with an income loss amounting to 6.9 percent of GNP.[106] More crucially, the good times would end because of changes in Washington.

From October 1979 onward, the US Federal Reserve, under its chair Paul Volcker, fought inflation (partly due to the oil crisis) by aggressively raising interest rates. In response, banks across the world raised rates and shortened payment schedules. From real lending rates hovering at close to zero in the 1970s, they shot up to 8 and 10 percent during the early 1980s.[107] The developing world is estimated to have lost as much as $141 billion due to higher interest rate payments from 1981 to 1982 alone.[108] In the Philippines, the rise in real interest rates was almost 12 percent from 1979 to 1980, adding 3.5 percentage points to GNP income loss.[109] "La Década Perdida" of the 1980s is primarily remembered as a Latin American crisis, with the Mexican default of 1982 signaling the start of the turmoil. However, Stuart Corbridge posits that the crisis had already started in sub-Saharan Africa, the Philippines, and Indonesia as early as 1981, though Western media ignored events in these countries.[110]

Though the crisis affected most developing economies, the Philippines was hit particularly hard (see table 4.2). The downturn it experienced was significantly more pronounced than those of its neighbors and even parts of Latin America, where the crisis was most acute. The country's real per capita growth rate of –1.9 percent from 1980 to 1986 (the last years of the Marcos regime) was worse than the average for all of South America (–0.19773 percent and significantly worse than the average for Southeast Asia (2.10429 percent).

Why did the Philippines experience the 1980s in a manner more like Guatemala than its neighbor Indonesia? The oft-repeated explanation from activists, media commentators, and academics is often a variation of the crony capitalism narrative. Indeed, the term "crony capitalism"—now a worldwide descriptor for corrupt regimes like Putin's Russia—was initially used to describe the Marcos regime in the 1980s.[111] As with the deflationary crisis of the 1920s, popular commentary often portrays the debt crisis of the 1980s as an exceptional domestic event occasioned by local mismanagement.[112] Because this commentary is critical of Marcos's policies, it de-emphasizes the global context and places blame on the regime's spending and corruption. The effect is to focus on the sin of debt accumulation instead of examining the anatomy of a world economic crisis.

Table 4.2 Real GDP growth rate percentage per capita (1971–1979)

| | 1980 | 1981 | 1982 | 1983 | 1984 | 1985 | 1986 | AVERAGE |
|---|---|---|---|---|---|---|---|---|
| Brunei Darussalam | -9.95115 | -22.3781 | 0.566832 | -2.83674 | -2.7521 | -4.78904 | -14.4377 | -8.08257 |
| El Salvador | -10.2277 | -9.0802 | -6.64268 | -1.15665 | 0.320088 | -000136 | -1.26907 | -4.00822 |
| Bolivia | -3.53324 | -1.25968 | -6.40458 | -6.48405 | -2.68914 | -3.03904 | -4.52945 | -3.99131 |
| Venezuela | -4.70764 | -3.03156 | -2.02918 | -8.12341 | -3.9353 | -2.39094 | 3.777109 | -2.92013 |
| Guatemala | 1.180743 | -1.83069 | -5.74945 | -4.87791 | -2.22053 | -3.26126 | -2.51496 | -2.75344 |
| Philippines | 2.451575 | 0.799596 | 1.134998 | -0.603 | -9.28939 | -9.06352 | 1.117667 | -1.92173 |
| Argentina | -0.1421 | -6.90019 | -4.67287 | 2.502406 | 0.449507 | -8.35362 | 5.536507 | -1.65439 |
| Cambodia | -7.90765 | -2.56055 | -3.85557 | 0.453579 | 1.226354 | 1.23338 | -0.06363 | -1.63916 |
| Nicaragua | 1.793275 | 2.437444 | -3.49334 | 1.907739 | -3.97413 | -6.33852 | -3.30385 | -1.56734 |
| Costa Rica | -1.96253 | -4.89991 | -9.80946 | 0.045215 | 5.076816 | -2.01467 | 2.698339 | -1.55231 |
| Honduras | -2.40258 | -0.56579 | -4.33577 | -3.84881 | 1.306461 | 1.201661 | -2.12966 | -1.53921 |
| Uruguay | 5.531872 | 1.475531 | -9.78990 | -6.29646 | -1.58445 | 0.939869 | 8.248558 | -0.21071 |
| Peru | 3.319518 | 2.962511 | -2.62304 | -12.5616 | 1.143797 | -0.32138 | 6.925231 | -0.16499 |
| Mexico | 5.552583 | 6.392015 | -2.70681 | -6.18594 | 1.612798 | 0.874799 | -5.4615 | 0.011135 |
| Chile | 6.387444 | 4.681082 | -14.8307 | -4.17445 | 4.392783 | 0.490668 | 4.009006 | 0.136546 |
| Ecuador | 0.989019 | 2.872122 | -1.96731 | -2.86662 | 0.042222 | 1.336916 | 0.894161 | 0.185787 |
| Paraguay | 8.563836 | 5.815477 | -3.67475 | -5.65755 | 0.237258 | 1.099238 | -2.75655 | 0.518137 |
| Colombia | 1.713944 | -0.05148 | -1.33248 | -0.73385 | 1.029071 | 0.8667 | 3.585244 | 0.72415 |
| Brazil | 6.6923 | -6.45287 | -1.4503 | -5.00835 | 3.108082 | 5.566858 | 5.28839 | 1.094783 |
| Myanmar | 5.011869 | 3.848569 | 2.964272 | 2.635207 | 1.753916 | -1.10307 | -4.31719 | 1.541939 |

| | | | | | | | |
|---|---|---|---|---|---|---|---|
| Malaysia | 4.674368 | 4.19357 | 3.261159 | 3.453294 | 4.873952 | -3.83656 | -1.82516 | 2.113202 |
| Vietnam | -5.56803 | 3.23979 | 5.522427 | 4.50212 | 5.807507 | 3.13941 | 0.977005 | 2.517176 |
| Thailand | 2.545048 | 3.664089 | 3.203247 | 3.479431 | 3.694001 | 2.66533 | 3.594504 | 3.263664 |
| Indonesia | 7.299031 | 5.441329 | -0.078752 | 6.340241 | 4.644762 | 0.326723 | 3.783478 | 3.964021 |
| Singapore | 8.163888 | 8.511289 | 4.731422 | 6.118614 | 6.321813 | -2.90283 | -1.00605 | 4.276878 |
| Laos | 7.874889 | 12.81804 | 4.519647 | 2.021427 | 4.338098 | 2.215533 | 1.974757 | 5.108913 |
| World | 0.085459 | 0.057253 | -1.40721 | 0.990892 | 2.809748 | 1.712164 | 1.436335 | 0.812091 |
| Latin America and the Caribbean | 3.42776 | -1.51992 | -2.66142 | -4.32569 | 1.402776 | 0.736019 | 1.944616 | -0.14227 |
| Central America | 4.75998 | 5.31743 | -3.04114 | -5.83138 | 1.3436421 | 0.51365 | -4.97955 | -0.27351 |
| South America | 3.105603 | -4.57742 | -2.91667 | -4.10637 | 1.311108 | 0.948417 | 4.851226 | -0.19773 |
| Asia | 1.05359 | 1.771033 | 0.350818 | 2.127162 | 3.171088 | 2.720502 | 2.555963 | 1.964308 |
| Southeastern Asia | 3.976554 | 3.387479 | 1.825721 | 3.747655 | 1.747915 | -1.63403 | 1.678736 | 2.10429 |
| Developing economies | 2.233336 | -0.48717 | -1.81137 | -1.30024 | 2.185639 | 1.270723 | 1.989167 | 0.582869 |

Source: uctad.uctadstat.org.

There is merit to this argument because of the proportion of the Marcos administration's debt. Yet the absolute debt was never as large as the worst cases in Latin America. Even when the full extent of the government indebtedness had been revealed in 1983 (the central bank had disingenuously excluded some of its foreign liabilities in earlier computations), *The Washington Post* still noted that "the Asian nation's roughly $24 billion in foreign debt—about two thirds of which is owed to commercial banks—pales before the $90 billion that Brazil and Mexico owe."[113] Relative to the size of the economy, however, Philippine debt was large. Figure 4.3 shows that, as a percentage of the country's income, its debt had grown rapidly ahead of that of Brazil and Mexico during the 1970s. And while the Suharto government in Indonesia was another example of high debt growth in Southeast Asia, it was not as vulnerable as the Philippines at the end of the decade. Indeed, the Philippines' vulnerability is partially explained by the fact that its debt position had peaked just as the Volcker shock was about to hit.

Hindsight is twenty-twenty when it comes to Marcos's debt. In retrospect, the country's debt levels seem shocking. But in the 1970s, creditors were bullish about the Philippines. As we have seen, the balance of payments was improving, real growth was steady, and the public sector was expanding. Although the debt ratio in 1978 was rising, growth projections made the IMF representative in the Philippines, according

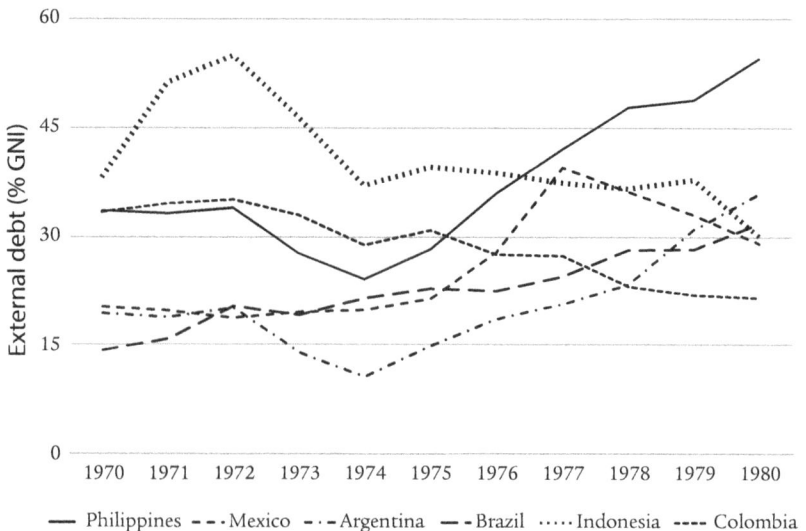

FIGURE 4.3. External debt as a percentage of gross national income

to the British Embassy, "cautiously bullish."[114] The 1970s was also a period when international banks were investing petrodollars from oil-producing states. In particular, the World Bank, under Robert McNamara, was increasing its influence on the Third World, favoring larger projects that it perceived would have long-term developmental outcomes. In the Philippines, the World Bank encouraged the Marcos government to invest in labor-intensive products like textiles, contributing to the rise and diversification of exports noted earlier.[115]

As for the technocrats, they were not only more fiscally expansive by disposition; they also had to use debt for countercyclical financing amid the two oil shocks.[116]

Yet, compared to the crisis of the 1920s, corruption was more of a factor in the 1980s. The monetary contraction brought into sharper focus the regime's perfidy. As early as 1978, another key technocrat, the minister of industry Vicente Paterno, had already noticed "increasing pressure from Marcos cronies to accommodate crooked projects," leading him to request an exit from the cabinet.[117] By the 1980s, the global downturn made crony businesses even more dependent on government largesse for survival. And these investments resulted in a marked decrease in capital productivity.

These were effectively bailouts that became unsustainable amid shrinking government coffers and more acute struggles at debt refinancing. The corruption of crony businesses is well documented, and we need not list multiple examples here.[118] The example of the Construction and Development Corporation (CDCP) of the Philippines, however, is illustrative. From 1981 to 1983, the government plowed over 6.2 billion pesos into the CDCP, about 25 percent of the money supply and 30 percent of the tax collected in 1981.[119] This kind of spending not only diverted money to Marcos allies but also distorted and blunted the broader program of countercyclical spending.[120]

At the high point of the crisis, moreover, currency management was no longer under the sole control of technocrats because of the emergence of a parallel banking system called the "Binondo Central Bank" (BCB, a reference to Manila's Chinatown in the Binondo district)—a group of businessmen that the Marcos regime organized to co-opt the black-market sale of dollars. Organized in 1983 by Trade Secretary Roberto Ongpin, the BCB sought to provide a steady stream of dollars to panicked importers purchasing expensive dollars on the black market.[121] This, too, would be an opportunity for businessmen close to the government to profit from the soaring rates of the illicit economy. Apart from Imelda Marcos's growing power, therefore, the technocrats were also being undercut by the Marcos family's close business associates. And while these trends predated the crisis, they became more visible amid the economic decay.

On the issue of corruption and the growing power of Marcos's cronies, the often-measured Sicat degenerates into a crass apologist, noting that "crony capitalism and other dispensations of power related to the public wealth was not a practice that could mainly be associated with Marcos."[122] Nevertheless, he is correct in contending that the regime's "debacle towards the end had many causes" and cannot be assessed simplistically by laying the blame exclusively on corruption, crony capitalism, and government largesse.[123]

Examining how a political crisis fed into an economic one is also crucial. Sicat is often taken to task by anti-Marcos economists for claiming that growth would have continued had it not been for the "Ninoy shock" of 1983, a reference to the assassination of the opposition senator Benigno "Ninoy" Aquino, which triggered the political crisis that led to Marcos's downfall.[124] Such assertions on Sicat's part are indeed dubious. As we have seen, many of the vulnerabilities of the Marcos economy were already evident in the early 1980s. Moreover, other events apart from the assassination could have exposed the economy's vulnerabilities. Still, Aquino's death precipitated the worst phase of the crisis. The sections in bold from table 4.2 show that the Philippines only went into negative growth from 1983 to 1985 (after Aquino's death) and that the bleeding stopped in 1986, the year of Marcos's fall.

The effect of Aquino's assassination was evident to observers from the time. Virata and central bank governor Jaime Laya requested a ninety-day payment moratorium a little less than two months after Aquino's assassination. This period was when the Philippine crisis began to look Latin American, as the Philippines became, according to *The New York Times*, "the first Asian country to request a change in its foreign debt repayment timetable since the international debt crisis intensified a year ago." The *Times* attributed the move to the "political crisis set off by the assassination in Manila on Aug. 21 of Benigno Aquino. . . . The impact of that event on business's confidence in the Marcos regime," it added, "brought on a 21 percent devaluation of the peso amid large-scale purchases of dollars."[125] Such a devaluation was sudden and rending. More than the devaluation of 1970, this was an unplanned devaluation and unstrategic depreciation—purely the effect of a deepening crisis.

AUSTERITY DEMOCRATIZED    143

It would further cement the idea that a decline in currency value equals a decline in economic health.

The central bank initially claimed that the capital flight after Aquino's assassination amounted to one billion dollars. Banks, however, discovered that the capital flight after the assassination had only been $400 million and that the central bank had fudged the numbers to obscure that its reserves were already dwindling in 1982. Still, the Aquino assassination ensured that capital flight would continue. Because there was a political crisis, bankers (mostly American) had decided, according to *The Washington Post*, that the government would be "reluctant to impose further belt-tightening measures on a disaffected population."[126] Even worse, the Mexican and Brazilian defaults of 1982 spooked investors in Third World markets and cut off lines of credit for countries like the Philippines. As Virata (then already prime minister) noted in late 1983, "The main reason why we are in this difficult situation is that normal financing was withdrawn in late 1982, when the Mexican and Brazilian defaults occurred. Many of our credit lines were cut and others were shortened. A one-year line was reduced to six months then three months, then one month."[127]

The *Post* summarized what a top US banker believed were the causes of the acute phase of the crisis. First, the chronic balance-of-trade deficit that began with "the oil crunches of 1974 and 1979." Second, the Marcos regime's propensity to take on short-term debt. And third, "political instability and growing disaffection with the military regime of Marcos, coupled with the perception during most of 1983 that the leader's wife, Imelda, was growing too strong and would succeed her husband."[128]

Such accounts from the period depart from today's emotionally and politically charged defenses and recriminations. They reinforce Caroline Hau's view of the crisis as a perfect storm that resulted from two oil shocks, the Volcker rate hike, increasing debt, a commodity price recession, corruption, and the political crisis.[129] Despite the various causes of the crisis, Hau shows how commentators have reduced it to a tale of crony capitalism.[130] The crisis thus cemented the view of the Philippines "as a model of the pathological excesses of the predatory, rent-seeking oligarchy-dominated weak state."[131] In other words, it reinforced the good-governance narrative of Philippine development that we have been tracing since chapter 2.

As we have seen, good-governance discourse is often the handmaiden of austerity. Like the PNB crisis of the 1920s, the crisis of the 1980s tainted the legacy of developmental spending and reminded potential profligate colonials of what the state should and should not do. Those who seek to "learn" from the lessons of the Marcos regime often derive conclusions that are now clearly recognizable as evincing modern neoliberal thought. For example, an article from a recent volume on the legacy of the Marcos regime notes that, post-Marcos, the Philippines still "offers even more opportunities for collusive rent-seeking, raising the importance of the State as a fair regulator rather than as a direct market actor (i.e. through state owned enterprises)."[132] Such are the views of more conservative economists. But they are not necessarily anathema to those of the contemporary left.

## Freedom from Debt, and Hawkish Central Banking

Given the trauma of dictatorship, measured assessments are understandably difficult to come by. The pain of the debt crisis impelled a righteous indignation not just from economic conservatives but also from the Philippine left. Debt became associated with the authoritarianism that the left sought to combat. As a history of the left-wing anti-debt movement notes, "To seek freedom from the dictatorship was to seek freedom from debt. The two issues were inseparable."[133] If the 1970s turned dear money into a left-wing case, the Third World debt crisis of the 1980s made the left critical of debt, even as the sudden depreciations made the left even more supportive of dear money.

Much of this early analysis was rigorous. In 1982, Marxist sociologist Walden Bello and reporters David Kinley and Elaine Elinson riffled through classified World Bank documents to show how the international financial community knowingly propped up a corrupt and violent dictatorship.[134] Their book was less about debt per se and more about the developmental models prescribed by global financial institutions. But its critique of World Bank aid contributed to a sense that debt was a foreign threat. Similarly, in 1984, the Maoist-aligned IBON databank published a data-driven booklet that remains one of the finest early accounts of the crisis. While it detailed the multiple factors that led to the crisis, its account of debt was moralizing, noting, "Borrowing can be addictive. The first 'sniff' is intoxicating. Add bigger doses and in no time at all, a country is hooked. Soon it finds itself caught in a vicious cycle of borrowing and repaying. But it's never too late to kick the habit."[135]

Then there was Alejandro Lichauco, who remained prolific in the 1980s. He, too, would develop an anti-debt position. Lichauco's hero and mentor, the nationalist senator Claro M. Recto, had been more open to foreign debt in the 1950s, viewing it as a better source of capital than foreign investments, which could displace local capitalists. For Lichauco, however, devaluation and debt were two sides of the same coin. In 1988, he argued that the US and the IMF made loans contingent on the peso's devaluation, concluding that "decontrol prodded the country to live beyond its means and fall into the debt trap."[136] Alongside his rewriting of the history of the 1950s and Cuaderno's regime of austerity (see previous chapter), Lichauco constructed a fall-from-Eden narrative: In the 1950s, Philippine policymaking was nationalist in its protection of its currency and its promotion of a so-called industrial class. It also maintained stable debt levels and stood firm against US interests through its strong central bank governor. The fall occurred when Macapagal repudiated Cuaderno, a process that climaxed under the regime of the dictator, who further depreciated the currency and sent the country spiraling into a debt trap. This remains a key narrative for many purportedly left-wing Filipino economists today.

In 1986, Marcos fell after a bloodless revolution.[137] Bereft of a common enemy, the already fractious left fractured even further, culminating in a major split of the CPP in 1992.[138] Amid the ideological and military squabbles, the left found a common cause in the anti-debt movement. Not only had Marcos accumulated so much foreign debt, but his democratic successor, Corazon Aquino (the assassinated Senator Aquino's widow), vowed to honor all those debts and refused to renegotiate them. In 1988, multiple left-wing organizations representing various political blocks, individuals, and sectors founded the Freedom from Debt Coalition (FDC). The grouping initially included Maoists, remnants of an old pro-Soviet Communist Party, social democrats, and independent socialists.[139] In many other countries, an organization with such a name would be coded as right-wing or libertarian. Still, after a debt crisis caused by fascistic authoritarianism, the name and its cause would prove unproblematic.

The FDC's initial advocacy involved calling for a moratorium on foreign debt-service payments, a selective repudiation of debts, particularly those tainted with corruption, and limiting debt-service payments to 10 percent of export earnings.[140] These demands were reasonable in the immediate aftermath of the Third World debt crisis; they were ways to stop the bleeding. However, the FDC had placed anti-debt discourse squarely within the left. Moreover, it had mainstreamed the notion that "debt-driven growth" was unsustainable. To this day, it is common for left-wing economists to look back at the Marcos era as a time of "debt-driven growth," as if growing by debt is exceptional (how many states have grown without issuing bonds?). And as we shall see in the conclusion, the threat of a new Marcos creating a new debt bomb remains a perennial fear of the left.

As external foreign debt declined in the 1990s, the debt issue became less salient, and the FDC had to broaden its agenda and began to focus on the neoliberalism of international financial institutions.[141] Today, its website claims that debt is "the prism that holds the wide spectra of issues" that involve the "imposition of neo-liberal policies."[142]

The first two decades after Marcos's fall were, indeed, years of high neoliberalism in the Philippines, as they were globally. Amid the multiple privatizations and the various WTO trade rounds that forcibly opened up the economy, the Philippine left took principled stances that placed it at odds with the technocrats of post-Marcos presidents. Yet there was one area where the left and the post-Marcos technocracy saw eye to eye: dear money and monetary austerity. In the 1990s, with the left's support, the Philippine legislature would abrogate the central bank's duty to foster growth and development.

When the first Philippine Central Bank was established after the war, it had, like many other central banks, multiple roles, which included the maintenance of price stability, the preservation of the peso's value, and the promotion of production, employment, and income. The Marcos regime modified the roles of the central bank after the declaration of martial law in 1972, placing (at least on paper) a greater premium on price stability. Still, it kept the bank's developmental role. Upon the restoration of democracy in 1986, however, bankers and civil society sought to "reform" central banking in the country. The inflation crisis of the 1980s, they believed, could have been blunted had there been a truly "independent" central bank immune to the overreach of a dictator like Marcos. The new constitution of 1987 thus instructed Congress to establish a new central bank. After a lengthy legislative grind, Congress passed the New Central Bank Act in 1993.[143]

Unlike previous iterations of the central bank, the new one would no longer have a developmental function. Its "primary function" would be to maintain price stability. And this priority shift had the support of the left and the right. In explaining the revised role of the bank, the reformist senator Raul Roco, one of the law's authors, noted that "economists, bankers, and even the Freedom from Debt Coalition, all of them were unanimous in stating that this should be the primary objective of monetary policy of the Bangko Sentral."[144] In emphasizing that *even the FDC* accepted this new vision of central banking, Roco gestured to the left-right consensus around monetary austerity. (Roco himself was one of the few mainstream politicians that many on the left saw as an ally.)

Despite fighting neoliberalism on other fronts, the FDC had failed to consider that this narrow notion of an inflation-fighting, "independent" central bank was a key part of the neoliberalism it stood against. As Adam Tooze explains, "If freedom of capital movement was the belt, then central bank independence was the buckle on the free-market Washington Consensus of the 1990s."[145] Both were ways to prevent democratic publics from participating in economic debates.

In endorsing the abrogation of the central bank's developmental duty, those who advocated for a new central bank were participating in a tradition of monetary overcorrection in the Philippines. As we saw in chapter 2, Leonard Wood imposed one of the world's strictest currency reserve requirements on the Philippines after the PNB crisis. In the wake of the 1980s debt crisis, hard money bankers and the miserly left created an extra-conservative central bank with a limited mandate. Like the 1920s overcorrection, the result was a Philippines that was more austere than its colonizer and its mentor in anti-profligacy. Today, the US Fed has a dual mandate of maintaining price stability and sustaining employment. And those who wish to change this setup to a Filipino-style single, anti-inflation mandate comprise traditional economic conservatives of the Republican Party, such as former Vice President Mike Pence.

But the single mandate is sacred in the Philippines. And central bankers embrace the de facto conservatism of the present-day Bangko Sentral ng Pilipinas (BSP). For example, in 2023, the dictator's son, President Ferdinand Marcos Jr., appointed as BSP governor the former New York Fed banker Eli Remolona.[146] Unlike his father's central bank governors, Marcos Jr.'s appointee would not be associated with profligacy. After his appointment, Remolona stated, "The BSP is an inflation-targeting bank—that means it is structurally hawkish when it comes to inflation."[147] Given a choice, then, between more jobs, higher wages, and more growth on the one hand and slowing inflation / preserving the peso's value on the other, the BSP is legally obligated to prioritize the former. Put another way, central banking in contemporary Philippines is inherently austere.

In 2023, as Remolona's BSP engaged in the most aggressive rate hikes in all of Asia, the director of the National Economic Development Authority, Arsenio Balisacan, complained that the bank's hawkishness would strengthen the peso and hurt growth and exports in the process.[148] But the BSP was independent of economic planners like Balisacan and would double down on its aggressive rate hikes. Forty years prior, the central bank would have found Balisacan's predecessor, Gerardo Sicat, more difficult to ignore.

In the previous chapter, we discussed the emergence of the central bank myth in the 1950s—the idea that an "independent" central bank should stand over democratic processes to maintain the value of rentier assets. In the 1950s, the central bank myth was upheld by dint of Cuaderno's antidemocratic personality; after Marcos, it had become legally enshrined. It was also enshrined in public discourse. In the 1950s, thinkers like Araneta could challenge the central bank, exposing the inherent politics embedded in the institution. Since the fall of Marcos, currency revaluation and inflation management have been the unchallenged goals of monetary policy. And after acquiescing to the creation of a structurally hawkish central bank, the left has mostly given up on questions of monetary policy, except to complain when the peso value drops—no doubt to hallelujahs from the hawks at the central bank.

The discourse of austerity in the Philippines has thus come full circle because of Marcos. When the US colonized the Philippines, it brought with it hard money, and the expensive peso became a symbol of American power. By the end of the century, the belief in a strong peso was held not just by conservative bankers but also by the left. Traumatized by the inflation and corrupt profligacy of the Marcos years, all Filipinos agreed that developmental goals had to take a back seat to price stability.

This dictator was many things—corrupt, venal, brutal, dishonest—but he was not austere. Opposing this dictator was the principled thing to do, but opposing him also led to the democratization of austerity.

# Conclusion
## Profligate Others Everywhere

The rhetoric that the miserly left developed during the Marcos years thrives to this day. I should know; I've used it myself. As a youth activist critical of a few post-Marcos administrations, I learned a simple formula for agitprop speeches: Check inflation rates, the peso's value, and the debt level. If the numbers looked bad, I'd make a comparison to the "dark days of the dictatorship" (you could also fudge the numbers by looking at the absolute debt—always a great way to induce sticker shock).[1] In a slow and affected Tagalog cadence, activists like me would complain that inflation was "cooking the poor in their own grease" (ginigisa ang mahirap sa sariling mantika) or of "our grandchildren being buried in debt" (mga apo nating nababaon sa utang). We could even take total debt, divide it by the population, and make it seem like individual Filipinos all owed foreign capitalists.[2] There were corollary strategies: condemn the administration for promoting "oligarchic democracy," abetting corruption, and condemning us to penury.

Ultimately, things would go back to Marcos. This was especially the case from roughly 2010 onward when pro-Marcos accounts started to crop up on social media and YouTube. Like American liberals who first confronted the alt-right online, I thought these were fringe accounts run by the ill-informed. It took a while for me to realize that this had become a well-oiled machine of historical distortion. It took me an even longer time to realize that this well-oiled machine appealed to other Filipinos, not because they were stupid, but because they had grown weary of the liberal-democratic status quo.

As a graduate student and eventually a young assistant professor in Manila, I started to be interviewed on national media as an "expert" on the Marcos regime. During these interviews, I would come armed with numbers I had memorized (I've forgotten them now). The number of tortured, killed, and incarcerated by the regime came first. Then I would recite an incantation of figures on the inflation, poverty, and debt of the early 1980s (largely neglecting the 1970s). I did not know what the Volcker shock was then, and I only had the faintest idea of what the oil crisis was, but I would confidently conclude that "we are still paying to this day for the debts Marcos incurred." When pro-Marcos trolls called me out for ignoring the context of the 1980s, I would be smug and dismiss them as deplorables.

Those who identify as progressives in the Philippines—liberals, socialists, social democrats, Communists—have lost the war of position against the Marcoses. Anti-Marcos intellectuals like me no longer tell the story of the nation. For the first two decades since the fall of Marcos, we were the victors, and we told a victor's history: The dark lord rose, we defeated him, and we restored our country's democracy. Now we are only victorious in the classrooms of elite universities and the newsrooms of increasingly marginal legacy media. Our first major defeat was in 2016 when our compatriots elected the murderous strongman Rodrigo Duterte. Of course, Duterte was John the Baptist for the coming Marcos restoration. In 2022, the Philippines elected Ferdinand Marcos Jr.

There are many reasons why we lost. But I suspect part of it has to do with our tired rhetoric. Many of us counseled good governance and macro-prudentialism while warning people of the threat of dictatorship. Liberal politicians and the socialists enamored with them believed the solution to the country's problems was simple: honest governance. All we needed to do was elect politicians who were not like the duplicitous, corrupt, and extravagant Marcos. Meanwhile, the electorate was slowly starting to believe that a government that could "do something" was more important than a clean one.[3]

Apart from a violent Communist rebellion from the countryside that would usher in a Maoist utopia, very few thought about alternative economic systems. The economy, after all, was doing well enough. In the 2010s, inflation was low. The balance-of-payments crises that had plagued the country since independence had been eased by overseas Fili-pino workers (OFWs) sending home foreign currency and by call center workers who attracted dollar investments. They were shouldering the burdens of a nonindustrialized, non-exporting, service-driven economy produced by decades of dear money policy. In the case of the call center workers, they shouldered this burden amid broken circadian rhythms and screaming Karens. For OFWs, dislocation from home and loved ones was the cost of foreign exchange. Many of these "new heroes"—a title bestowed on OFWs by former President Corazon Aquino—voted for Duterte and Marcos Jr.[4]

The immediate post-Marcos period was the Philippines' end of his-tory. Elite liberal democracy held sway, and progressives believed we could open new spaces for the left as long as we kept pushing. But Duterte pressed the play button on history and resumed where Marcos had left off, paving the way for the dictator's son. Like Marcos, Duterte was murderous. But, like Marcos, he also promised a golden age of infrastructural development, telling the people that he would "build, build, build." He also spent more on social services than any of his post-Marcos predecessors.[5]

Right-wing populism outflanks the left by appropriating some of its strategies—bold spending, the promotion of social services, the rhetoric of grassroots empowerment—while combining these with dark impulses like racism and authoritarianism. And in the case of Duterte, bloodlust. Given how austere Filipino progressives had become, this outflanking was an easy move for the murderous mayor-turned-president.

In the middle of Duterte's term—a time when the Philippine debt-to-GDP ratio was at its most stable in over thirty years and tax collec-tion was at a twenty-year high[6]—Rene Ofreneo, president of the Freedom from Debt Coalition, insisted that public infrastructure spending must ensure "debt sustainability" lest a "debt bomb" explode. To the conten-tion that the debt-to-GDP ratio was low, Ofreneo did not offer a rebut-tal but merely asked, "Is there an assurance that this scenario of debt sustainability shall be the case in the coming years?" Policymaking is, of course, not about assurances but about probabilities, and given the trends, the likelihood of the "debt bomb" was doubtful. But Ofreneo insisted that debt could balloon overnight because of "the experience of the Philippines during the Marcos period" when "the debt bomb exploded because of the failure of the real economic sectors to grow, at a pace enough to strengthen the capacity of the country to service the growing debt."[7] The threat of the Marcos regime was eternal.

The more hard-line Maoist-aligned left struck a miserly tone as well. In 2018, also amid Duterte's increased spending, the Maoist-aligned IBON Foundation's executive director, Sonny Africa, wrote a 2018 year-end review that condemned "the country's neoliberal economic managers" for inflation and other perceived injustices in economic policy. For Africa, one of the faults of these "neoliberal" managers was the belief that they "could spend their way" out of economic slowdowns—curious, since one of neoliberalism's main goals is reducing state spending. More curious still, Africa believed that these "neoliberals" needed to be condemned since "the budget deficit is already at its worst in seven years."[8] But Duterte's supporters did not care about debt or the budget deficit because many benefited from the mass murderer's largesse. Duterte's approval hovered at roughly 80 percent for his entire term.

Though less obvious, progressives worldwide had also become austere enough to be outflanked by populists. In the United States, Donald Trump capitalized on the decline of manufacturing and the Democratic Party's neglect of unions to turn himself into a hero of the white working class. Extravagant in his consumption and extravagant in his false promises of American greatness, Trump was like a profligate Filipino politician. Like Marcos, he promised that his country would be "great again" (a line from Marcos's inauguration speech in 1965) and even had the old Filipino dictator's election adviser, Paul Manafort, run his campaign.[9] Finally, our colonizers were learning from us.

The Philippine left's extreme attraction to austerity makes it challenging to compare it with other movements. But stories of ostensibly progressive political groups falling prey to austerity's vampiric allure are all too common, from the dependence on "third way" liberals like Bill Clinton, Tony Blair, and Gerhard Schroeder in the 1990s and 2000s to a Malaysian opposition that found its voice in an old neoliberal like Anwar Ibrahim. No wonder people believe There Is No Alternative (TINA).

If the political dilemmas around austerity I have described thus far resonate with struggles in other places, it is because the story of how austerity unfolded in the Philippines provides us with broader insights into its history. Austerity roots itself by becoming normalized, so much so that even liberals and leftists take it for granted. When they do, however, they expose themselves to populist backlash. In this regard, the story of the Philippines is the story of the world. And some of its experiences are generalizable.

## Austerity in the Colonies

I began this book by claiming that austerity plus colonialism equals something different. I end it by teasing out some of these differences and identifying the attributes of austerity in colonial contexts. These attributes are, naturally, provisional, as they are based on one case study. However, as I noted in the introduction, the Philippines is an ideal case study because austerity's hegemony in that country lays bare its logic. Simultaneously, its hidden nature allows us to trace its contradiction-ridden history.

While this conclusion attempts broad theorizing, I leave it to the reader to assess how my initial findings apply to other cases, especially because the Philippine case is difficult to compare. At this point, the reader has also hopefully noticed that I find my country weird. Much of the country's history is anomalous: the poor little rich country of the postcolonial world with a miserly left that is as, or even more, zealous about hard money as its imperialists. Admittedly, it requires hindsight and analytical license to argue that such an exceptional case has broad theoretical importance. However, the fact that the Philippines experienced and, many times, even presaged many of the historical changes of the twentieth century leads me to think that some of my reflections apply elsewhere. The Philippines contracted austerity from the United States amid the initial stirrings of a Pax Americana and the decline of Pax Britannica. It was the first country in Asia to be placed under an American blanket of gold, and it was there that Progressive Era debates about American money started to be globalized. It was a preview of our present world of dollar supremacy.

During the First World War, the Philippine colonial state briefly experimented with developmentalism, like its neighbors, French Indochina and the Dutch East Indies. As in these other colonies, the postwar great deflation led to a quick repudiation of an expansive state and the implementation of austerity. This era of high austerity arrived in Asia at the same time it came to Europe—a period when conservative economists rejected wartime economic experiments.

In the immediate postwar period, the Philippines became the Third World symbol of "responsible" central banking. As Miguel Cuaderno often pointed out, the IMF held out his policies as examples for other developing nations to imitate. Regardless of economic circumstances, Filipinos trumpeted their expensive currency, earning them the moniker of the "poor little rich country" in Asia.

The implications of the rise and fall of the Marcos regime were likewise global in scale. As we saw in chapter 4, the global discourse on "crony capitalism" was born after the dictator's downfall. During events like the Asian Financial Crisis, conservative economists bandied about the specter of crony capitalism to spurn developmental and industrial policy. Thus, a state investing in its economy became equated with corrupt politicians rewarding their cronies. In the aftermath of the Marcos regime, the Philippines became the prototypical "anti-developmental" state—proof that expansive government policy led to corruption.[10] Its story, therefore, became part of modern neoliberalism's morality tale against the state becoming an engine of economic growth.

The story I have tried to tell has, thus, been a global one. And many of the conclusions we derive from this story may also be global.

I propose five traits of colonial austerity grounded on the Philippine experience.

We begin with the most obvious observation: *Colonial austerity is tied to civilizational discourse.* Of course, viewing allegedly profligate individuals or societies as others is not exclusive to colonies. The same pro-gold Republicans who imposed the gold standard on the Philippines also looked down on "spendthrift" southern farmers. For the first two decades of this century, much of Europe condescended to Greece for failing to reduce its spending on social services. And, globally, but especially in the United States, the rich blame people on welfare. In these cases, austerity is tied to notions of morality and sometimes racial superiority. But this dynamic is more pronounced in colonies.

In the Philippines, austerity arrived alongside the violence of imperialism—an imperialism that was highly classificatory. Within the US's civilizational matrix, one had to split hairs: Filipinos were not civilized because they were racially inferior, but Hispanicized Filipinos were slightly more civilized than Muslims or animists; an economy tied to the Anglo-Asian silver trade was not barbaric, but it could be elevated to a higher degree of refinement. The exceptional American empire styled itself as the exceptional avatar of economic rectitude, more austere than previous empires. Americans prided themselves on being the global ambassadors of civilized hard money, manlier and more consistent than the informal British empire it sought to replace.

Filipinos soon sought to share their pride, internalizing the civilizational logic of colonial austerity. This shift manifested in absurd moments when Filipinos sought to out-austere their colonial masters, like when legislators looked down on the Roosevelt administration for devaluing the dollar during the Depression, or when the Commonwealth government-in-exile bragged to the US Treasury Department about the strength of the peso amid widespread destruction, or when Cuaderno "talked back" to the US for recommending depreciation in 1958. On the surface, these were cases of Filipinos evincing nationalist pride. More profoundly, they were testaments to the success of imperialist austerity. Frantz Fanon's now clichéd description of the postcolonial condition where the colonized wear "white masks" applies here.[11] Austerity was a white mask Filipinos donned early in the twentieth century. It is a mask they continue to wear today.

Second: *Colonial austerity is a joint project between the colonizer and the colonized.* If colonial austerity is internalized by the colonized, it is unsurprising that they participate in its rearticulation, reification, and implementation. Today, commentators talk about neoliberalism and how neoliberal institutions impose austerity on the Third World from the outside. This story not only neglects the agency of policymakers in the developing world but also absolves them of their complicity. When Cuaderno designed his system of controls alongside the IMF money doctor George Luthringer, he did so willingly; and when the US and the IMF proposed to reverse these policies, Cuaderno actively resisted. When international financial institutions and the US were austere, the Philippines supported them. When they were less austere, the Philippines rejected them.

Eventually, the end of free-trade agreements between the United States and the Philippines meant the US had less reason to raise the price of Philippine exports by imposing an expensive currency. Nevertheless, from the 1970s onward, "left wing" nationalists like Alejandro Lichauco continued to press for dear money. In the wake of the Marcos dictatorship, almost all Filipinos agreed that a stable currency, anti-inflation, and low debt were preferable to aggressive development.

This consensus leads to a poverty of economic thought in the country, where we all argue over short-term indicators like inflation, currency strength, and debt levels. Critics of the government, especially the left, use these indicators to condemn the government. But they do not challenge the thinking that leads us to prioritize these indicators over indicators like the poverty rate, employment, wages, unionization rates, or inequality levels. Like mainstream economists, left-wing economists conceive of Filipinos primarily as consumers who need to be protected from higher prices. Rarely do they think of them as producers and workers who get paid. Anti-inflation becomes more important than organizing for better wages. Colonial austerity constrains our national conversations and puts limits on our imaginations.

Third: *Colonial austerity hides in plain sight.* When one reads economic news in the US, one knows who is for and against austerity. And those who organize around austerity—the Tea Party and the now defunct Paul Ryan wing of the Republican Party—make explicit what they are arguing for. Similarly, if we read European news, it is clear enough that German central bankers are more austere than Scandinavian social democrats.[12]

However, all our macroeconomic regimes in the Philippines were built on austerity. In 1902, Americans built a colonial economy on the gold standard—a standard they would defend and turn even more restrictive after the great deflation of the 1920s. In the 1950s, Miguel Cuaderno inaugurated the central bank as a beacon for global austerity in the Third World. And after 1986, the left and the right sought to forge an economic order that repudiated the corrupt state spending of the Marcos regime. Austerity is, thus, the economic air that we breathe. And we rarely think about the air.

The result of this neglect is that Filipinos (except, in his day, the zealot Cuaderno) rarely call austerity by its name. Sometimes, commentators use near-antonyms to describe austere policies, such as when the left calls for reflation or massive debt reduction, claiming they are fighting "neoliberalism." In the case of monetary policy, few Filipinos note that a "hawkish" central bank is a euphemism for an austere central bank. And because Filipinos are so inflation-averse, calling one's policies anti-inflation instead of austerity is always a better way to persuade the public.

The inability to name austerity leads to its hegemony. Indeed, this vagueness allows even ostensibly progressive groups to defend its tenets. It therefore behooves us to call austerity by its name.

Fourth: *Colonial austerity presents itself as good governance.* We saw this most clearly in chapter 2 when we examined the PNB "crisis." In that instance, we examined how William Cameron Forbes and Leonard Wood repudiated developmental spending by portraying Filipinos as profligate and corrupt. Today, many analysts of Philippine politics tacitly endorse austerity by rehearsing the themes of the good-governance discourse that emerged in the early twentieth century. They no longer claim Filipinos are too barbaric or effeminate to spend. Instead, they argue that the "weakness" of Philippine "institutions" dooms us to fail. For example, the historian Alfred McCoy, who has spent decades writing important critiques of the Philippine elite, blames the country's "recurring crises" on "the fusion of political power and rent-seeking" that leads to corruption, the concentration of wealth, and weak institutions.[13] This is typical of a mainstream line of political-economic analysis in the Philippines that I was, unfortunately, also previously and naively a champion of.[14]

In response to McCoy, economists have pointed out that crony capitalism is more rampant in the wealthier economies of Singapore, Malaysia, and Hong Kong.[15] More broadly, if weak and corrupt institutions doom countries to be poor, what explains China's rapid growth amid widespread corruption and rent-seeking?[16] Beyond being empirically false, however, quick conclusions like McCoy's lead to implicit, sometimes explicit, endorsements of austerity. If the state is corrupt, why fund it? And if institutions are inherently weak, what is the point of large-scale developmental planning and spending? Politicians will just use this money to enrich themselves and weaken institutions further.

The discourse around "weak institutions" being the cause of underdevelopment is global.[17] And, as Ha-Joon Chang points out, this explanation became au courant after the neoliberal reforms (which included austerity) of the 1980s and 1990s had failed. Those who advocated these reforms needed something else to blame for their failures. They thus concluded that inherently weak institutions doom countries to fail.[18] Yet this idea neglects that economic growth may precede the maturation of institutions. Such was the case in the United States, a hotbed of rent-seeking and corruption during the Progressive Era. And something similar may be said of developmental states in East Asia, which used their wealth to clean up their corrupt bureaucracies. In other words, they strengthened their institutions by being un-austere.

There is a sense, however, that nothing can be done in the Philippines. For instance, political scientist Paul Hutchcroft and economist Emmanuel de Dios believe that "the power of the particularistic demands of the oligarchy" ruins "sound policy agenda at the national level."[19] (What, then, is the use of policy?) And as we saw in chapter 4, economists who seek to "learn" from the Marcos regime have advocated cutting back on state investments. Such thinking would not have been foreign to imperialists like Forbes and Wood, who also believed corruption precluded rational spending.

In response to this cynicism, we should note that *any* combination of liberal democracy and capitalism produces incentives for rent-seeking and crony capitalism.[20] And in these systems, one will always find examples of deplorable and exploitative corruption by the elite. Indeed, some of the most advanced liberal capitalist democracies, like today's United States, have the most advanced forms of influence-peddling. The Philippines is undoubtedly an elite democracy, and its elites are rapacious. But rapacious elites influence democracies everywhere. This does not mean that nothing can be done. Unfortunately, austerity, cynicism, and quiescence dovetail in the Philippines.

Fifth and finally: *Colonial patterns of dependency can obscure austerity's worst effects.* Austerity has thrived in the Philippines not because of its benefits but because of colonial Band-Aids. When the Americans first implemented the gold exchange standard, they averted a balance-of-payments crisis because of congressional appropriations and because the military sent dollars to fight a war of occupation. After the great deflation, Governor-General Leonard Wood imposed possibly the world's most restrictive currency system on the colony. Yet the colony survived, and its bureaucrats even grew to love this currency system because preferential trading between the Philippines and the United States kept Philippine exports afloat.

As the preferential trade window closed in the 1970s, the Philippine economy required reorientation. The Marcos government's attempt to diversify the country's exports through its incipient developmentalism had some success but ultimately failed during the debt crisis of the 1980s. Although we have not discussed this issue at length, any reader with passing familiarity with the Philippines knows that we responded by exporting people instead of goods. Our capacity to send our labor abroad has been the most significant exhaust valve of an economy that has failed to experiment with bold alternatives. And the growth of the service industry—specifically the business processing outsourcing sector—allows government officials to neglect industrial policy, even as a neighbor like Vietnam keeps its currency cheap and produces more tradable goods.

How long can the country mask and blunt the worst effects of austerity? How long can these effects continue to be hidden? I hope that we will not need to answer these questions.

## Back to the Philippines

Try as I might to sketch broad conclusions about austerity, I am hopelessly attached to my country. Writing this book has been frustrating. It was frustrating enough to document a history of our losing out on chances for economic growth because of the conservatism of our colonizers and our postwar policymakers. It was even more frustrating to see that few people, except for visionary elites like Salvador Araneta, knew what was happening. That alternatives to austerity have been articulated mostly by a modernizing elite and not a vibrant labor movement betrays the lack of imagination in the Philippine left. But it also presents opportunities.

My modest goal for Filipino readers is to make them aware of what has happened and what continues to happen. Unfortunately, we have let austerity gaslight us. Because the arguments are forwarded by left-wing critics or principled academics who disdain our truly rotten oligarchy, we have trouble accepting that these arguments aid austerity. I have done many double-takes while writing this book, struggling with the fact that many individuals I admire effectively defend an economic rationality that I find destructive. There are reasons—sometimes even good—why progressives support austerity in the postcolony. Understanding these reasons, however, does not mean giving austerity and its defenders a free pass.

Ambitiously, I hope this book does more than alert readers to a neglected history. I hope to help shift the tenor of left-wing economic criticism in my country. We have noted that because the contemporary left was born during the anti-Marcos struggle and anchors its identity on this struggle, it is difficult to depart from the binaries of the time. It is even more difficult today with another Marcos in power. Yet the left, broadly defined, cannot challenge the status quo if it accepts the terms of economic debate. It is tempting and easy to ape conservative economists and spread fear about debt and inflation. These short-term indicators are great ways of scoring political points (something I know from my agitprop days). Especially when we don't like the politicians in power. But what are the long-term effects of feeding into such a rationality? If progressives are serious and hope to one day govern the Philippines, we must imagine ambitious programs anchored on social justice. These programs will be criticized for being inflationary and increasing debt.

Should we feed into an economic rationality that will ultimately delegitimize our vision? Or should we begin to outline a vision of the future where stable unionized jobs, a strong redistributive state, and social safety nets make inflation less of a concern? And can we envision ways in which sovereign debt—primarily obtained from the bonds sold to Filipino citizens and not foreign capital—can be used for growth and the promotion of human thriving?

This book is less about outlining alternatives and more about exposing roadblocks that have prevented Filipinos from imagining something different. Yet, I hope that between the polemics, spaces to articulate new ideas may be found.

As frustrating as our history may be, alternatives may still take root in the Philippines.

# Acknowledgments

This book started almost as a dare from the leading critic of Philippine literature. While on a postdoctoral fellowship at Kyoto University, Carol Hau and I chatted in her office, and she showed me a shelf full of macroeconomics books—all of which she had read. Carol explained her frustration with humanities scholars who claim to write materialist work while relying exclusively on critical theory, bereft of any knowledge of basic economics. She had taken economics seriously in her literary and historical criticism and suggested I do the same.

The concept of a textually driven yet economically sound project—one that would prove interesting to both humanities scholars and economists—intrigued me, but the prospect was always daunting. So the first person I want to express my gratitude to is Carol. She sparked the idea for this project and provided valuable feedback as it developed.

Apart from Carol, Jojo Abinales, Mike Montesano, Jun Aguilar, and Leia Castañeda Anastacio commented on various chapters. Jackie Teoh, my editor at Cornell University Press, believed in this project early in its writing. Her structural editing felt like mind reading; the book would be much less cogent without her.

While writing the book, I needed tutoring from actual economists. Thank you to Vinny Tagle and my father-in-law, Alex Herrin, for putting up with my badgering. Thank you also to Men Sta. Ana and everyone at Action for Economic Reforms for cultivating my interest in economics and allowing me to interact with and learn from jukebox economists. Any errors are, of course, my own and not theirs.

In Manila, JM Poso helped me collect a few documents. Wogie Pacala and the late Lina Araneta-Santiago provided me access to the files of Salvador Araneta and let me examine the preliminary research done by Don Badong's estate.

I conducted most of the primary research for this book while I was at the Center for Southeast Asian Studies at Kyoto University. Research continued during short stints at Ateneo de Manila University and De La Salle University, Manila. My thanks to colleagues from these three institutions who provided institutional, intellectual, and emotional support: Jayeel Cornelio, Kat Gutierrez, Ronnie Holmes, Armin Luistro, Julio Teehankee, Chris Collantes, Jeremey De Chavez, Jazmin Llana, Gen Asenjo, Caloy Piocos, Jafar Suryomenggolo, Mario Lopez, Yasuyuki Kono, Masaaki Okamoto, Jowel Canuday, Fernie Santiago, Nandy Aldaba, and anyone who let me talk their heads off about this project.

I finally found the time and space to write this book after joining the University of California, Berkeley. Thank you to colleagues and graduate students (former and present) here: Peter Zinoman, Munis Faruqi, Alexandra Dalferro, Vincent Pacheco, Paula Varsano, Joseph Scalice, Sarah Maxim, Johaina Crisostomo, Nancy Peluso, Josh Acosta, Paul Salamanca, Jenny Pham, Thomas Kingston, Vasugi Kailasam, Penny Edwards, Sylvia Tiwon, Alex von Rospatt, Jake Dalton, Rahul Parson, and Luther Obrock.

Outside these institutions, thank you to colleagues and friends Mark Thompson, Richard Heydarian, Marco Garrido, Nicole Curato, Jonathan Ong, Stephen Acabado, Nicole CuUnjieng Aboitiz, and Mara Coson for the conversations that have filtered into this book.

A very preliminary and significantly shorter version of chapter 4 was previously published in *The Marcos Era: A Reader* from Ateneo de Manila University Press. I am grateful to the editors (Leia and Jojo) and the press for allowing me that rough, initial foray into my material.

My acknowledgments are growing less sentimental as I transition from youth to a cantankerous middle age. But my family and friends—especially my spouse, Christine, my parents, and my brothers—know what they continue to mean to me.

# NOTES

## Introduction

1. Richard Bensel, *Passion and Preferences: William Jennings Bryan and the 1896 Democratic National Convention* (New York: Cambridge University Press, 2008), xii.

2. William Jennings Bryan, "The Issue in the Presidential Campaign," *North American Review* 170, no. 523 (1900): 758.

3. See Jackson Lears, *Rebirth of a Nation* (New York: Harper Collins, 2009) for an account of how these debates intersected during this period.

4. Bryan, "Issue in the Presidential Campaign," 759.

5. Bryan, 759.

6. Bryan, 759.

7. Bryan, 765.

8. Bryan, 766.

9. Bryan, 767.

10. Bryan, 767.

11. See Bensel, *Passion and Preferences*, for the history and the legacy of the "cross of gold" speech.

12. Barry Eichengreen, Arnaud Mehl, and Livia Chitu, *How Global Currencies Work: Past, Present, and Future* (Princeton, NJ: Princeton University Press, 2018), 43.

13. Eichengreen et al., 30.

14. Donald Lorenzo Kemmerer, *The Life and Times of Professor Edwin Walter Kemmerer, 1875–1945, and How He Became an International "Money Doctor"* (Donald L. Kemmerer, 1993), 17.

15. Quoted in Emily S. Rosenberg, *Financial Missionaries to the World: The Politics and Culture of Dollar Diplomacy, 1900–1930* (Durham, NC: Duke University Press, 2003), 22.

16. Daniel Immerwahr, *How to Hide an Empire: A History of the Greater United States* (New York: Farrar, Straus and Giroux, 2019).

17. Calixto V. Chikiamco, "Time for Jukebox Economics," *BusinessWorld*, June 14, 2020, https://www.bworldonline.com/time-for-jukebox-economics/.

18. Raul V. Fabella, *Capitalism and Inclusion Under Weak Institutions* (Quezon City: University of the Philippines Center for Integrative and Development Studies, 2018), 63. The jukebox economists were proven right when the portfolio investment was revealed to be a bubble during the Asian Financial Crisis.

19. Fabella, 63.

20. Sonny Africa, "PH Peso: Catch Me I'm Falling," *IBON Foundation* (blog), October 6, 2022, https://www.ibon.org/ph-peso-catch-me-im-falling/. The title

of Africa's article is a reference to Teri DeSario's radio classic (at least in the Philippines) "Fallin'." The singer claims that someone must catch her because she fears falling in love. In contrast to Africa's and DeSario's cynicism, we must view love and a weak currency as things we can fall into when the time and circumstances are right.

21. "IBON Research Head on Pres. Marcos Jr Just Monitoring Peso Weakening," *IBON Foundation* (blog), September 30, 2022, https://www.ibon.org/ibon-research-head-on-pres-marcos-jr-just-monitoring-peso-weakening/.

22. "P57.43/$: Where Do We Go from This Record Low?," *BusinessWorld*, September 18, 2022, https://www.bworldonline.com/opinion/2022/09/18/475216/.

23. Wilson Sy, "Defending the Peso," *Philippine Star*, October 24, 2022, https://www.philstar.com/business/2022/10/24/2218788/defending-peso.

24. After the talk, I excitedly chatted with Professor Paderanga, and we agreed to talk the next time I visited Manila. Unfortunately, he passed away in January 2016.

25. Rosenberg, *Financial Missionaries*, 33–34.

26. Mitsuru Obe and Francesca Regalado, "The Money Blizzard: Asia's Central Banks Reckon with the Aftermath of COVID-19," *Nikkei Asia*, October 5, 2022, https://asia.nikkei.com/Spotlight/The-Big-Story/The-money-blizzard-Asia-s-central-banks-reckon-with-the-aftermath-of-COVID-19.

27. Mark Blyth, *Austerity: The History of a Dangerous Idea* (New York: Oxford University Press, 2013); Clara E. Mattei, *The Capital Order: How Economists Invented Austerity and Paved the Way to Fascism* (Chicago: University of Chicago Press, 2022); David Stuckler and Sanjay Basu, *The Body Economic: Why Austerity Kills* (New York: Basic Books, 2013); Suzanne J. Konzelmann, "The Political Economics of Austerity," *Cambridge Journal of Economics* 38, no. 4 (2014).

28. I thank the poet Kael Co for a back-and-forth conversation about the best way to translate these words.

29. What will likely add more confusion to the term is a recent online trend of political liberals, who identify as "neoliberal" and forward the values of global cooperation and technocratic knowledge amid a populist challenge to these principles. See, for example, the website theneoliberalproject.org.

30. Wendy Brown, *Undoing the Demos: Neoliberalism's Stealth Revolution* (New York: Zone Books, 2016).

31. Mattei, *Capital Order*, 128–29.

32. Mattei, 129.

33. Paul Krugman, *Arguing with Zombies: Economics, Politics, and the Fight for a Better Future* (New York: W. W. Norton, 2020), 17.

34. Blyth, *Austerity*, 2

35. Blyth, 9.

36. The only time another election issue was more salient than inflation was during a brief period in 2016 when Rodrigo Duterte ran on a popular law-and-order platform. His campaign made criminality and illegal drugs the top electoral concern. Readers interested in tracking these trends may consult the website of one of the country's top two polling firms, Pulse Asia, pulsasia.ph. As a longtime fellow of Pulse Asia, I have tracked this data closely.

I thank Pulse Asia's president Ronald Holmes for always answering my questions about the data.

37. Even the maverick economist Raul Fabella, while defending peso depreciation and offering alternatives to inflation-phobia, has to pay obeisance to this rhetoric, noting, "Inflation is not just anti-poor but also weakens the social fabric, apart from eroding the approval ratings of the authorities." See Raul Fabella, "The Policy Dilemma of Our Time: Growth First vs Inflation First," *BusinessWorld*, October 23, 2022, https://www.bworldonline.com/opinion/2022/10/23/482241/.

38. Blyth, *Austerity*, 9.

39. Blyth, 9.

40. Mattei, *Capital Order*, 130.

41. Ha-Joon Chang, *23 Things They Don't Tell You About Capitalism* (London: Allen Lane, 2010), 61.

42. I have firsthand experience in this regard. After I summarized arguments against inflation-phobia, a University of the Philippines economist condemned me as a nonexpert who did not understand economics. My comments also got me trolled. A noneconomist friend and collaborator of mine, Richard Heydarian, defended some of my views and got into even more trouble on Twitter. For a summary of this minor, annoying, but revealing incident see Richard Heydarian, "Time for Economic Revolution Under Marcos Jr.," *Philippine Daily Inquirer*, October 18, 2022, https://opinion.inquirer.net/157951/.

43. Barry Eichengreen, *Golden Fetters: The Gold Standard and the Great Depression, 1919–1939* (New York: Oxford University Press, 1992); Rosenberg, *Financial Missionaries*. Rosenberg's account discusses the Philippines only in the introduction.

44. Mark Metzler, *Lever of Empire: The International Gold Standard and the Crisis of Liberalism in Prewar Japan* (Berkeley: University of California Press, 2006).

45. There are too many works to cite here, but one important edited volume gives one a sense of the scope of this research and which areas it examines. See Alfred W. McCoy and Francisco A. Scarano, eds., *Colonial Crucible: Empire in the Making of the Modern American State* (Quezon City: Ateneo de Manila University Press, 2010).

46. Leia Castañeda Anastacio, *The Foundations of the Modern Philippine State: Imperial Rule and the American Constitutional Tradition, 1898–1935* (New York: Cambridge University Press, 2016).

47. Warwick Anderson, *Colonial Pathologies: American Tropical Medicine, Race, and Hygiene in the Philippines*, E-Duke Books Scholarly Collection (Durham, NC: Duke University Press, 2006).

48. Sarah Steinbock-Pratt, *Educating the Empire: American Teachers and Contested Colonization in the Philippines* (Cambridge: Cambridge University Press, 2019).

49. Alfred W. McCoy, *Policing America's Empire: The United States, the Philippines, and the Rise of the Surveillance State* (Quezon City: Ateneo de Manila University Press, 2009).

50. Patricio N. Abinales, *Making Mindanao: Cotabato and Davao in the Formation of the Philippine Nation-State* (Quezon City: Ateneo de Manila University Press, 2000); Michael Hawkins, *Making Moros: Imperial Historicism and*

*American Military Rule in the Philippines Muslim South* (DeKalb, IL: Northern Illinois University Press, 2013); Oliver Charbonneau, *Civilizational Imperatives: Americans, Moros, and the Colonial World* (Ithaca, NY: Cornell University Press, 2020); Rebecca Tinio McKenna, *American Imperial Pastoral: The Architecture of US Colonialism in the Philippines* (Quezon City: Ateneo de Manila University Press, 2017); Gerard A. Finin, *The Making of the Igorot: Ramut Ti Panagkaykaysa Dagiti Taga Cordillera (Contours of Cordillera Consciousness)* (Quezon City: Ateneo de Manila University Press, 2005).

51. See Willem G. Wolters, "From Silver Currency to the Gold Standard in the Philippine Islands," *Philippine Studies* 51, no. 3 (2003): 375–404; Allan E. S. Lumba, *Monetary Authorities: Capitalism and Decolonization in the American Colonial Philippines* (Durham, NC: Duke University Press, 2022); Ponciano S. Jr. Intal, *Essays on Philippine Colonial Economy: Balance of Payments and Trade, 1870s to 1930s* (Manila: De La Salle University Press, 2003); Yoshiko Nagano, *State and Finance in the Philippines, 1898–1941: The Mismanagement of an American Colony* (Quezon City: Ateneo de Manila University Press, 2015). While I agree with Wolters and Intal (I consider Intal's work an underrated classic) and see their works as necessary, empirically grounded introductions to the topic, I fundamentally depart from Lumba's and Nagano's. Lumba's focus on an ill-defined conception of "capital accumulation" makes it seem as if the gold standard was implemented to increase liquidity for a fledgling state so that it would have more money for violence against Filipinos (p. 62). This is a fundamental misunderstanding of the gold standard and the goals of American colonial policy, as I detail in chapter 1. Meanwhile, while I find Nagano's archival work rigorous, I disagree with her explicit endorsement of the gold standard. As we shall see in chapter 2, her defense of the American gold exchange standard is oddly antiquated and highly conservative by today's standards.

52. Anthony Reid, *Southeast Asia in the Age of Commerce, 1450–1680*, vol. 2, *Expansion and Crisis* (New Haven, CT: Yale University Press, 1993).

53. Gregg Huff, *World War II and Southeast Asia: Economy and Society Under Japanese Occupation* (Cambridge: Cambridge University Press, 2020).

54. Takashi Shiraishi, "The Third Wave: Southeast Asia and Middle-Class Formation in the Making of a Region," in *Beyond Japan: The Dynamics of East Asian Regionalism*, ed. Peter Katzenstein and Takashi Shiraishi (Ithaca, NY: Cornell University Press, 2006), 237–71.

55. David A. Steinberg, *Demanding Devaluation: Exchange Rate Politics in the Developing World* (Ithaca, NY: Cornell University Press, 2015).

56. Vicente Rafael, *Contracting Colonialism: Translation and Christian Conversion in Tagalog Society Under Early Spanish Rule* (Quezon City: Ateneo de Manila University Press, 1988).

## 1. Austerity Contracted

1. Barry Eichengreen, *Exorbitant Privilege: The Rise and Fall of the Dollar* (Oxford: Oxford University Press, 2011), 12.

2. This quote is from de Gaulle's finance minister, Valéry Giscard d'Estaing. Eichengreen, 4.

3. William J. Taft, "The Government of the Philippine Islands, Executive Bureau, Executive Order No. 66" (1903), *The United States and Its Territories, 1870–1925: The Age of Imperialism*, University of Michigan Special Collections, https://quod.lib.umich.edu/p/philamer/ACD6603.1903.001/91.

4. Barry Eichengreen, Arnaud Mehl, and Livia Chitu, *How Global Currencies Work: Past, Present, and Future* (Princeton. NJ: Princeton University Press, 2018), 1.

5. Raymond Williams, *Marxism and Literature* (Oxford: Oxford University Press, 1977), 128-35.

6. Anthony Reid, *Southeast Asia in the Age of Commerce, 1450–1680*, vol. 2, *Expansion and Crisis* (New Haven, CT: Yale University Press, 1993).

7. Reid, 2:23.

8. Dennis Flynn and Arturo Giraldez, "Born with a 'Silver Spoon': The Origin of World Trade in 1571," *Journal of World History* 6, no. 2 (1995): 214.

9. Flynn and Giraldez, 204.

10. Rafael Díaz Arenas, *Report on the Commerce and Shipping of the Philippine Islands*, trans. Encarnacion Alzona (Manila: National Historical Institute of the Philippines, 1979), 40-41.

11. Arenas, 40.

12. P. J. Drake, "Southeast Asian Monies and the Problem of a Common Measure, with Particular Reference to the Nineteenth Century," *Australian Economic History Review* 31, no. 1 (1991): 92.

13. Ponciano S. Intal Jr., *Essays on Philippine Colonial Economy: Balance of Payments and Trade, 1870s to 1930s* (Manila: De La Salle University Press, 2003), 1.

14. Richard Bensel, *Passion and Preferences: William Jennings Bryan and the 1896 Democratic National Convention* (New York: Cambridge University Press, 2008), 24.

15. Intal, *Essays on Philippine Colonial Economy*, 2.

16. Frank A. Branagan, "Memorandum Concerning the Currency of the Philippine Islands," n.d., Dean C. Worcester's Philippine Collection, University of Michigan Library Special Collections Research Center, box 1, folder 1.22, p. 1.

17. Scholars, in fact, trace the origins of the contemporary Philippine "weak state" to this period. See Patricio N. Abinales and Donna J. Amoroso, *State and Society in the Philippines*, 2nd ed. (Quezon City: Ateneo de Manila University Press, 2017), 66.

18. Intal, *Essays on Philippine Colonial Economy*, 5.

19. Abinales and Amoroso, *State and Society*, 66-67.

20. Takashi Shiraishi, *Empire of the Seas* (Tokyo: Japan Publishing Industry Foundation for Culture, 2021), 50.

21. Shiraishi, 66.

22. Abinales and Amoroso, *State and Society*, 82-83; Benito J. Legarda, *After the Galleons: Foreign Trade, Economic Change and Entrepreneurship in the Nineteenth Century Philippines* (Madison: Center for Southeast Asian Studies, University of Wisconsin-Madison, 1999), 125-35; Caroline S. Hau, *Elites and Ilustrados in Philippine Culture* (Quezon City: Ateneo de Manila University Press, 2017), 27.

23. Caroline S. Hau, *The Chinese Question: Ethnicity, Nation, and Region in and Beyond the Philippines* (Singapore: NUS Press and Kyoto University Press, 2014), 294.

24. Charles Arthur Conant, "Currency in the Philippines: Statement of Charles A. Conant," § United States Senate Subcommittee on the Philippines (1902), 6.

25. Michael D. Pante, "The 'Cocheros' of American-Occupied Manila: Representations and Persistence," *Philippine Studies: Historical & Ethnographic Viewpoints* 60, no. 4 (2012): 452.

26. Michael Cullinane, *Arenas of Conspiracy and Rebellion in the Late Nineteenth-Century Philippines: The Case of the April 1898 Uprising in Cebu* (Quezon City: Ateneo de Manila University Press, 2014).

27. Branagan, "Memorandum Concerning the Currency," 2.

28. Intal, *Essays on Philippine Colonial Economy*, 2.

29. Francis Burton Harrison to Moorefield Storey, copy, April 30, 1917, box 1, Irving Winslow Papers, Special Collections Research Center, University of Michigan.

30. John N. Schumacher, *The Making of a Nation: Essays on Nineteenth-Century Philippine Nationalism* (Quezon City: Ateneo de Manila University Press, 1991), 17.

31. John N. Schumacher, *The Propaganda Movement, 1880–1895: The Creation of a Filipino Consciousness, the Making of a Revolution* (Quezon City: Ateneo de Manila University Press, 1997), 17.

32. W. Arthur Lewis, "The Export Stimulus," in *Tropical Development: 1880–1913*, ed. W. Arthur Lewis (London: George Allen & Unwin, 1970), 13.

33. Intal, *Essays on Philippine Colonial Economy*, 17.

34. Conant, "Currency in the Philippines," 59.

35. Benito Legarda, "The Economic Background of Rizal's Time," *Philippine Review of Economics* 48, no. 2 (2011): 10.

36. Nick Joaquin, *A Question of Heroes* (Pasig City: Anvil, 2005), 38.

37. Hau, *Elites and Ilustrados*, 26–27; Schumacher, *Propaganda Movement*, 17; Schumacher, *Making of a Nation*, 17; Joaquin, *Question of Heroes*, 26; Legarda, "Economic Background of Rizal's Time," 13; Lisandro E. Claudio, *Jose Rizal: Liberalism and the Paradox of Coloniality*, Global Political Thinkers (Singapore: Palgrave Macmillan, 2019), 8.

38. Legarda, *After the Galleons*, 328–29.

39. Legarda, "Economic Background of Rizal's Time," 16.

40. Beverly J. Silver and Giovanni Arrighi, "Polanyi's 'Double Movement': The Belle Époques of British and US Hegemony Compared," *Politics & Society* 31, no. 2 (2003): 338.

41. Utsa Patnaik, "Imperialism, Gold Standard and the Colonised," *Social Scientist* 49, no. 9/10 (580–81) (2021): 50.

42. Utsa Patnaik, "Aspects of India's Colonial Economic History," *Economic and Political Weekly* 49, no. 5 (2014): 31–32.

43. Glenn A. May, "Why the United States Won the Philippine-American War, 1899-1902," *Pacific Historical Review* 52, no. 4 (1983): 356.

44. Quoted in Clarence R. Edwards, "Memorandum for the Secretary of War on Currency and Exchange in the Philippines" (Washington, DC: Government Printing Office, 1900), 15, Files of the Senate Committee on the Philippines, 56th Congress, NARA.

45. Edwards, 7–8.

46. Edwards, 11.

47. Quoted in Edwards, 15.

48. Quoted in Edwards, 16.

49. *Reports of the Taft Philippine Commission* (Washington, DC: Government Printing Office, 1901), 86–87.

50. Conant, "Currency in the Philippines," 8.

51. Conant, 9.

52. *Reports of the Taft Philippine Commission*, 87.

53. Edwards, "Memorandum for the Secretary of War," 31.

54. Quoted in Edwards, 33.

55. Edwards, 34.

56. Quoted in Edwards, 22.

57. Bonifacio Salamanca, *The Filipino Reaction to American Rule, 1901–1913* (Hamden, CT: Shoe String, 1968), 3.

58. Conant, "Currency in the Philippines," 3.

59. Allan E. S. Lumba, *Monetary Authorities: Capitalism and Decolonization in the American Colonial Philippines* (Durham, NC: Duke University Press, 2022), 43–44.

60. Lumba, 52–53.

61. Rebecca Tinio McKenna, *American Imperial Pastoral: The Architecture of US Colonialism in the Philippines* (Quezon City: Ateneo de Manila University Press, 2017), 115–17; Lumba, *Monetary Authorities*, 44–45.

62. Conant, "Currency in the Philippines," 17.

63. Conant, 18.

64. Conant, 48.

65. Conant, 16.

66. Conant, 43.

67. Conant, 42.

68. Conant, 44.

69. Conant, 48.

70. Conant, 59.

71. Conant, 60.

72. Conant, 62.

73. Conant, 62.

74. Conant, 66.

75. Conant, 65.

76. Edwin Walter Kemmerer, *Modern Currency Reforms: A History and Discussion of Recent Currency Reforms in India, Porto Rico, Philippine Islands, Straits Settlements and Mexico* (New York: Macmillan, 1916), 309.

77. Frank H. Golay, *Face of Empire: United States–Philippine Relations, 1898–1946* (Quezon City: Ateneo de Manila University Press, 1997), 88; Yoshiko Nagano, *State and Finance in the Philippines, 1898–1941: The Mismanagement of an American Colony* (Quezon City: Ateneo de Manila University Press, 2015), 25–26; Lumba, *Monetary Authorities*, 60–61.

78. "Gold Standard for Filipinos: Senate Committee Agrees on a Currency Bill Drafted by Senators Lodge and Allison," *New York Times*, December 19, 1902.

79. Golay, *Face of Empire*, 108.

80. "Gold Standard for Filipinos."
81. Kemmerer, *Modern Currency Reforms*, 313.
82. Golay, *Face of Empire*, 98.
83. Kemmerer, *Modern Currency Reforms*, 301.
84. Rep. Hamilton (NY), "Banking and Coinage," Congressional Record 35, Pt. 7 (June 20, 1902), 7106.
85. Hamilton, 7107.
86. Rep. Fowler (NJ), "Philippine Coinage," Congressional Record 36, Pt. 1 (January 22, 1903), 1070.
87. Quoted in Fowler, 1070.
88. Rebecca L. Spang, "The Rise of Inflation: Bursting the Bubble," *Cabinet*, no. 50 (2013), https://cabinetmagazine.org/issues/50/spang.php.
89. Like Kemmerer's 1916 magisterial history of currency "reforms" in India, Puerto Rico, the Philippines, the Straits Settlements, and Mexico, the work was published by the Macmillan Company. Fisher's work is advertised at the end of Kemmerer's book. See the advertisements section of Kemmerer, *Modern Currency Reforms*.
90. Irving Fisher, *Appreciation and Interest* (New York: American Economic Association, 1896), 35–36.
91. "Gold Standard in the Philippines; Tait to Delay Setting a Time for Its Establishment. Preparations Must First Be Made to Maintain Parity—to Guard Against Inflation," *New York Times*, May 12, 1903.
92. Donald Lorenzo Kemmerer, *The Life and Times of Professor Edwin Walter Kemmerer, 1875–1945, and How He Became an International "Money Doctor"* (Donald L. Kemmerer, 1993), 29.
93. Bruce G. Carruthers and Sarah Babb, "The Color of Money and the Nature of Value: Greenbacks and Gold in Postbellum America," *American Journal of Sociology*, October 15, 2015: 1572-73.
94. Carruthers and Babb, 1570.
95. Kashia Amber Arnold, "Yellow Money: China, the Silver Question, and the Rise of the American West" (Northridge: California State University, 2013), 46–47, https://scholarworks.calstate.edu/downloads/qr46r338t.
96. Annie L. Cot, "'Breed Out the Unfit and Breed In the Fit,'" *American Journal of Economics and Sociology* 64, no. 3 (2005): 793-826.
97. Emily S. Rosenberg, *Financial Missionaries to the World: The Politics and Culture of Dollar Diplomacy, 1900–1930* (Durham, NC: Duke University Press, 2003), 34.
98. Edward Rosenberg, "Filipinos as Workmen," *American Federationist* 10, no. 10 (1903): 1028.
99. Greg Bankoff, "Wants, Wages, and Workers," *Pacific Historical Review* 74, no. 1 (2005): 73.
100. Conant, "Currency in the Philippines," 51.
101. Kemmerer, *Modern Currency Reforms*, 313.
102. Kemmerer, 314.
103. Kemmerer, 315.
104. Alvita Akiboh, "Pocket-Sized Imperialism: U.S. Designs on Colonial Currency," *Diplomatic History* 41, no. 5 (2017): 875.

105. Quoted in "HR 13445–57th Congress (1901–1903): Administration of Civil Affairs in the Philippines Islands," August 10, 1902, BIA General Classified Files 1898–1945, box 180b, RG 350, NARA.

106. Conant, "Currency in the Philippines," 51.

107. Kemmerer, *Modern Currency Reforms*, 315.

108. Kemmerer, 318.

109. Kemmerer, 327.

110. Nagano, *State and Finance in the Philippines*, 26.

111. Quoted in D. Kemmerer, *Life and Times*, 9.

112. D. Kemmerer, 9, 14.

113. Edwin Walter Kemmerer, "The Progress of the Filipino People Toward Self-Government," *Political Science Quarterly* 23, no. 1 (1908): 74.

114. Kemmerer, 14.

115. Kemmerer, *Modern Currency Reforms*, 299.

116. Kemmerer, 298–99.

117. Kemmerer, 299.

118. Kemmerer, 328.

119. Akiboh, "Pocket-Sized Imperialism," 885–87.

120. Quoted in Kemmerer, *Modern Currency Reforms*, 332.

121. Quoted in Kemmerer, 331.

122. Kemmerer, 329.

123. Kemmerer, 330.

124. Kemmerer, 340.

125. D. Kemmerer, *Life and Times*, 19.

126. Kemmerer, *Modern Currency Reforms*, 345.

127. Kemmerer, 346.

128. Rosenberg, *Financial Missionaries*, 53.

129. Rosenberg, 53.

130. Kim A. Wagner, *Massacre in the Clouds: An American Atrocity and the Erasure of History* (New York: PublicAffairs, 2024), 69.

131. Patricio N. Abinales, *Orthodoxy and History in the Muslim-Mindanao Narrative* (Quezon City: Ateneo de Manila University Press, 2010), 2–3.

132. Edwin Walter Kemmerer, *Gold and the Gold Standard: The Story of Gold Money, Past, Present and Future* (New York: McGraw-Hill, 1944), 153.

133. Golay, *Face of Empire*, 109.

134. Golay, 109.

135. Rosenberg, "Filipinos as Workmen," 1026.

136. The locus of the early American state was the relatively peaceful Manila. Consequently, nonmilitary spending had to rise as the colonial state expanded to the newly pacified provincial areas. For an account of this early Manila-centric state see Michael Cullinane, *Ilustrado Politics: Filipino Elite Responses to American Rule, 1898–1908* (Quezon City: Ateneo de Manila University Press, 2003), 73–142.

137. McKenna, *American Imperial Pastoral*, 4.

138. Salamanca, *Filipino Reaction to American Rule*, 122.

139. Salamanca, 123.

140. Intal, *Essays on Philippine Colonial Economy*, 41.

141. Journal of Cameron Forbes, series 1, vol. 5, p. 75, W. Cameron Forbes Papers, Houghton Library, Harvard University.

142. Lumba, *Monetary Authorities*, 62.

143. Allan E. S. Lumba and Nicole Curato, "Monetary Authorities," New Books in Southeast Asian Studies Podcast, July 1, 2023, https://newbooksnetwork.com/monetary-authorities.

144. Forbes journal, series 1, vol. 5, 75–76.

145. *Report of the Philippine Commission to the Secretary of War* (Washington, DC: Government Printing Office, 1912), 10.

146. Gerard A. Finin, *The Making of the Igorot: Ramut Ti Panagkaykaysa Dagiti Taga Cordillera (Contours of Cordillera Consciousness)* (Quezon City: Ateneo de Manila University Press, 2005), 27.

147. Most Filipinos today know it as Kennon Road, named after its builder, Colonel Lyman Kennon of the US Army Corps of Engineers.

148. McKenna, *American Imperial Pastoral*, 55.

149. Forbes journal, series 1, vol. 5, 87.

150. Forbes journal, 75.

151. *Report of the Philippine Commission to the Secretary of War*, 31.

152. Forbes journal, series 1, vol. 5, 111.

153. McKenna, *American Imperial Pastoral*, 170–71.

154. Maximo Kalaw, *Self-Government in the Philippines* (New York: Century, 1919), 47.

155. Kalaw, 47.

156. Golay, *Face of Empire*, 179.

157. Golay, 180.

158. Golay, 181.

159. Vicente Angel S. Ybiernas, "Philippine Financial Standing in 1921: The First World War Boom and Bust," *Philippine Studies* 55, no. 3 (2007): 254.

## 2. Austerity Defended

1. Leonard Wood and W. Cameron Forbes, *Report of the Special Mission on the Investigation to the Philippine Islands to the Secretary of War* (Washington, DC: Government Printing Office, 1921), 38.

2. Philippines v. Concepcion, L-19190 (Supreme Court of the Philippines, 1922), https://www.chanrobles.com/scdecisions/jurisprudence1922/nov1922/gr_l-19190_1922.php.

3. "The Bank's Staggering Loss," *Philippines Free Press*, July 1, 1922, box 6769-a, BIA General Classified Files (1914–1945).

4. Allan E. S. Lumba, *Monetary Authorities: Capitalism and Decolonization in the American Colonial Philippines* (Durham, NC: Duke University Press, 2022), 94.

5. Clara Mattei, *The Capital Order: How Economists Invented Austerity and Paved the Way to Fascism* (Chicago: University of Chicago Press, 2022), 1–73.

6. Allan Lumba, "Monetary Authorities: Market Knowledge and Imperial Government in the Colonial Philippines, 1892–1942" (PhD diss., University of Washington, 2013), 236, https://digital.lib.washington.edu:443/researchworks/handle/1773/23423.

7. Yoshiko Nagano, *State and Finance in the Philippines, 1898–1941: The Mismanagement of an American Colony* (Quezon City: Ateneo de Manila University Press, 2015).

8. For a discussion of the implications of being an unincorporated territory, particularly on what it meant to be a Filipino citizen, see Filomeno V. Aguilar, "The Riddle of the Alien-Citizen: Filipino Migrants as US Nationals and the Anomalies of Citizenship, 1900s–1930s," *Asian and Pacific Migration Journal* 19, no. 2 (2010): 203–36; Rick Baldoz and César Ayala, "The Bordering of America: Colonialism and Citizenship in the Philippines and Puerto Rico," *Centro Journal* 25, no. 1 (2013): 76–105.

9. Yoshiko Nagano, "The Philippine Currency System During the American Colonial Period: Transformation from the Gold Exchange Standard to the Dollar Exchange Standard," *International Journal of Asian Studies* 7, no. 1 (2010): 41.

10. "To Head Philippine Bank; H. Parker Willis, Secretary of Federal Reserve Board, Chosen," *New York Times*, February 20, 1916.

11. Nagano, *State and Finance in the Philippines*, 30–31.

12. Shirley Jenkins, *American Economic Policy Towards the Philippines* (Stanford, CA: Stanford University Press, 1954), 110.

13. Nagano, "Philippine Currency System," 41.

14. Patricio N. Abinales and Donna J. Amoroso, *State and Society in the Philippines*, 2nd ed. (Quezon City: Ateneo de Manila University Press, 2017), 140.

15. Vicente Angel S. Ybiernas, "Philippine Financial Standing in 1921: The First World War Boom and Bust," *Philippine Studies* 55, no. 3 (2007): 357–58.

16. Leia Castañeda Anastacio, *The Foundations of the Modern Philippine State: Imperial Rule and the American Constitutional Tradition, 1898–1935* (New York: Cambridge University Press, 2016), 183.

17. Anastacio, 181.

18. Mattei, *Capital Order*, 21.

19. Ruth T. McVey, *The Rise of Indonesian Communism* (Ithaca, NY: Cornell University Press, 1965), 109.

20. Martin Thomas, "Albert Sarraut, French Colonial Development, and the Communist Threat, 1919–1930," *Journal of Modern History* 77, no. 4 (2005): 917–55.

21. Francis Burton Harrison, "Copy of a Letter to a Mr. Storey," April 30, 1917, Erving Winslow Papers, Special Resources Center, University of Michigan, box 1.

22. Frank H. Golay, *Face of Empire: United States–Philippine Relations, 1898–1946* (Quezon City: Ateneo de Manila University Press, 1997), 218.

23. O. D. Corpuz, *An Economic History of the Philippines* (Quezon City: University of the Philippines Press, 1997), 247.

24. Corpuz, 247.

25. Corpuz, 247.

26. Corpuz, 247.

27. Yoshihara Kunio, *Philippine Industrialization* (Quezon City: Ateneo de Manila University Press, 1985), 31.

28. Jim Richardson, *Komunista: The Genesis of the Philippine Communist Party, 1902–1935* (Quezon City: Ateneo de Manila University Press, 2011), 40.

29. Adam Tooze, *The Deluge: The Great War and the Remaking of Global Order, 1916–1931* (London: Allen Lane, 2014), 262.

30. Barry Eichengreen, *Golden Fetters: The Gold Standard and the Great Depression, 1919–1939* (New York: Oxford University Press, 1992), 121.

31. Christina D. Romer, "World War I and the Postwar Depression: A Reinterpretation Based on Alternative Estimates of GNP," *Journal of Monetary Economics* 22, no. 1 (1988): 110–11.

32. Romer, 111.

33. Mark Metzler, *Lever of Empire: The International Gold Standard and the Crisis of Liberalism in Prewar Japan* (Berkeley: University of California Press, 2006), 117.

34. Metzler, 135.

35. Metzler, 136.

36. Ybiernas, "Philippine Financial Standing in 1921," 360.

37. Richardson, *Komunista*, 69.

38. "Pass Philippine Debt Bill: Senate Sends to Conference Measure Doubling Loan Limit," *New York Times*, July 7, 1921, 10.

39. "Pass Philippine Debt Bill," 10.

40. These debates over the colonial debt ceiling foreshadowed today's debates in the US, where Republicans blame Democrats for having blown up the debt and then hold the government hostage by refusing to adjust the debt ceiling.

41. Quoted in Frederick G. Hoyt, "The Wood-Forbes Mission to the Philippines, 1921" (PhD diss., Claremont Graduate School and University Center, 1963), 307.

42. Quoted in Hoyt, 308.

43. Paul D. Hutchcroft, *Booty Capitalism: The Politics of Banking in the Philippines* (Ithaca, NY: Cornell University Press, 1998), 67; John T. Sidel, *Republicanism, Communism, Islam: Cosmopolitan Origins of Revolution in Southeast Asia* (Ithaca, NY: Cornell University Press, 2021), 65; Alfred W. McCoy, *Policing America's Empire: The United States, the Philippines, and the Rise of the Surveillance State* (Quezon City: Ateneo de Manila University Press, 2009), 272; Peter W. Stanley, *A Nation in the Making: The Philippines and the United States, 1899–1921* (Cambridge, MA: Harvard University Press, 1974), 24.

44. Hutchcroft, *Booty Capitalism*, 67.

45. Sidel, *Republicanism, Communism, Islam*, 65.

46. McCoy, *Policing America's Empire*, 272.

47. Joe Studwell, *Asian Godfathers: Money and Power in Hong Kong and South-East Asia* (London: Profile, 2007), 103.

48. Kim A. Wagner, *Massacre in the Clouds: An American Atrocity and the Erasure of History* (New York: PublicAffairs, 2024), 162–97.

49. Hoyt, "Wood-Forbes Mission to the Philippines," 9.

50. Quoted in Hoyt, 11.

51. Hoyt, 11.

52. Hoyt, 13.

53. Journal of Cameron Forbes, series 1, vol. 1, p. 5, W. Cameron Forbes Papers.

54. Warwick Anderson, *Colonial Pathologies: American Tropical Medicine, Race, and Hygiene in the Philippines* (Durham, NC: Duke University Press, 2006), 189, 1.

55. "Philippines in Chaos; Big Harding Task," *New-York Tribune*, February 26, 1916.

56. Untitled document, unbound and scattered papers from "Printed and Miscellaneous Materials on the Philippines," box 4, W. Cameron Forbes Papers. This note/draft was likely written while Forbes was governor-general, since he references being in the Philippines and defending government policy. We are unsure as to which "indecencies" Taft was referring.

57. W. H. Taft to Leonard Wood, April 5, 1921, letter reproduced in the Journal of Cameron Forbes, series 2, vol. 2, p. 334.

58. Taft, 335.

59. Wood and Forbes, *Report of the Special Mission*, 10–11.

60. Ambeth R. Ocampo, "'Birds of Prey,'" *Philippine Daily Inquirer*, August 2, 2019, https://opinion.inquirer.net/123002/birds-of-prey.

61. Leonard Wood, "Letter to Dean C. Worcester," July 13, 1921, Dean Conant Worcester Papers 1900–1924, Bentley Historical Library, box 1.

62. Dean C. Worcester, "Letter to the Special Mission to the Philippine Islands," August 4, 1921, Worcester Papers, box 1.

63. "Banking and Hemp in the Philippines," *Journal of Commerce and Commercial Bulletin*, January 17, 1922, 12.

64. "Banking and Hemp," 12.

65. "The Bank's Staggering Loss," *Philippines Free Press*, July 1, 1922, box 6769-a, BIA General Classified Files (1914–1945).

66. "Bank's Staggering Loss."

67. Philippine Press Bureau, press release, August 20 [probably 1922], box 6769-a, BIA General Classified Files (1914–1945).

68. Philippine Press Bureau. For an account of Osias's career see Lisandro E. Claudio, "Beyond Colonial Miseducation: Internationalism and Deweyan Pedagogy in the American-Era Philippines," *Philippine Studies: Historical and Ethnographic Viewpoints* 63, no. 2 (2015): 193–220.

69. Many early Filipino socialists clustered around *El Debate*, making it a hub for Asian radical thought. In 1925, for example, the Indonesian Communist and Comintern representative, Tan Malaka, would serve as a correspondent for the newspaper. Helen Jarvis, "Tan Malaka: Revolutionary or Renegade?," *Bulletin of Concerned Asian Scholars* 19, no. 1 (1987): 46.

70. BIA English translation of "Public Exposé of the Bank's Losses: Are Those Now Alleged Much Exaggerated?," *El Debate*, August 23, 1923, box 6769-a, BIA General Classified Files (1914–1945).

71. BIA English translation of "The Effects of the Present Crisis Will Be Felt Until 1923," *El Ideal*, June 29, 1921, box 6769-a, BIA General Classified Files (1914–1945).

72. "Gen. Wood Gives Out Rejected Message," *New York Times*, August 19, 1923, 1; "The Governor General's Message," *New York Times*, August 19, 1923, 7.

73. "Gen. Wood Gives Out Rejected Message," 1.

74. "Banks Interests Safe, Says Wilson," *Manila Daily Bulletin*, July 28, 1922, box 6769-A, BIA General Classified Files (1914–1945).

75. "Bank Foreclosing on Oil Mills to Protect Big Loans," *Manila Daily Bulletin*, September 2, 1922, box 6769-A, BIA General Classified Files (1914–1945).

76. "Philippine Bank's New Policies Promise Bright Future," *Washington Times*, October 25, 1922, box 6769-a, NARA, BIA General Classified Files (1914–1945).

77. BIA English translation of "The National Bank Grants a Loan to the Bank of the Philippine Islands of 6,000,000 Pesos in Place of Helping Farmers," *El Ideal*, November 18, 1921, box 6769-a, BIA General Classified Files (1914–1945).

78. Barry Eichengreen and Peter Temin, "The Gold Standard and the Great Depression," *Contemporary European History* 9, no. 2 (2000): 187.

79. George Francis Luthringer, *The Gold-Exchange Standards in the Philippines* (Princeton, NJ: Princeton University Press, 1934), 118.

80. Luthringer, 119.

81. Luthringer, 119.

82. Luthringer, 119.

83. Luthringer, 137.

84. Nagano, *State and Finance in the Philippines*, 137.

85. Nagano, 29.

86. Willis was also a major anti-imperialist. Box 1 of the Erving Winslow papers at the Special Collections Resource Center of the University of Michigan contains various letters in which Winslow, the secretary of the Anti-Imperialist League, lobbies various US officials to appoint Parker vice governor-general of the Philippines based on his credentials as an anti-imperialist. See, in particular, Winslow's correspondences with Parker, where Winslow updates Parker on his efforts.

87. Dean C. Worcester, "Letter to the Special Mission to the Philippine Islands," August 4, 1921, Worcester Papers, box 1.

88. Venancio Concepcion, *"La Tragedia" del Banco Nacional Filipino* (Manila: s.n., 1927), 41.

89. Concepcion, 4.

90. Concepcion, 4.

91. Fred Block, "Swimming Against the Current: The Rise of a Hidden Developmental State in the United States," *Politics & Society* 36, no. 2 (2008): 169–206.

92. Ha-Joon Chang, *Kicking Away the Ladder: Development Strategy in Historical Perspective* (London: Anthem, 2003), 25.

93. Chang, 25.

94. Filomeno V. Aguilar, *Clash of Spirits: The History of Power and Sugar Planter Hegemony on a Visayan Island* (Quezon City: Ateneo de Manila University Press, 1998), 197.

95. Aguilar, 203.

96. Abinales and Amoroso, *State and Society*, 142.

97. Philippine National Bank, "Summary of the Transactions Had from the Date the Securities Listed in the Attached Exhibits Were Accepted To," July 31, 1919, box 676, BIA General Files (1914–1945).

98. The best I can surmise is that these are preliminary notes written by Wood, Forbes, or both. They were, however, more likely penned by Forbes, since he was the banking expert. For convenience, I shall hereafter refer to these notes as authored by Forbes.

99. Unbound and scattered papers from "Printed and Miscellaneous Materials on the Philippines," box 2, Forbes Papers.

100. Note with the title "Economic Conditions" from the same scattered papers.

101. Concepcion, *"La Tragedia,"* 34.

102. Concepcion, 29.

103. Concepcion, 29.

104. Concepcion, 30.

105. Eichengreen, *Golden Fetters*, 188–90.

106. Eichengreen, 190.

107. Wasana Wongsurawat, *The Crown and the Capitalists: The Ethnic Chinese and the Founding of the Thai Nation* (Seattle: University of Washington Press, 2019), 102.

108. Eichengreen, *Golden Fetters*, 188.

109. W. G. Huff, "Boom-or-Bust Commodities and Industrialization in Pre–World War II Malaya," *Journal of Economic History* 62, no. 4 (2002): 1080.

110. Eichengreen, *Golden Fetters*; Pierre van der Eng, "The Silver Standard and Asia's Integration into the World Economy, 1850–1914," *Review of Asian and Pacific Studies*, no. 18 (1999): 66.

111. Huff, "Boom-or-Bust Commodities," 128.

112. Takashi Shiraishi, *Empire of the Seas: Thinking About Asia* (Tokyo: Japan Publishing Industry Foundation for Culture, 2021), 50–67.

113. Mattei, *Capital Order*, 30.

114. Eichengreen, *Golden Fetters*, 8.

115. "Philippines in Chaos; Big Harding Task."

116. W. Cameron Forbes to the Secretary of War, November 16, 1921, letter reproduced in the Journal of William Cameron Forbes, series 2, vol. 2, p. 351, Forbes Papers.

117. Eichengreen, *Golden Fetters*, 17.

118. Quoted in Anastacio, *Foundations of the Modern Philippine State*, 197.

119. Michael P. Onorato, "Leonard Wood: His First Year as Governor General," *Asian Studies* 4, no. 2 (1966): 356.

120. Luthringer, *Gold-Exchange Standards*, 206.

121. Luthringer, 203.

122. Luthringer, 219.

123. Jenkins, *American Economic Policy*, 112.

124. Luthringer, *Gold-Exchange Standards*, 234.

125. Thomas, "Albert Sarraut," 927.

126. McVey, *Rise of Indonesian Communism*, 109.

127. Untitled document, unbound and scattered papers from "Printed and Miscellaneous Materials on the Philippines," box 2, Forbes Papers.

128. "Note on Exhibit 3—Report on Legislation," unbound and scattered papers from "Printed and Miscellaneous Materials on the Philippines," box 2, Forbes Papers.

129. "Message Squelched Gov. Wood Charges: Filipino Politicians Unwilling to Reveal Bad Condition of Bank," *Hartford (CT) Courant*, August 19, 1923, p. X6.

130. Vicente Angel S. Ybiernas, "Governor-General Leonard Wood's Neoliberal Agenda of Privatizing Public Assets Stymied, 1921-1927," *Social Science Diliman* 8, no. 11 (2012): 63-82.

131. Stanley, *Nation in the Making*, 24.

132. Chang, *Kicking Away the Ladder*, 10-11.

133. Chang, 78-79.

134. Chang, 115-16.

135. Nagano, *State and Finance in the Philippines*, 120.

136. Golay, *Face of Empire*, 219.

## Interlude

1. Also, why be so parochial as to only care about the United States?

2. I thank Joshua Acosta for pointing this out to me during one of our graduate seminars.

3. Ian Brown, "The Philippine Economy During the Depression of the 1930s," *Philippine Studies* 40, no. 3 (1992): 385.

4. Brown, 381. One way to think about the Great Depression in the Philippines is to consider that the earlier great deflation had already done most of the damage. Something similar happened to the Philippines in the 1980s and 1990s. The downturn during the Asian Financial Crisis of the 1990s was less pronounced for the Philippines than its neighbors. Part of this was because the Philippines had already undergone a major crisis during the Third World debt crisis of the 1980s. As we shall see in chapter 4, the Philippines was the Southeast Asian economy most hurt by that Third World debt crisis.

5. Brown, 383.

6. Allan E. S. Lumba, *Monetary Authorities: Capitalism and Decolonization in the American Colonial Philippines* (Durham, NC: Duke University Press, 2022), 128.

7. Lumba, 130-31.

8. Lumba, 133-35.

9. Frank H. Golay, *Face of Empire: United States–Philippine Relations, 1898–1946* (Quezon City: Ateneo de Manila University Press, 1997), 372-73.

10. Gregg Huff, *World War II and Southeast Asia: Economy and Society Under Japanese Occupation* (Cambridge: Cambridge University Press, 2020), 374.

11. Huff, 388, 387.

12. Huff, 99.

13. Gregg Huff and Shinobu Majima, "Financing Japan's World War II Occupation of Southeast Asia," *Journal of Economic History* 73, no. 4 (2013): 954.

14. Teodoro A. Agoncillo, *History of the Filipino People*, 8th ed. (Quezon City: R. P. Garcia, 1990), 402.

15. Frank H. Golay, *The Philippines: Public Policy and National Economic Development* (Ithaca, NY: Cornell University Press, 1961), 60.

16. Huff, *World War II*, 103-4.

17. Eric Helleiner, *Forgotten Foundations of Bretton Woods: International Development and the Making of the Postwar Order* (Ithaca, NY: Cornell University Press, 2014), 201.

18. *American Economic Policy Towards the Philippines* (Stanford, CA: Stanford University Press, 1954), 110.

19. Huff, *World War II*, 387.

20. Huff, 388.

21. Golay, *Philippines: Public Policy*, 66.

22. Golay, 64.

23. Vicente B. Valdepeñas Jr., "Turning Points in Central Banking: A Retrospective Essay," *Bangko Sentral [Central Bank] Review*, January 2009, 5, https://www.bsp.gov.ph/Media_And_Research/Publications/BS09_A1.pdf.

24. Quoted in Cheryl Ann Payer, "Exchange Controls and National Capitalism: The Philippines Experience," *Journal of Contemporary Asia* 3, no. 1 (1973): 56.

25. Patricio N. Abinales and Donna J. Amoroso, *State and Society in the Philippines*, 2nd ed. (Quezon City: Ateneo de Manila University Press, 2017), 172.

26. Steven Dale MacIsaac, "Nationalists, Expansionists and Internationalists: American Interests and the Struggle for National Economic Development in the Philippines, 1937–1950" (PhD diss., University of Washington, 1993), 519.

## 3. Austerity Nationalized

1. "President Garcia's Second Austerity Speech Delivered at the Independence Grandstand, Saturday Afternoon," January 18, 1958, *Official Gazette of the Philippines Online*, https://www.officialgazette.gov.ph/1958/01/18/second-austerity-speech-of-president-garcia/.

2. Quoted in Patricio N. Abinales and Donna J. Amoroso, *State and Society in the Philippines*, 2nd ed. (Quezon City: Ateneo de Manila University Press, 2017), 183.

3. Miguel Cuaderno, *Guideposts to Economic Stability and Progress: A Selection of the Speeches and Articles of Miguel Cuaderno, Sr., Governor of the Central Bank of the Philippines*, 2nd ed. (Manila: Central Bank of the Philippines, 1960), 90.

4. Cuaderno, 91.

5. Abinales and Amoroso, *State and Society*, 184.

6. Adam Tooze, "The Death of the Central Bank Myth," *Foreign Policy* (blog), May 13, 2020, https://foreignpolicy.com/2020/05/13/european-central-bank-myth-monetary-policy-german-court-ruling/.

7. Clara Mattei, *The Capital Order: How Economists Invented Austerity and Paved the Way to Fascism* (Chicago: University of Chicago Press, 2022), 130.

8. Frank H. Golay, Ralph Anspach, and Eliezer B. Ayal, *Underdevelopment and Economic Nationalism in Southeast Asia* (Ithaca, NY: Cornell University Press, 1969), 42, n. 17.

9. Martin Galan, introduction to "The Human Side of Miguel Cuaderno Sr.," 1978, Accession Number OHT0018, Marcelino A. Foronda Oral Histories Collection, De La Salle University.

10. Enrique T. Galan, "The Human Side of Miguel Cuaderno Sr.," interview by Martin Galan, October 4, 1978, Accession Number OHT00182, Marcelino A. Foronda Oral Histories Collection, De La Salle University. Cuaderno may have dressed with slightly too much sartorial flair. In pictures, one sees him wearing suits with wide peaked lapels (as opposed to more casual notched lapels) that dwarfed his slender frame. In other photos, he wears three-piece suits, inappropriate for Manila's tropical weather and ostentatious for a government official.

11. Miguel Cuaderno, "The Central Bank and Economic Planning," in *Planning for Progress: The Administration of Economic Planning in the Philippines*, ed. R. S. Milne (Manila: Institute of Public Administration and Institute of Economic Development and Research, University of the Philippines, 1960), 104.

12. Yusuke Takagi, *Central Banking as State Building* (Singapore: National University of Singapore Press, 2016), 99.

13. Miguel Cuaderno, *Problems of Economic Development (The Philippines: A Case Study)* (Manila: n.p., 1964), 91.

14. Takagi, *Central Banking*, 74.

15. Shirley Jenkins, *American Economic Policy Towards the Philippines* (Stanford, CA: Stanford University Press, 1954), 111.

16. Cuaderno, *Problems of Economic Development*, 27.

17. James A. Storer and Teresita L. de Guzman, "Philippine Economic Planning and Progress," in *Planning for Progress: The Administration of Economic Planning in the Philippines*, ed. R. S. Milne (Manila: Institute of Public Administration and Institute of Economic Development and Research, University of the Philippines, 1960), 9–10.

18. Cuaderno, *Problems of Economic Development*, 35; Vicente B. Valdepeñas Jr., "Turning Points in Central Banking: A Retrospective Essay," *Bangko Sentral [Central Bank] Review*, January 2009, 8, https://www.bsp.gov.ph/Media_And_Research/Publications/BS09_A1.pdf; Robert E. Baldwin, *Foreign Trade Regimes and Economic Development: Philippines* (New York: National Bureau of Economic Research, 1975), 31.

19. For a typical account see Rene E. Ofreneo, "Six Decades of Debt-Driven Economic Governance: What Is the Scorecard?," *BusinessMirror*, February 27, 2023, https://businessmirror.com.ph/2023/02/27/six-decades-of-debt-driven-economic-governance-what-is-the-scorecard/.

20. Paul D. Hutchcroft, *Booty Capitalism: The Politics of Banking in the Philippines* (Ithaca, NY: Cornell University Press, 1998), 30.

21. Cuaderno, *Problems of Economic Development*, 24.

22. Cuaderno, 25.

23. Lisandro E. Claudio, *Liberalism and the Postcolony: Thinking the State in 20th-Century Philippines* (Singapore: NUS Press, 2017), 48–49.

24. See my earlier summary of this literature in Claudio, 50.

25. Emmanuel de Dios, "From Sancianco to Encarnacion: Footnotes to a Genealogy of Economics in the Philippines," *Philippine Review of Economics* 37, no. 2 (2000): 32.

26. See Yusuke Takagi, "Politics of the Great Debate in the 1950s: Revisiting Economic Decolonization in the Philippines," *Kasarinlan: Philippine Journal of Third World Studies* 23, no. 1 (2008): 91–114.

27. Takagi, 54.

28. Jose V. Abueva, *Ramon Magsaysay: A Political Biography* (Manila: Solidaridad, 1971), 341.

29. Claudio, *Liberalism and the Postcolony*, 54.

30. Claudio, 49.

31. Salvador Araneta, *Economic Re-Examination of the Philippines: A Review of Economic Policies Dictated by Washington* (Malabon: Sahara Heritage Foundation, 1953), 331.

32. Cuaderno, *Problems of Economic Development*, 38.

33. Mark R. Thompson, *The Anti-Marcos Struggle: Personalistic Rule and Democratic Transition in the Philippines* (New Haven, CT: Yale University Press, 1995), 24–25.

34. Frank H. Golay, "The Quirino Administration in Perspective," *Far Eastern Survey* 28, no. 3 (1959): 43.

35. Jorge R. Coquia, *The Philippines Presidential Election of 1953* (Manila: Philippine Education Foundation, 1955), 102.

36. Valdepeñas, "Turning Points in Central Banking," 3.

37. Thompson, *Anti-Marcos Struggle*, 28–29. See also Eva-Lotta E. Hedman, *In the Name of Civil Society: From Free Election Movements to People Power in the Philippines* (Quezon City: Ateneo de Manila University Press, 2006), 44–66.

38. Cuaderno, *Problems of Economic Development*, 54.

39. Cuaderno, 134.

40. Jose D. Soberano, "The Fiscal Policy Controversy," in *Patterns in Decision-Making: Case Studies in Philippine Public Administration*, ed. Raul P. De Guzman (Manila: Graduate School of Public Administration, University of the Philippines, 1963), 336.

41. Cuaderno, *Problems of Economic Development*, 55.

42. Cuaderno, 121.

43. Cuaderno, 120.

44. Baldwin, *Foreign Trade Regimes*, 37.

45. Cuaderno, *Problems of Economic Development*, vi.

46. Miguel Cuaderno, *Guideposts to Economic Stability and Progress* (Manila: Central Bank of the Philippines, 1955), 77.

47. Abueva, *Ramon Magsaysay*, 320.

48. Abueva, 343–44.

49. Cuaderno, *Problems of Economic Development*, 55.

50. Cuaderno, "Central Bank and Economic Planning," 108.

51. Lisandro E. Claudio, *Taming People's Power: The EDSA Revolutions and Their Contradictions* (Quezon City: Ateneo de Manila University Press, 2013), 92. The Cojuangco family continues to own the bulk of Hacienda Luisita, and because Jose Cojuangco's daughter, Corazon Cojuangco Aquino, and grandson Benigno Cojuangco Aquino, became presidents of the Philippines, it remains the most potent symbol of landlord power in the country.

52. Cuaderno, *Guideposts to Economic Stability*, 308.

53. Soberano, "Fiscal Policy," 337; Abueva, *Magsaysay*, 341.

54. Filemon C. Rodriguez, "The National Economic Council, Past and Present," in *Planning for Progress: The Administration of Economic Planning in the*

*Philippines*, ed. R. S. Milne (Manila: Institute of Public Administration and Institute of Economic Development and Research, University of the Philippines, 1960), 38.

55. Rodriguez, 40.

56. Hermenegildo B. Reyes, "The National Economic Council, Planning and Private Enterprise," in Milne, *Planning for Progress*, 50.

57. Rodriguez, "National Economic Council," 40.

58. Reyes, "National Economic Council," 51–53.

59. Quoted in Soberano, "Fiscal Policy," 350.

60. Cuaderno, *Guideposts to Economic Stability*, 2nd ed., 239.

61. Cuaderno, 238.

62. Cuaderno, 53.

63. Cuaderno, *Problems of Economic Development*, 96.

64. Cuaderno, 140.

65. Cuaderno, 53.

66. Salvador Araneta, *Christian Democracy for the Philippines: A Re-Examination of Attitudes and Views* (Malabon, Rizal: Araneta University Press, 1958), 371.

67. Abueva, *Ramon Magsaysay*, 347.

68. Soberano, "Fiscal Policy," 344.

69. Abueva, *Ramon Magsaysay*, 354.

70. Quoted in Soberano, "Fiscal Policy," 362.

71. Quoted in Abueva, *Ramon Magsaysay*, 352.

72. Teodoro M. Locsin, "Economic Challenge: Recto on Economics," *Philippines Free Press*, October 13, 1956, 2.

73. Quoted in Abueva, *Ramon Magsaysay*, 353.

74. Cuaderno, "Central Bank and Economic Planning," 100.

75. Cuaderno, 121.

76. National Security Council, "April 2, 1958: Operations Coordinating Board Report," in *Managing Nationalism: United States National Security Documents on the Philippines*, ed. Nick Cullather (Quezon City: New Day, 1992), 112.

77. Cuaderno, *Problems of Economic Development*, 120–21.

78. Cuaderno, 121.

79. Cuaderno, 124.

80. Amado A. Castro, "The Central Bank of the Philippines: The First Twenty Years," Discussion Paper (Institute of Economic Development and Research, School of Economics, University of the Philippines, May 26, 1972), 5.

81. Baldwin, *Foreign Trade Regimes*, 37.

82. Cuaderno, *Problems of Economic Development*, 78.

83. Cuaderno, *Guideposts to Economic Stability*, 2nd ed., 106. He did not name Schacht but merely referred to a foreign expert whom he assumed that audience knew.

84. Baldwin, *Foreign Trade Regimes*, 37.

85. Teodoro M. Locsin, "Economic Re-Examination," *Philippines Free Press*, October 6, 1956, 5.

86. Quoted in Locsin.

87. Locsin.

88. Cuaderno, *Guideposts to Economic Stability*, 2nd ed., 57.

89. Frank H. Golay, *The Philippines: Public Policy* and National Economic Development (Ithaca, NY: Cornell University Press, 1961), 121–22.

90. Golay, 124.

91. Golay, 123–24, n. 9.

92. John T. Caroll, "Philippine Labor Unions," *Philippine Studies* 9, no. 2 (1961): 240.

93. Jenkins, *American Economic Policy*, 163.

94. Caroll, "Philippine Labor Unions," 243; Leopoldo J. Dejillas, *Trade Union Behavior in the Philippines, 1946–1990* (Quezon City: Ateneo de Manila University Press, 1994), 34.

95. Caroll, "Philippine Labor Unions," 253.

96. Gonzalo M. Jurado, Ricardo D. Ferrer, and Emmanuel F. Esguerra, "Trade Policy, Growth and Employment: A Study of the Philippines" (International Labour Organisation: International Division of Labour Programme, October 1983), 13, http://www.ilo.org/public/libdoc/ilo/1983/83B09_511_engl.pdf.

97. Amando Doronila, *The State, Economic Transformation, and Political Change in the Philippines: 1946–1972* (Singapore: Oxford University Press, 1992), 63.

98. Cuaderno, *Problems of Economic Development*, 130.

99. Araneta, *Economic Re-Examination*, 259.

100. Cuaderno, *Guideposts to Economic Stability*, 309.

101. Cuaderno, *Guideposts to Economic Stability*, 2nd ed., 92.

102. Christina D. Romer, "What Ended the Great Depression?," *Journal of Economic History* 52, no. 4 (1992): 782.

103. Cuaderno, *Guideposts to Economic Stability*, 309.

104. Quoted in Golay et al., *Underdevelopment and Economic Nationalism*, 43.

105. Renato Constantino, "The Mis-Education of the Filipino," *Journal of Contemporary Asia* 1, no. 1 (1970): 20. That Filipino First was enshrined in this essay speaks to its rhetorical hold over a generation of nationalist commentators, mostly baby boomers raised on the works of scholars like Constantino. This essay may be the most important in defining a left-wing nationalism I have labeled elsewhere as the "Diliman Consensus"—a reference to the Diliman campus of the University of the Philippines. See Claudio, *Liberalism and the Postcolony*, 25–27. For a discussion of the significance of Constantino's essay see Vicente L. Rafael, "Mis-Education, Translation and the Barkada of Languages: Reading Renato Constantino with Nick Joaquin," *Kritika Kultura*, no. 21/22 (2013): 40–68.

106. This pattern is best explained in Henry Schwalbenberg, "Class Conflict and Economic Stagnation in the Philippines: 1950–1972," *Philippines Studies* 37, no. 4 (1989): 440–50.

107. "Inside Congress: Dangerous Decision," *Philippines Free Press*, June 6, 1959, 5.

108. "Thanks to the NPs!," *Philippines Free Press*, June 6, 1959, 8.

109. Golay, *Philippines: Public Policy*, 77.

110. "Buy Your Dollars, Mister?," *Philippines Free Press*, May 30, 1959, 41.

111. "Editorial: Decontrol," *Philippines Free Press*, April 30, 1960, 8.

112. Quoted in Abinales and Amoroso, *State and Society*, 183.

113. Cheryl Ann Payer, "Exchange Controls and National Capitalism: The Philippines Experience," Journal of Contemporary Asia 3, no. 1 (1973): 63.

114. Baldwin, *Foreign Trade Regimes*, 50.

115. "Editorial: The Cuaderno Exchange 'Decontrol' Plan," *Journal of the American Chamber of Commerce* 36, no. 5 (1960): 248.

116. Cuaderno, *Problems of Economic Development*, 82–83.

117. Cuaderno, 58.

118. Vicente B. Valdepeñas Jr. and Germilino M. Bautista, *The Emergence of the Philippine Economy* (Manila: Papyrus, 1977), 183.

119. Raul Fabella, "The BSP and Inflation: What Mission Creep?," Opinion, *BusinessWorld*, July 9, 2018, http://www.bworldonline.com/the-bsp-and-inflation-what-mission-creep/.

120. David G. Timberman, *A Changeless Land: Continuity and Change in Philippine Politics* (Armonk, NY: M. E. Sharpe, 1991), 47–48.

121. Cayetano Paderanga, "The Macroeconomic Dimensions of Philippine Development," keynote lecture, Philippine Studies Conference in Japan, Center for Southeast Asian Studies, Kyoto University, February 28, 2014, 23.

122. Fumitaka Furuoka, Qaiser Munir, and Hanafiah Harvey, "Does the Phillips Curve Exist in the Philippines?," *Economics Bulletin* 33, no. 3 (2013): 2001–16; Paderanga, "Macroeconomic Dimensions."

123. Castro, "Central Bank of the Philippines," 4.

124. Hideyoshi Sakai, "An Overview: Postwar Economic Development Experience in the Philippines: Thrust, Zeal and Achievement," in *Philippine Macroeconomic Perspective: Developments and Policies*, ed. Manuel F. Montes and Hideyoshi Sakai (Tokyo: IDE-JETRO, 1989), 4.

125. Paderanga, "Macroeconomic Dimensions," 22.

126. Francisco G. Dakila Jr., Vic K. Delloro, and Jade Eric T. Redoblado, "Economic Crises in the Philippines: 1950s–1970s," in *Central Banking in Challenging Times: The Philippine Experience*, ed. Vicente B. Valdepeñas Jr. and Amando M. Tetangco (Manila: Bangko Sentral ng Pilipinas, 2009), 176.

127. Dakila et al., 169.

128. Golay, *Philippines: Public Policy*, 40.

129. Ichiro Otani, "Inflation in an Open Economy: A Case Study of the Philippines," *IMF Economic Review* 22, no. 3 (1975): 768.

130. Takagi, *Central Banking*, 135, 134, 181.

131. Ofreneo, "Six Decades."

132. Miguel Cuaderno, "The Anti-Capitalist Attitude," in *Private Investment: The Key to International Industrial Development* (New York: McGraw-Hill, 1958), 61.

133. Cuaderno, *Problems of Economic Development*, 111.

134. Cuaderno, 128.

135. Paul M. Sweezy and Harry Magdoff, introduction to *The Lichauco Paper: Imperialism in the Philippines*, by Alejandro Lichauco (New York: Monthly Review Press, 1973), xi.

136. Sweezy and Magdoff, xi–xii.

137. Alejandro Lichauco, *Nationalist Economics: History, Theory and Practice* (Quezon City: Institute for Rural Industrialization, 1988), 161, 163–64.

138. Lichauco, *Lichauco Paper*, 22, 56.

139. Alejandro Lichauco, "Preface: What 'Economic Re-Examination' Is About," in Araneta, *Economic Re-Examination of the Philippines*, xxx–xxxvi.

140. This latter contradiction was not atypical of "progressives" from this period. As a recent account has shown, the defining feature of Philippine communism (which he prefers to label "Stalinism") has been its tendency to subordinate anticapitalism in favor of creating united, anti-imperial fronts with the domestic bourgeoisie. See Joseph Scalice, *The Drama of Dictatorship: Martial Law and the Communist Parties of the Philippines* (Ithaca, NY: Cornell University Press, 2023).

141. Lichauco, *Lichauco Paper*, 37, 39.

142. Barry Eichengreen, *Globalizing Capital: A History of the International System*, 3rd ed. (Princeton, NJ: Princeton University Press, 2019), 88.

143. Jacques J. Polak, "The Changing Nature of IMF Conditionality," *Essays in International Finance*, no. 184 (1991): 18, https://ies.princeton.edu/pdf/E184.pdf.

144. Lichauco, *Nationalist Economics*, 145.

145. Quoted in Lichauco, 145.

146. On the misinterpretation of this episode see Lisandro E. Claudio, "The Father of Filipino Austerity: Central Bank Governor Miguel Cuaderno and Anti-Inflationary Ideology in the 1950s," *Philippine Studies, Historical & Ethnographic Viewpoints* 69, no. 4 (2021): 539–45.

147. Cuaderno, *Guideposts to Economics Stability*, 2nd ed., 313.

148. See Takagi, *Central Banking*, 134, and Doronila, *State, Economic Transformation*, 114.

149. Kim Scipes, "Global Economic Crisis, Neoliberal Solutions, and the Philippines," *Monthly Review*, December 1, 1999, https://monthlyreview.org/1999/12/01/global-economic-crisis-neoliberal-solutions-and-the-philippines/; Miguel Antonio Jimenez, "Views on the Philippine Economy Through the Nationalist Lens: 1945–1992," *TALA: An Online Journal of History* 1, no. 1 (2018): 39–57.

150. Claudio, *Liberalism and the Postcolony*, 57.

## 4. Austerity Democratized

1. Bobby Benedicto, "The Queer Afterlife of the Postcolonial City: (Trans) Gender Performance and the War of Beautification," *Antipode* 47, no. 3 (2015): 538.

2. See Gerard Lico, *Edifice Complex: Power, Myth, and Marcos State Architecture* (Quezon City: Ateneo de Manila University Press, 2003).

3. Benedicto, "Queer Afterlife," 585.

4. Salim Lakha and Michael Pinches, "Poverty and the 'New Society' in Manila," *Australian Journal of International Affairs* 31, no. 3 (1977): 372.

5. Caroline S. Hau, *Elites and Ilustrados in Philippine Culture* (Quezon City: Ateneo de Manila University Press, 2017), 214.

6. Teresa Encarnacion Tadem, *Philippine Politics and the Marcos Technocrats: The Emergence and Evolution of a Power Elite* (Quezon City: Ateneo de Manila University Press, 2019), 27.

7. It is also likely that the intellectual aura of the Marcos administration appealed to them. More than any other president, Marcos had a knack for appealing to academics and intellectuals. See Rommel Curaming, *Power and Knowledge in Southeast Asia: State and Scholars in Indonesia and the Philippines* (London: Routledge, 2020).

8. Lisandro E. Claudio, *Liberalism and the Postcolony: Thinking the State in 20th-Century Philippines* (Singapore: NUS Press), 113.

9. Claudio, 113.

10. Salvador Araneta, *Salvador Araneta: Reflections of a Filipino Exile*, ed. Michael P. Onorato (Fullerton: Oral History Program, California State University, 1979), 32.

11. Cecilia P. Serrano, *Beating the Odds: The Life, the Times, and the Politics of Diosdado P. Macapagal* (Quezon City: New Day, 2005), 53.

12. Robert E. Baldwin, *Foreign Trade Regimes and Economic Development: Philippines* (New York: National Bureau of Economic Research, 1975), 56.

13. Amado A. Castro, "The Central Bank of the Philippines: The First Twenty Years," Discussion Paper (Institute of Economic Development and Research, School of Economics, University of the Philippines, May 26, 1972), 40–41.

14. Sixto K. Roxas, interview by Teresa Encarnacion Tadem, November 26, 2007, JSPS Technocracy Project Interviews, 17.

15. Sixto K. Roxas, "Exchange Decontrol in the Philippines," *Philippines Studies*, no. 2 (1962): 199.

16. Baldwin, *Foreign Trade Regimes*, 65–66.

17. Baldwin, 73.

18. Baldwin, 73.

19. Patricio N. Abinales and Donna J. Amoroso, *State and Society in the Philippines*, 2nd ed. (Quezon City: Ateneo de Manila University Press, 2017), 198.

20. Robert S. Dohner and Ponciano S. Intal Jr., "The Marcos Legacy: Economic Policy and Foreign Debt in the Philippines," in *Developing Country Debt and Economic Performance*, vol. 3, *Country Studies—Indonesia, Korea, Philippines, Turkey*, ed. Jeffrey D. Sachs and Susan M. Collins (Chicago: University of Chicago Press, 1989), 382.

21. Amando Doronila, "The Transformation of Patron-Client Relations and Its Political Consequences in Postwar Philippines," *Journal of Southeast Asian Studies* 16, no. 1 (1985): 111–12.

22. Hau, *Elites and Ilustrados*, 203.

23. Quoted in Dohner and Intal, "Marcos Legacy," 382.

24. "Diary of Ferdinand E. Marcos," January 1970, Philippine Diary Project, https://philippinediaryproject.com/1970/01/18/sunday-january-18-1970/ 37.

25. "Diary of Ferdinand E. Marcos."

26. Placido Mapa, interview by Yutaka Katayama, Teresa Encarnacion Tadem, Cayetano Paderanga, and Temario Rivera, 2009, JSPS Technocracy

Project Interviews, 17. My thanks to Tesa Tadem for providing access to these interviews.

27. Jose F. Lacaba, *Days of Disquiet, Nights of Rage: The First Quarter Storm and Related Events*, new ed. (Pasig City: Anvil, 2003).

28. "Diary of Augusto Ceasar Espiritu," September 5, 1972, Philippine Diary Project, https://philippinediaryproject.wordpress.com/1972/09/05/tuesday-september-5-1972/.

29. Leia Castañeda Anastacio, "Hard Cases, Bad Law: The Martial Law Cases and the Judicial Legitimation of Constitutional Authoritarianism," in *The Marcos Era: A Reader*, ed. Leia Castañeda Anastacio and Patricio N. Abinales (Quezon City: Bughaw, 2022), 61–62.

30. Ma. Lina Araneta Santiago, *Salvador Araneta: A Man Ahead of His Time* (Malabon, Metro Manila: AIA, 1986), 11.

31. This information is from the unpublished preliminary research of Wogie Pacala, head archivist of Salvador Araneta's estate.

32. Santiago, *Salvador Araneta*, 11.

33. Araneta, *Reflections of a Filipino Exile*, 22.

34. Cesar E. Virata, email to Lisandro E. Claudio, December 4, 2020.

35. Tadem, *Philippine Politics and the Marcos Technocrats*, 113.

36. Diplomatic report of the British Ambassador in the Philippines to the Secretary for Foreign and Commonwealth Affairs, "Philippines: Annual Review for 1970," January 1, 1971, FCO 15/1439, Foreign Office files for South East Asia, 1967–1980 (digital).

37. After a 1978 constitutional amendment, legislative and executive powers were fused through the office of the president. Marcos thus simultaneously became president and prime minister. In 1981, he relinquished the powers of the prime minister to Virata.

38. Cesar E. Virata, interview by Lisandro E. Claudio, Zoom recording, September 9, 2020.

39. "Floating Rate for the Peso Announced by the Philippines," *New York Times*, February 22, 1970.

40. Gerardo P. Sicat, *Cesar Virata: Life and Times; Through Four Decades of Philippine Economic History* (Diliman, Quezon City: University of the Philippines Press, 2014), 198.

41. Sicat, 237.

42. Sicat, 113–14.

43. Gerardo P. Sicat, interview by Lisandro E. Claudio, Zoom recording, July 10, 2020.

44. Sicat interview.

45. Gerardo P. Sicat, "A Memoir of the Young UP School of Economics," *Philippine Review of Economics* 54, no. 2 (2017): 156.

46. Sicat, 167.

47. Sicat, 168.

48. Gerardo P. Sicat, *Economic Policy and Philippine Development* (Quezon City: University of the Philippines Press, 1972), vii.

49. John H. Power and Gerardo P. Sicat, *The Philippines: Industrialization and Trade Policies* (London: Oxford University Press, 1971).

50. Emmanuel de Dios, "From Sanciano to Encarnacion: Footnotes to a Genealogy of Economics in the Philippines," *Philippine Review of Economics* 37, no. 2 (2000): 50.

51. Power and Sicat, *Philippines*, 51.

52. Gerardo Sicat, "A Historical and Current Perspective of Philippine Economic Problems," Philippine Institute for Development Studies, 1986, 12, https://dirp4.pids.gov.ph/ris/ms/pidsms86-11.pdf.

53. Gerardo Sicat, "Forex Controls in the 1950s: Philippine Economic History," *Philippine Star*, October 24, 2018, https://www.philstar.com/business/2018/10/24/1862529/forex-controls-1950s-philippine-economic-history.

54. Amando Doronila, *The State, Economic Transformation, and Political Change in the Philippines: 1946–1972* (Singapore: Oxford University Press, 1992), 68.

55. Kim Scipes, "Global Economic Crisis, Neoliberal Solutions, and the Philippines," *Monthly Review*, December 1, 1999, https://monthlyreview.org/1999/12/01/global-economic-crisis-neoliberal-solutions-and-the-philippines/.

56. Sicat, *Economic Policy*, 33.

57. Sicat, 421.

58. Chalmers Johnson, *MITI and the Japanese Miracle: The Growth of Industrial Policy, 1925–1975* (Stanford, CA: Stanford University Press, 1982), 18. See Hau, *Elites and Ilustrados*, 214–16, for an extended analysis of why it is inadequate to refer to Marcos's attempt at developmentalism as simply neoliberal.

59. As Paul Hutchcroft notes, during this period the central bank governor Gregorio Licaros became "a master at bringing in the foreign loans that both sustained the entire system of crony privilege and fed the growth of the local banking system." Paul Hutchcroft, *Booty Capitalism: The Politics of Banking in the Philippines* (Ithaca, NY: Cornell University Press, 1998), 120.

60. De Dios, "From Sanciano," 50.

61. United States Embassy, Philippines, airgram to US Department of State, "An Assessment of Progress Toward the New Society," February 2, 1979, the Philippines: U.S. policy during the Marcos years, 1965–1986, Digital National Security Archive.

62. United States Embassy, 8–9.

63. In any case, the technocrats were either out of power or sidelined by the 1980s. During this time there was a widespread perception that an ailing Marcos (he was later revealed to have lupus) could no longer shelter the technocrats from politics and that First Lady Imelda Marcos had gained greater power.

64. G. S. Licaros to Ferdinand E. Marcos, January 4, 1971, C6: box 1, roll 001, folder 6, Presidential Commission on Good Government (PCGG) files.

65. Licaros to Marcos.

66. Bangko Sentral ng Pilipinas [Central Bank of the Philippines], "Foreign Exchange Transactions-Developments and Prospects: February 1970–February, 1973," n.d. [almost certainly 1973], C6: box 23, roll 023, folder 52, PCGG files.

67. Licaros to Marcos.

68. Licaros to Marcos.

69. Cayetano Paderanga, "The Macroeconomic Dimensions of Philippine Development," keynote lecture, Philippine Studies Conference in Japan (PSCJ), Center for Southeast Asian Studies, Kyoto University, 2014, 6.

70. Gerardo Sicat, "The Economic Legacy of Marcos," in *UPSE Discussion Papers*, vol. 2011-11 (University of the Philippines, School of Economics, Quezon City, 2011), 28, https://ideas.repec.org/p/phs/dpaper/201111.html.

71. Diplomatic report of the British Ambassador in the Philippines to the Secretary for Foreign and Commonwealth Affairs, "Philippines: Annual Review for 1979," January 7, 1980, FCO 15/2728, Foreign Office files for South East Asia.

72. Dohner and Intal, "Marcos Legacy," 434.

73. Emmanuel S. de Dios, Maria Socorro Gochoco-Bautista, and Jan Carlo Punongbayan, "Martial Law and the Philippine Economy," *UP School of Economics Discussion Papers*, no. 2021-07 (2021): 21.

74. Sicat, "Historical and Current Perspective," 10.

75. Sicat, 11.

76. Sicat, 12.

77. Paderanga, "Macroeconomic Dimensions," 2.

78. Robert Wade, *Governing the Market: Economic Theory and the Role of Government in East Asian Industrialization* (Princeton, NJ: Princeton University Press, 1990), 118.

79. See Lacaba, *Days of Disquiet*, for the best reporting from and about this period. For a comprehensive scholarly account see Joseph Scalice, *The Drama of Dictatorship: Martial Law and the Communist Parties of the Philippines* (Ithaca, NY: Cornell University Press, 2023), 60–109.

80. Lisandro E. Claudio, *Taming People's Power: The EDSA Revolutions and Their Contradictions* (Quezon City: Ateneo de Manila University Press, 2013), 124–26; Scalice, *Drama of Dictatorship*, 36–43.

81. KM Economic Research Bureau, "Devaluation and IMF Dictation," *Philippine Collegian*, March 12, 1970. My thanks to Joseph Scalice for sending me a copy of this op-ed.

82. I have confirmed from two MDP members that although Lichauco may not have drafted the MDP statements in discussion, they were reflections of his views.

83. Movement for a Democratic Philippines, "The True State of the Nation," January 24, 1972, reel 5, box 11/18.22, Philippine Radical Papers, University of the Philippines Diliman Main Library.

84. Alejandro Lichauco, *The Lichauco Paper: Imperialism in the Philippines* (New York: Monthly Review Press, 1973), 42.

85. Lichauco, 41.

86. Lichauco, 42.

87. Alejandro Lichauco, *Nationalist Economics: History, Theory and Practice* (Quezon City: Institute for Rural Industrialization, 1988), 189.

88. David A. Steinberg, "Developmental States and Undervalued Exchange Rates in the Developing World," *Review of International Political Economy* 23, no. 3 (2016): 418.

89. Lichauco, *Lichauco Paper*, 42.

90. Lichauco, 42.

91. Lichauco worked for Araneta and Araneta-owned companies in various capacities. At one point he was himself Araneta's lawyer. My thanks to Wogie Pacala, head archivist of Salvador Araneta's estate, for this information.

92. Lichauco, 42.

93. Movement for a Democratic Philippines, "Ang Tunay na Kalagayan ng Bansa" [The true state of the nation], January 25, 1971, reel 5, box 11/18.23, Radical Papers.

94. Martin Daunton, *Just Taxes: The Politics of Taxation in Britain, 1914–1979* (Cambridge: Cambridge University Press, 2002), 344.

95. This two-step theory of revolution posits that Communists must first ally with so-called "progressive" segments of the domestic bourgeois to combat the imperialism of foreign capital. The most compelling critique of how this policy has been implemented by Maoists in the Philippines is Scalice, *Drama of Dictatorship*.

96. Eduardo C. Tadem, "Beyond the Grains: The Political Economy of the Rice Industry in the Philippines, 1965–1985," in *The Marcos Era: A Reader*, ed. Leia Castañeda Anastacio and Patricio N. Abinales (Quezon City: Bughaw, 2022), 259.

97. Scalice, *Drama of Dictatorship*, 118. The romantic way the movement conceived of the transport sector is evident in my father's history of activism. My father was a student activist during the early 1970s and dropped out of the University of the Philippines to engage in full-time activist work with the CPP. To become closer to the masses, he studied to become a mechanic.

98. Scalice, 118. The Maoist strategy of infiltrating strikes to elicit a violent response from the state is called "kiskis" (scratches) and has become a common strategy for the CPP. For other examples of kiskis see Dominique Caouette, "Persevering Revolutionaries: Armed Struggle in the 21st Century; Exploring the Revolution of the Communist Party of the Philippines" (PhD diss., Cornell University, 2004), 463, and Claudio, *Taming People's Power*, 137.

99. Scalice, *Drama of Dictatorship*, 145.

100. "Intelligence Summary NR 71-01," January 1971, C6: box 1, roll 001, folder 6, PCGG files. The report also noted that KM leaders had asked Philippine Science High School students to obtain explosive chemicals from the laboratory.

101. Caeser Z. Lanuza to Ferdinand E. Marcos, January 12, 1971, C6: box 1, roll 001, folder 6, PCGG files.

102. Scalice, *Drama of Dictatorship*, 140–44.

103. Scalice, 146.

104. Martial law was effectively an *autogolpe* or self-coup. To create his dictatorship, Marcos used the military to destroy the constitutional order he was leading.

105. Dohner and Intal, "Marcos Legacy," 391.

106. Dohner and Intal, 396.

107. Tyler Cowen, "Paul Volcker Death: He Left a Complicated Legacy in Latin America," *Bloomberg*, December 10, 2019, https://www.bloomberg.com/opinion/articles/2019-12-10/paul-volcker-death-he-left-a-complicated-legacy-in-latin-america.

108. Stuart Corbridge, "From Riches to Rags: The International Debt Crisis," in *Companion Encyclopedia of Geography: The Environment and*

*Humankind,* ed. Ian Douglas, Richard Huggett, and Mike Robinson (London: Routledge, 1996), 415.

109. Dohner and Intal, "Marcos Legacy," 396.

110. Corbridge, "From Rags to Riches," 417.

111. Hau, *Elite and Ilustrdos,* 170.

112. The most vocal in this regard is the anti-Marcos economist JC Punong-bayan, who uses his columns, social media posts, and popular book to debunk economic myths about the Marcos regime. See JC Punongbayan, "Correcting Misleading Claims by Ex-President Marcos' Technocrats," *Rappler,* May 19, 2023, https://www.rappler.com/voices/thought-leaders/analysis-correcting-mislead ing-claims-by-ex-president-ferdinand-marcos-technocrats/; JC Punongbayan, *False Nostalgia: The Marcos "Golden Age" Myths and How to Debunk Them* (Bughaw, 2023); Kevin Mandrilla and JC Punongbayan, "Marcos Years Marked 'Golden Age' of PH Economy? Look at the Data," *Rappler,* March 5, 2016, https://www.rappler.com/voices/imho/marcos-economy-golden-age-philippines.

113. James C. Rowe, "Philippines Faces Foreign Debt Crisis," *Washington Post,* December 25, 1983, https://www.washingtonpost.com/archive/business/1983/12/25/philippines-faces-foreign-debt-crisis/14d99c52-aa57-486d-8985-10d682d25c19/.

114. Diplomatic report of the British Ambassador in the Philippines to the Secretary for Foreign and Commonwealth Affairs, "Philippines: Annual Review for 1978," January 1, 1979, FCO 15/2532, Foreign Office files for South East Asia, 1967–1980 (digital).

115. Patrick Allan Sharma, *Robert McNamara's Other War: The World Bank and International Development* (Philadelphia: University of Pennsylvania Press, 2017), 132.

116. Dohner and Intal, "Marcos Legacy," 405–8.

117. Vicente Tirona Paterno, *On My Own Terms: The Autobiography of Vicente Tirona Paterno* (Mandaluyong City: Anvil, 2014), 270.

118. See Ricardo Manapat, *Some Are Smarter Than Others: The History of Marcos' Crony Capitalism,* annotated ed. (Quezon City: Bughaw, 2020), and Belinda A. Aquino, *Politics of Plunder: The Philippines Under Marcos,* 2nd ed. (Diliman, Quezon City: University of the Philippines, National College of Public Administration and Governance, 1999).

119. Charles W. Lindsey, "Economic Crisis in the Philippines," *Asian Survey* 24, no. 12 (1984): 1187.

120. Lindsey, 1187.

121. Dohner and Intal, "Marcos Legacy," 525–27.

122. Sicat, "Economic Legacy of Marcos," 42.

123. Sicat, 11.

124. Emmanuel S. de Dios, "The Truth About the Economy Under the Marcos Regime," *BusinessWorld,* November 17, 2015, https://econ.upd.edu.ph/perse/?p=5058; Punongbayan, "Correcting Misleading Claims."

125. Kenneth Gilpin, "Philippine Debt Delay Is Granted," *New York Times,* October 15, 1983.

126. Rowe, "Philippines Faces."

127. "Interview with Cesar Virata," *Third World Quarterly* 6, no. 2 (1984): 274.

128. "Interview with Cesar Virata."

129. Hau, *Elites and Ilustrados*, 196–97.

130. Hau, 97.

131. Hau, 200.

132. Ronald U. Mendoza, Oscar Bulaong Jr., and Gabrielle Ann S. Mendoza, "Cronyism, Oligarchy, and Economic Governance in the Philippines: 1970s vs. 2020s," in *Martial Law in the Philippines: Lessons and Legacies, 1972–2022*, ed. Edilberto C. de Jesus and Ivyrose S. Baysic (Quezon City: Bughaw, 2023), 349.

133. Joel F. Ariate Jr. and Ronald C. Molmisa, "More Than Debt Relief: Two Decades of the Freedom from Debt Coalition," in *Global Civil Society Movements in the Philippines*, ed. Teresa Encarnacion Tadem (Manila: Anvil, 2011), 29.

134. Walden Bello, David Kinley, and Elaine Elinson, *Development Debacle: The World Bank in the Philippines* (San Francisco: Institute for Food and Development Policy, 1982).

135. IBON Databank, *What Crisis: Highlights of the Philippine Economy 1983* (Manila: IBON Databank Phils., 1984).

136. Lichauco, *Nationalist Economics*, 172.

137. See Claudio, *Taming People's Power*, for my assessment of the legacies of this conjunctural event.

138. See Patricio N. Abinales, ed., *The Revolution Falters: The Left in Philippine Politics After 1986*, Southeast Asia Program Series, no. 15 (Ithaca, NY: Southeast Asia Program Publications, Cornell University, 1996); Joel Rocamora, *Breaking Through: The Struggle Within the Communist Party of the Philippines* (Pasig: Anvil, 1994).

139. Ariate and Molmisa, "More Than Debt Relief," 33.

140. Ariate and Molmisa, 34

141. Ariate and Molmisa, 43.

142. Freedom from Debt Coalition, "The History," https://fdcphils.org/about/the-history-of-fdc/, n.d.

143. Mario B. Lamberte, "Central Banking in the Philippines: Then, Now and the Future," Working Paper, PIDS Discussion Paper Series, 2002, 9–10, https://www.econstor.eu/handle/10419/127797.

144. Quoted in Lamberte, 7.

145. Adam Tooze, "The Death of the Central Bank Myth," *Foreign Policy* (blog), May 13, 2020, https://foreignpolicy.com/2020/05/13/european-central-bank-myth-monetary-policy-german-court-ruling/.

146. As I write this chapter early into the new Marcos administration, my sense is that the president is trying to rhetorically tap into the authoritarian nostalgia for his father's period, while subtly signaling that he will avoid the martial law regime's worst excesses. The appointment of a highly qualified and "independent" central banker like Remolona is part of this process.

147. Niña Myka Pauline Arceo, "Extended Pause Likely; Cuts to Be Considered," *Manila Times*, July 7, 2023, https://www.manilatimes.net/2023/07/07/business/top-business/extended-pause-likely-cuts-to-be-considered/1899511.

148. "Further Rate Hikes in Philippines Could Hurt Consumers, Economics Minister Says," Asian Markets, Reuters, October 6, 2023, https://www.reuters.com/markets/asia/further-policy-tightening-could-hurt-philippine-consumers-says-economic-minister-2023-10-06/.

## Conclusion

1. My first agitprop speech was sometime in 2007, during the administration of the corrupt Gloria Macapagal-Arroyo (president from 2001 to 2010). It was a baptism by fire. I spoke in the famous Plaza Miranda, the site of various anti-Marcos protests in the 1970s and hallowed ground of political activists. It was a rare moment when various squabbling left-wing organizations got together to protest not only the corruption but the budding authoritarianism of the Arroyo regime. I recall attending the event with my first-ever hangover and being coached by older activists about how to speak and what economic data to use. My anxiety over delivering the speech doubled when I was told I would be speaking after a particularly charismatic youth leader from one of the major Maoist youth groups.

2. It is technically true that future generations pay for our current state debt, but states do not die as quickly as people, so they can just keep lending and paying money. This is how modern states work. In fact, as Paul Krugman has shown, the British people today have yet to repay the debts of the Napoleonic Wars. See "Wonking Out: Death, Napoleon and Debt," Opinion, *New York Times*, May 19, 2023, https://www.nytimes.com/2023/05/19/opinion/government-debt-pay-off.html.

3. I document this shift in electoral attitudes in Lisandro E. Claudio, "Philippine Elections 2022: The End of Good Governance Discourse," *Contemporary Southeast Asia* 44, no. 3 (2022): 382–88.

4. See Jean Encinas-Franco, "Overseas Filipino Workers (OFWs) as Heroes: Discursive Origins of the 'Bagong Bayani' in the Era of Labor Export," Humanities Diliman 12, no. 2 (2015): 56–78, for an analysis of the new heroism rhetoric of the government.

5. Charmaine G. Ramos, "Change Without Transformation: Social Policy Reforms in the Philippines Under Duterte," *Development and Change* 51, no. 2 (2020): 485–505.

6. Rene Ofreneo, "Dissecting Data: PH Gov't Debt Hits Record P7.7-Trillion," *ABS-CBN News Channel*, March 12, 2020, https://www.youtube.com/watch?v=SbI42y2AJeg&t=144s.

7. Rene Ofreneo, "Are We Building Another Debt Bomb?," Opinion, *BusinessMirror*, March 7, 2019, https://businessmirror.com.ph/2019/03/07/are-we-building-another-debt-bomb/.

8. Sonny Africa, "2018 Yearender: Are You High? The Economy Isn't," *IBON Foundation* (blog), December 31, 2018, https://www.ibon.org/2018-yearender-are-you-high-the-economy-isnt/.

9. Kenneth P. Vogel, "Paul Manafort's Wild and Lucrative Philippine Adventure," *Politico Magazine*, June 10, 2016, https://www.politico.com/magazine/story/2016/06/2016-donald-trump-paul-manafort-ferinand-marcos-philippines-1980s-213952.

10. Caroline S. Hau, *Elites and Ilustrados in Philippine Culture* (Quezon City: Ateneo de Manila University Press, 2017), 171.

11. Frantz Fanon, *Black Skin, White Masks* (New York: Grove Atlantic, 2008).

12. After reading parts of this book and interviewing me for an article, a *New York Times* reporter told me, "Your work makes it seem like the Philippines is the Germany of Asia." I couldn't agree more.

13. "A Tale of Two Families: Generational Succession in Filipino and American Family Firms," *TRaNS: Trans-Regional and -National Studies of Southeast Asia* 3, no. 2 (2015): 185.

14. Lisandro E. Claudio, "Postcolonial Fissures and the Contingent Nation: An Antinationalist Critique of Philippine Historiography," *Philippine Studies: Historical and Ethnographic Viewpoints* 61, no. 1 (2013): 45–75; Lisandro E. Claudio, *Taming People's Power: The EDSA Revolutions and Their Contradictions* (Quezon City: Ateneo de Manila University Press, 2013), 89–116. It was writing this book that caused me to do a 180.

15. Ramon L. Clarete, Emmanuel F. Esguerra, and Hal Hill, "The Philippine Economy: An Overview," in *The Philippine Economy: No Longer the East Asian Exception?*, ed. Ramon L. Clarete, Emmanuel F. Esguerra, and Hal Hill (Singapore: ISEAS-Yusof Ishak Institute, 2018), 14–15.

16. The finest work on this uncomfortable reality is Yuen Yuen Ang, *China's Gilded Age: The Paradox of Economic Boom and Vast Corruption* (Cambridge: Cambridge University Press, 2020).

17. See Daron Acemoglu and James A. Robinson, *Why Nations Fail: The Origins of Power, Prosperity, and Poverty* (New York: Crown, 2012).

18. Ha-Joon Chang, "Are Some Countries Destined for Under-Development?," lecture, University of Manchester Global Development Institute, February 6, 2018, http://blog.gdi.manchester.ac.uk/gdi-lecture-series-ha-joon-chang/.

19. Paul Hutchcroft and Emmanuel de Dios, "Political Economy," in *The Philippine Political Economy: Development, Policies, and Challenges*, ed. Arsenio M. Balisacan and Hal Hill (New York: Oxford University Press, 2003), 70.

20. This rarely stated (but, in hindsight, obvious) truth was pointed out to me by Paul Salamanca during a graduate student seminar.

# BIBLIOGRAPHY

## Archival Collections

### National Archives and Records Administration (NARA) of the United States

Bureau of Insular Affairs, General Classified Files 1898–1945, Record Group 350, NARA, College Park, MD

Files of the Senate Committee on the Philippines, 56th Congress, NARA, Washington, DC

### Personal Papers

W. Cameron Forbes Papers, Houghton Library, Harvard University

Marcelino A. Foronda Oral Histories Collection, De La Salle University, Manila

Irving Winslow Papers, Special Collections Research Center, University of Michigan

Dean Conant Worcester Papers 1900–1924, Bentley Historical Library, University of Michigan

Dean Conant Worcester's Philippine Collection, Special Collections Research Center, University of Michigan

### Online Collections

Chan Robles Virtual Law Library, Chan Robles Law Firm, Manila

*Congressional Record*, Proceedings and Debates of the US Congress

Foreign Office (United Kingdom) Files for South East Asia, 1967–1980 (digital)

*Official Gazette of the Philippines*

Philippine Diary Project

Presidential Commission on Good Government (PCGG) Files (digital scans of the entire archive shared with various scholars after the election of Ferdinand Marcos Jr.)

The United States and Its Territories, 1870–1925: The Age of Imperialism, University of Michigan Special Collections
United States Digital National Security Archive

## Other Collections

Japan Society for the Promotion of Science (JSPS) Technocracy Project Interviews (c/o Teresa Tadem)
Philippine Radical Papers, Main Library, University of the Philippines, Diliman

## Newspapers and Online News Sites

*Bloomberg*
*BusinessMirror*
*BusinessWorld*
*El Debate*
*El Ideal*
*Foreign Policy*
*Hartford Courant*
IBON Foundation
*Journal of Commerce and Commercial Bulletin (Philippines)*
*Journal of the American Chamber of Commerce (Philippines)*
*Manila Daily Bulletin*
*Manila Times*
*Monthly Review*
*New York Times*
*New-York Tribune*
*Nikkei Asia*
*Philippine Collegian*
*Philippine Daily Inquirer*
*Philippine Star*
*Philippines Free Press*
*Politico*
*Rappler*
Reuters
*Washington Post*
*Washington Times*

## Government Reports

Arenas, Rafael Díaz. *Report on the Commerce and Shipping of the Philippine Islands.* Translated by Encarnacion Alzona. Manila: National Historical Institute of the Philippines, 1979.

Conant, Charles Arthur. "Currency in the Philippines: Statement of Charles A. Conant." Washington, DC: Government Printing Office, March 24, 1902.

*The Philippines 1950: A Handbook of Trade and Economic Facts and Figures.* Manila: Department of Commerce and Industry, 1950.

*Report of the Philippine Commission to the Secretary of War.* Washington, DC: Government Printing Office, 1912.

*Reports of the Taft Philippine Commission.* Washington, DC: Government Printing Office, 1901.

United States Department of State, Office of the Historian. Milestones: 1899–1913, "The Philippine-American War, 1899–1902." https://history.state.gov/milestones/1899-1913/war.

Wood, Leonard, and W. Cameron Forbes. *Report of the Special Mission on the Investigation to the Philippine Islands to the Secretary of War.* Washington, DC: Government Printing Office, 1921.


## Interviews

Lumba, Allan E. S. Interview by Nicole Curato. "*Monetary Authorities.*" New Books in Southeast Asian Studies podcast, July 1, 2023. https://newbooksnetwork.com/monetary-authorities.

Sicat, Gerardo P. Interview by Lisandro E. Claudio. Zoom recording, September 9, 2020.

Virata, Cesar E. Interview by Lisandro E. Claudio. Zoom recording, September 9, 2020.

——. "Interview with Cesar Virata." *Third World Quarterly* 6, no. 2 (1984): 272–81.


## Secondary Sources

Abinales, Patricio N. *Fellow Traveler: Essays on Filipino Communism.* Quezon City: University of the Philippines Press, 2001.

——. *Making Mindanao: Cotabato and Davao in the Formation of the Philippine Nation-State.* Quezon City: Ateneo de Manila University Press, 2000.

——. *Orthodoxy and History in the Muslim-Mindanao Narrative.* Quezon City: Ateneo de Manila University Press, 2010.

——, ed. *The Revolution Falters: The Left in Philippine Politics After 1986.* Southeast Asia Program Series, no. 15. Ithaca, NY: Southeast Asia Program Publications, Cornell University, 1996.

Abinales, Patricio N., and Donna J. Amoroso. *State and Society in the Philippines.* 2nd ed. Quezon City: Ateneo de Manila University Press, 2017.

Abueva, Jose V. *Ramon Magsaysay: A Political Biography.* Manila: Solidaridad, 1971.

Acemoglu, Daron, and James A. Robinson. *Why Nations Fail: The Origins of Power, Prosperity, and Poverty.* New York: Crown, 2012.

Agoncillo, Teodoro A. *History of the Filipino People.* 8th ed. Quezon City: R. P. Garcia, 1990.

Aguilar, Filomeno V. *Clash of Spirits: The History of Power and Sugar Planter Hegemony on a Visayan Island.* Quezon City: Ateneo de Manila University Press, 1998.

——. "The Riddle of the Alien-Citizen: Filipino Migrants as US Nationals and the Anomalies of Citizenship, 1900s–1930s." *Asian and Pacific Migration Journal* 19, no. 2 (2010): 203–36.

Akiboh, Alvita. "Pocket-Sized Imperialism: U.S. Designs on Colonial Currency." *Diplomatic History* 41, no. 5 (2017): 874–902.

Anderson, Warwick. *Colonial Pathologies: American Tropical Medicine, Race, and Hygiene in the Philippines.* Durham, NC: Duke University Press, 2006.

Ang, Yuen Yuen. *China's Gilded Age: The Paradox of Economic Boom and Vast Corruption.* Cambridge: Cambridge University Press, 2020.

Araneta, Salvador. *Christian Democracy for the Philippines: A Re-Examination of Attitudes and Views.* Malabon: Araneta University Press, 1958.

——. *Economic Re-Examination of the Philippines: A Review of Economic Policies Dictated by Washington.* Malabon: Sahara Heritage Foundation, 1953.

——. *Salvador Araneta: Reflections of a Filipino Exile.* Edited by Michael P. Onorato. Fullerton: Oral History Program, California State University, 1979.

Araneta Santiago, Ma. Lina. *Salvador Araneta: A Man Ahead of His Time.* Malabon: AIA, 1986.

Ariate, Joel F. Jr., and Ronald C. Molmisa. "More Than Debt Relief: Two Decades of the Freedom from Debt Coalition." In *Global Civil Society Movements in the Philippines*, edited by Teresa Encarnacion Tadem, 25–60. Manila: Anvil, 2011.

Arnold, Ashia Amber. "Yellow Money: China, the Silver Question, and the Rise of the American West." California State University, 2013. https://scholarworks.calstate.edu/downloads/qr46r338t.

Baldoz, Rick, and César Ayala. "The Bordering of America: Colonialism and Citizenship in the Philippines and Puerto Rico." *Centro Journal* 25, no. 1 (2013): 76–105.

Baldwin, Robert E. *Foreign Trade Regimes and Economic Development: Philippines.* New York: National Bureau of Economic Research, 1975.

Bankoff, Greg. "Wants, Wages, and Workers." *Pacific Historical Review* 74, no. 1 (2005): 59–86.

Bello, Walden, David Kinley, and Elaine Elinson. *Development Debacle: The World Bank in the Philippines.* San Francisco: Institute for Food and Development Policy, 1982.

Benedicto, Bobby. "The Queer Afterlife of the Postcolonial City: (Trans)Gender Performance and the War of Beautification." *Antipode* 47, no. 3 (2015): 580–97.

Bensel, Richard Franklin. *Passion and Preferences: William Jennings Bryan and the 1896 Democratic National Convention*. New York: Cambridge University Press, 2008.

Block, Fred. "Swimming Against the Current: The Rise of a Hidden Developmental State in the United States." *Politics & Society* 36, no. 2 (2008): 169–206.

Blyth, Mark. *Austerity: The History of a Dangerous Idea*. New York: Oxford University Press, 2013.

Brown, Ian. "The Philippine Economy During the Depression of the 1930s." *Philippine Studies* 40, no. 3 (1992): 381–87.

Brown, Wendy. *Undoing the Demos: Neoliberalism's Stealth Revolution*. New York: Zone Books, 2016.

Bryan, William Jennings. "The Issue in the Presidential Campaign." *North American Review* 170, no. 523 (June 1900): 753–71.

Caroll, John T. "Philippine Labor Unions." *Philippine Studies* 9, no. 2 (1961): 220–54.

Carruthers, Bruce G., and Sarah Babb. "The Color of Money and the Nature of Value: Greenbacks and Gold in Postbellum America." *American Journal of Sociology*, October 15, 2015.

Castañeda Anastacio, Leia. *The Foundations of the Modern Philippine State: Imperial Rule and the American Constitutional Tradition, 1898–1935*. New York: Cambridge University Press, 2016.

——. "Hard Cases, Bad Law: The Martial Law Cases and the Judicial Legitimation of Constitutional Authoritarianism." In *The Marcos Era: A Reader*, edited by Leia Castañeda Anastacio and Patricio N. Abinales, 55–90. Quezon City: Bughaw, 2022.

Castro, Amado A. "The Central Bank of the Philippines: The First Twenty Years." Discussion paper. Institute of Economic Development and Research, School of Economics, University of the Philippines, May 26, 1972.

Chang, Ha-Joon. "Are Some Countries Destined for Under-Development?" Lecture, University of Manchester Global Development Institute, February 6, 2018. http://blog.gdi.manchester.ac.uk/gdi-lecture-series-ha-joon-chang/.

——. *Kicking Away the Ladder: Development Strategy in Historical Perspective*. London: Anthem, 2003.

——. *23 Things They Don't Tell You About Capitalism*. London: Allen Lane, 2010.

Charbonneau, Oliver. *Civilizational Imperatives: Americans, Moros, and the Colonial World*. Ithaca, NY: Cornell University Press, 2020.

Clarete, Ramon L., Emmanuel F. Esguerra, and Hal Hill. "The Philippine Economy: An Overview." In *The Philippine Economy: No Longer the East Asian Exception?*, edited by Ramon L. Clarete, Emmanuel F. Esguerra, and Hal Hill, 1–52. Singapore: ISEAS-Yusof Ishak Institute, 2018.

Claudio, Lisandro E. "Beyond Colonial Miseducation: Internationalism and Deweyan Pedagogy in the American-Era Philippines." *Philippine Studies: Historical and Ethnographic Viewpoints* 63, no. 2 (2015): 193–220.

——. "The Father of Filipino Austerity: Central Bank Governor Miguel Cuaderno and Anti-Inflationary Ideology in the 1950s." *Philippine Studies: Historical & Ethnographic Viewpoints* 69, no. 4 (2021): 527–60. https://doi.org/10.1353/phs.2021.0027.

——. *Jose Rizal: Liberalism and the Paradox of Coloniality.* Global Political Thinkers. Singapore: Palgrave Macmillan, 2019.

——. *Liberalism and the Postcolony: Thinking the State in 20th-Century Philippines.* Singapore: NUS Press, 2017.

——. "Philippine Elections 2022: The End of Good Governance Discourse." *Contemporary Southeast Asia* 44, no. 3 (2022): 382–88.

——. *Taming People's Power: The EDSA Revolutions and Their Contradictions.* Quezon City: Ateneo de Manila University Press, 2013.

Concepcion, Venancio. *"La Tragedia" del Banco Nacional Filipino.* Manila: s.n., 1927.

Constantino, Renato. "The Mis-Education of the Filipino." *Journal of Contemporary Asia* 1, no. 1 (1970): 20–36.

Coquia, Jorge R. *The Philippines Presidential Election of 1953.* Manila: Philippine Education Foundation, 1955.

Corbridge, Stuart. "From Riches to Rags: The International Debt Crisis." In *Companion Encyclopedia of Geography: The Environment and Humankind,* edited by Ian Douglas, Richard Huggett, and Mike Robinson. London: Routledge, 1996.

Corpuz, O. D. *An Economic History of the Philippines.* Quezon City: University of the Philippines Press, 1997.

Cot, Annie L. "'Breed Out the Unfit and Breed In the Fit.'" *American Journal of Economics and Sociology* 64, no. 3 (2005): 793–826.

Cuaderno, Miguel. "The Anti-Capitalist Attitude." In *Private Investment: The Key to International Industrial Development,* 52–61. New York: McGraw-Hill, 1958.

——. "The Central Bank and Economic Planning." In *Planning for Progress: The Administration of Economic Planning in the Philippines,* edited by R. S. Milne, 92–108. Manila: Institute of Public Administration and Institute of Economic Development and Research, University of the Philippines, 1960.

——. *Guideposts to Economic Stability and Progress.* Manila: Central Bank of the Philippines, 1955.

——. *Guideposts to Economic Stability and Progress: A Selection of the Speeches and Articles of Miguel Cuaderno, Sr., Governor of the Central Bank of the Philippines.* 2nd ed. Manila: Central Bank of the Philippines, 1960.

——. *Problems of Economic Development (The Philippines: A Case Study).* Manila: n.p., 1964.

Cullather, Nick, ed. *Managing Nationalism: United States National Security Documents on the Philippines.* Quezon City: New Day, 1992.

Cullinane, Michael. *Arenas of Conspiracy and Rebellion in the Late Nineteenth-Century Philippines: The Case of the April 1898 Uprising in Cebu.* Quezon City: Ateneo de Manila University Press, 2014.

——. *Ilustrado Politics: Filipino Elite Responses to American Rule, 1898–1908.* Quezon City: Ateneo de Manila University Press, 2003.

Curaming, Rommel. *Power and Knowledge in Southeast Asia: State and Scholars in Indonesia and the Philippines*. London: Routledge, 2020.

Dakila, Francisco G. Jr., Vic K. Delloro, and Jade Eric T. Redoblado. "Economic Crises in the Philippines 1950s–1970s." In *Central Banking in Challenging Times: The Philippine Experience*, edited by Vicente B. Valdepeñas Jr. and Amando M. Tetangco, 156–207. Manila: Bangko Sentral ng Pilipinas, 2009.

Daunton, Martin. *Just Taxes: The Politics of Taxation in Britain, 1914–1979*. Cambridge: Cambridge University Press, 2002.

de Dios, Emmanuel S. "From Sancianco to Encarnacion: Footnotes to a Genealogy of Economics in the Philippines." *Philippine Review of Economics* 37, no. 2 (2000): 26–67.

de Dios, Emmanuel S., Maria Socorro Gochoco-Bautista, and Jan Carlo Punongbayan. "Martial Law and the Philippine Economy." *UP School of Economics Discussion Papers*, no. 2021–07, November 2021.

de Dios, Emmanuel S., and Paul D. Hutchcroft. "Political Economy." In *The Philippine Political Economy: Development, Policies, and Challenges*, edited by Arsenio M. Balisacan and Hal Hill, 45–76. New York: Oxford University Press, 2003.

Dejillas, Leopoldo J. *Trade Union Behavior in the Philippines, 1946–1990*. Quezon City: Ateneo de Manila University Press, 1994.

Dohner, Robert S., and Ponciano S. Intal Jr. "Book 3: The Marcos Legacy: Economic Policy and Foreign Debt in the Philippines." In *Developing Country Debt and Economic Performance, vol. 3, Country Studies—Indonesia, Korea, Philippines, Turkey*, edited by Jeffrey D. Sachs and Susan M. Collins, 371–614. Chicago: University of Chicago Press, 1989.

Doronila, Amando. *The State, Economic Transformation, and Political Change in the Philippines: 1946–1972*. Singapore: Oxford University Press, 1992.

——. "The Transformation of Patron-Client Relations and Its Political Consequences in Postwar Philippines." *Journal of Southeast Asian Studies* 16, no. 1 (1985): 99–116.

Drake, P. J. "Southeast Asian Monies and the Problem of a Common Measure, with Particular Reference to the Nineteenth Century." *Australian Economic History Review* 31, no. 1 (1991): 90–96.

Eichengreen, Barry. *Globalizing Capital: A History of the International System*. 3rd ed. Princeton, NJ: Princeton University Press, 2019.

——. *Golden Fetters: The Gold Standard and the Great Depression, 1919–1939*. New York: Oxford University Press, 1992.

Eichengreen, Barry, Arnaud Mehl, and Livia Chitu. *How Global Currencies Work: Past, Present, and Future*. Princeton, NJ: Princeton University Press, 2018.

Eichengreen, Barry, and Peter Temin. "The Gold Standard and the Great Depression." *Contemporary European History* 9, no. 2 (2000): 183–207.

Encinas-Franco, Jean. "Overseas Filipino Workers (OFWs) as Heroes: Discursive Origins of the 'Bagong Bayani' in the Era of Labor Export." *Humanities Diliman* 12, no. 2 (2015): 56–78.

Eng, Pierre van der. "The Silver Standard and Asia's Integration into the World Economy, 1850–1914." *Review of Asian and Pacific Studies*, no. 18 (1999): 59–85.

Fabella, Raul V. *Capitalism and Inclusion Under Weak Institutions.* Quezon City: University of the Philippines Center for Integrative and Development Studies, 2018.

Fanon, Frantz. *Black Skin, White Masks.* New York: Grove Atlantic, 2008. First published in French in 1952.

Finin, Gerard A. *The Making of the Igorot: Ramut Ti Panagkaykaysa Dagiti Taga Cordillera (Contours of Cordillera Consciousness).* Quezon City: Ateneo de Manila University Press, 2005.

Fisher, Irving. *Appreciation and Interest.* New York: American Economic Association, 1896.

Flynn, Dennis, and Arturo Giraldez. "Born with a 'Silver Spoon': The Origin of World Trade in 1571." *Journal of World History* 6, no. 2 (1995): 201–21.

Furuoka, Fumitaka, Qaiser Munir, and Hanafiah Harvey. "Does the Phillips Curve Exist in the Philippines?" *Economics Bulletin* 33, no. 3 (2013): 2001–16.

Golay, Frank H. *Face of Empire: United States–Philippine Relations, 1898–1946.* Quezon City: Ateneo de Manila University Press, 1997.

——. *The Philippines: Public Policy and National Economic Development.* Ithaca, NY: Cornell University Press, 1961.

——. "The Quirino Administration in Perspective." *Far Eastern Survey* 28, no. 3 (1959): 40–43.

Golay, Frank H., Ralph Anspach, and Eliezer B. Ayal. *Underdevelopment and Economic Nationalism in Southeast Asia.* Ithaca, NY: Cornell University Press, 1969.

Hau, Caroline S. *The Chinese Question: Ethnicity, Nation, and Region in and Beyond the Philippines.* Singapore: NUS Press, 2014.

——. *Elites and Ilustrados in Philippine Culture.* Quezon City: Ateneo de Manila University Press, 2017.

Hedman, Eva-Lotta E. *In the Name of Civil Society: From Free Election Movements to People Power in the Philippines.* Quezon City: Ateneo de Manila University Press, 2006.

Helleiner, Eric. *Forgotten Foundations of Bretton Woods: International Development and the Making of the Postwar Order.* Ithaca, NY: Cornell University Press, 2014.

Hoyt, Frederick G. "The Wood-Forbes Mission to the Philippines, 1921." PhD diss., Claremont Graduate School and University Center, 1963.

Huff, W. Gregg. "Boom-or-Bust Commodities and Industrialization in Pre-World War II Malaya." *Journal of Economic History* 62, no. 4 (2002): 1074–1115.

——. "Currency Boards and Chinese Banks in Malaya and the Philippines Before World War II." *Australian Economic History Review* 43, no. 2 (2003): 125–39.

——. *World War II and Southeast Asia: Economy and Society Under Japanese Occupation.* Cambridge: Cambridge University Press, 2020.

Huff, Gregg, and Shinobu Majima. "Financing Japan's World War II Occupation of Southeast Asia." *Journal of Economic History* 73, no. 4 (2013): 937–77.

Hutchcroft, Paul D. *Booty Capitalism: The Politics of Banking in the Philippines.* Ithaca, NY: Cornell University Press, 1998.

IBON Databank. *What Crisis? Highlights of the Philippine Economy 1983.* Manila: IBON Databank Phils., 1984.

Immerwahr, Daniel. *How to Hide an Empire: A History of the Greater United States.* New York: Farrar, Straus and Giroux, 2019.

Intal, Ponciano S. Jr. *Essays on Philippine Colonial Economy: Balance of Payments and Trade, 1870s to 1930s.* Manila: De La Salle University Press, 2003.

Jarvis, Helen. "Tan Malaka: Revolutionary or Renegade?" *Bulletin of Concerned Asian Scholars* 19, no. 1 (1987): 41-54.

Jenkins, Shirley. *American Economic Policy Towards the Philippines.* Stanford, CA: Stanford University Press, 1954.

Jimenez, Miguel Antonio. "Views on the Philippine Economy Through the Nationalist Lens: 1945-1992." *TALA: An Online Journal of History* 1, no. 1 (2018): 39-57.

Joaquin, Nick. *A Question of Heroes.* Pasig City: Anvil, 2005.

Johnson, Chalmers. *MITI and the Japanese Miracle: The Growth of Industrial Policy, 1925-1975.* Stanford, CA: Stanford University Press, 1982.

Jurado, Gonzalo M., Ricardo D. Ferrer, and Emmanuel F. Esguerra. "Trade Policy, Growth and Employment: A Study of the Philippines." International Labour Organisation: International Division of Labour Programme, October 1983. http://www.ilo.org/public/libdoc/ilo/1983/83B09_511_engl.pdf.

Kalaw, Maximo. *Self-Government in the Philippines.* New York: Century, 1919.

Kemmerer, Donald Lorenzo. *The Life and Times of Professor Edwin Walter Kemmerer, 1875-1945, and How He Became an International "Money Doctor."* Donald L. Kemmerer, 1993.

Kemmerer, Edwin Walter. *Gold and the Gold Standard: The Story of Gold Money, Past, Present and Future.* New York: McGraw-Hill, 1944.

——. *Modern Currency Reforms: A History and Discussion of Recent Currency Reforms in India, Porto Rico, Philippine Islands, Straits Settlements and Mexico.* New York: Macmillan, 1916.

——. "The Progress of the Filipino People Toward Self-Government." *Political Science Quarterly* 23, no. 1 (1908): 47-74.

Konzelmann, Suzanne J. "The Political Economics of Austerity." *Cambridge Journal of Economics* 38, no. 4 (2014): 701-41.

Krugman, Paul R. *Arguing with Zombies: Economics, Politics, and the Fight for a Better Future.* New York: W. W. Norton, 2020.

Kunio, Yoshihara. *Philippine Industrialization.* Quezon City: Ateneo de Manila University Press, 1985.

Lacaba, Jose F. *Days of Disquiet, Nights of Rage: The First Quarter Storm & Related Events.* New ed. Pasig City: Anvil, 2003.

Lakha, Salim, and Michael Pinches. "Poverty and the 'New Society' in Manila." *Australian Journal of International Affairs* 31, no. 3 (1977): 371-78.

Lamberte, Mario B. "Central Banking in the Philippines: Then, Now and the Future." Working paper. PIDS Discussion Paper Series, 2002. https://www.econstor.eu/handle/10419/127797.

Lears, Jackson. *Rebirth of a Nation: The Making of Modern America, 1877–1920*. New York: Harper Collins, 2009.

Legarda, Benito J. *After the Galleons: Foreign Trade, Economic Change and Entrepreneurship in the Nineteenth-Century Philippines*. Madison: Center for Southeast Asian Studies, University of Wisconsin–Madison, 1999.

——. "The Economic Background of Rizal's Time." *Philippine Review of Economics* 48, no. 2 (2011).

Lewis, W. Arthur. "The Export Stimulus." In *Tropical Development: 1880–1913*, edited by W. Arthur Lewis, 13–45. London: George Allen & Unwin, 1970.

Lichauco, Alejandro. *The Lichauco Paper: Imperialism in the Philippines*. New York: Monthly Review Press, 1973.

——. *Nationalist Economics: History, Theory and Practice*. Quezon City: Institute for Rural Industrialization, 1988.

——. "Preface: What 'Economic Re-Examination' Is About." In *Economic Re-Examination of the Philippines: A Review of Economic Policies Dictated by Washington*, by Salvador Araneta, xxx–xxxvi. Malabon: Sahara Heritage Foundation and Araneta Institute of Agriculture, 2000.

Lico, Gerard. *Edifice Complex: Power, Myth, and Marcos State Architecture*. Quezon City: Ateneo de Manila University Press, 2003.

Lindsey, Charles W. "Economic Crisis in the Philippines." *Asian Survey* 24, no. 12 (1984): 1185–1208.

Lumba, Allan E. S. *Monetary Authorities: Capitalism and Decolonization in the American Colonial Philippines*. Durham, NC: Duke University Press, 2022.

——. "Monetary Authorities: Market Knowledge and Imperial Government in the Colonial Philippines, 1892–1942." PhD diss., University of Washington, 2013. https://digital.lib.washington.edu:443/researchworks/handle/1773/23423.

Luthringer, George Francis. *The Gold-Exchange Standards in the Philippines*. Princeton, NJ: Princeton University Press, 1934.

MacIsaac, Steven Dale. "Nationalists, Expansionists and Internationalists: American Interests and the Struggle for National Economic Development in the Philippines, 1937–1950." PhD diss., University of Washington, 1993.

Manapat, Ricardo. *Some Are Smarter Than Others: The History of Marcos' Crony Capitalism*. Annotated ed. Quezon City: Bughaw, 2020.

Mattei, Clara E. *The Capital Order: How Economists Invented Austerity and Paved the Way to Fascism*. Chicago: University of Chicago Press, 2022.

May, Glenn A. "Why the United States Won the Philippine-American War, 1899–1902." *Pacific Historical Review* 52, no. 4 (1983): 353–77.

McCoy, Alfred W. *Policing America's Empire: The United States, the Philippines, and the Rise of the Surveillance State*. Quezon City: Ateneo de Manila University Press, 2009.

——. "A Tale of Two Families: Generational Succession in Filipino and American Family Firms." *TRaNS: Trans-Regional and -National Studies of Southeast Asia* 3, no. 2 (2015): 159–90.

McCoy, Alfred W., and Francisco A. Scarano, eds. *Colonial Crucible: Empire in the Making of the Modern American State*. Quezon City: Ateneo de Manila University Press, 2010.

McKenna, Rebecca Tinio. *American Imperial Pastoral: The Architecture of US Colonialism in the Philippines.* Quezon City: Ateneo de Manila University Press, 2017.

McVey, Ruth Thomas. *The Rise of Indonesian Communism.* Ithaca, NY: Cornell University Press, 1965.

Mendoza, Ronald U., Oscar Bulaong Jr., and Gabrielle Ann S. Mendoza. "Cronyism, Oligarchy, and Economic Governance in the Philippines: 1970s vs. 2020s." In *Martial Law in the Philippines: Lessons and Legacies, 1972–2022,* edited by Edilberto C. de Jesus and Ivyrose S. Baysic, 347–88. Quezon City: Bughaw, 2023.

Metzler, Mark. *Lever of Empire: The International Gold Standard and the Crisis of Liberalism in Prewar Japan.* Berkeley: University of California Press, 2006.

Nagano, Yoshiko. "The Philippine Currency System During the American Colonial Period: Transformation from the Gold Exchange Standard to the Dollar Exchange Standard." *International Journal of Asian Studies* 7, no. 1 (2010): 29–50.

——. *State and Finance in the Philippines, 1898–1941: The Mismanagement of an American Colony.* Quezon City: Ateneo de Manila University Press, 2015.

Onorato, Michael P. "Leonard Wood: His First Year as Governor General." *Asian Studies* 4, no. 2 (1966): 353–61.

Otani, Ichiro. "Inflation in an Open Economy: A Case Study of the Philippines." *IMF Economic Review* 22, no. 3 (1975): 750–74.

Paderanga, Cayetano. "The Macroeconomic Dimensions of Philippine Development." Keynote lecture, Philippine Studies Conference in Japan, Center for Southeast Asian Studies, Kyoto University, February 28, 2014.

Pante, Michael D. "The 'Cocheros' of American-Occupied Manila: Representations and Persistence." *Philippine Studies: Historical & Ethnographic Viewpoints* 60, no. 4 (2012): 429–62.

Paterno, Vicente Tirona. *On My Own Terms: The Autobiography of Vicente Tirona Paterno.* Mandaluyong City: Anvil, 2014.

Patnaik, Utsa. "Aspects of India's Colonial Economic History." Edited by Amiya Kumar Bagchi. *Economic and Political Weekly* 49, no. 5 (2014): 31–39.

——. "Imperialism, Gold Standard and the Colonised." *Social Scientist* 49, no. 9/10 (2021): 45–58.

Payer, Cheryl Ann. "Exchange Controls and National Capitalism: The Philippines Experience." *Journal of Contemporary Asia* 3, no. 1 (1973): 54–69.

Polak, Jacques J. "The Changing Nature of IMF Conditionality." *Essays in International Finance,* no. 184 (1991). https://ies.princeton.edu/pdf/E184.pdf.

Power, John H., and Gerardo P. Sicat. *The Philippines: Industrialization and Trade Policies.* London: Oxford University Press, 1971.

Punongbayan, JC. *False Nostalgia: The Marcos "Golden Age" Myths and How to Debunk Them.* Quezon City: Bughaw, 2023.

Rafael, Vicente L. *Contracting Colonialism: Translation and Christian Conversion in Tagalog Society Under Early Spanish Rule.* Quezon City: Ateneo de Manila University Press, 1988.

——. "Mis-Education, Translation and the Barkada of Languages: Reading Renato Constantino with Nick Joaquin." *Kritika Kultura*, no. 21/22 (2013): 40–68.

——. "White Love: Census and Melodrama in the United States Colonization of the Philippines." *History and Anthropology* 12, no. 1 (1999): 265–98.

Ramos, Charmaine G. "Change Without Transformation: Social Policy Reforms in the Philippines Under Duterte." *Development and Change* 51, no. 2 (2020): 485–505.

Reid, Anthony. *Southeast Asia in the Age of Commerce, 1450–1680. Vol. 2, Expansion and Crisis.* New Haven, CT: Yale University Press, 1993.

Reyes, Hermenegildo B. "The National Economic Council, Planning and Private Enterprise." In *Planning for Progress: The Administration of Economic Planning in the Philippines*, edited by R. S. Milne, 48–61. Manila: Institute of Public Administration and Institute of Economic Development and Research, University of the Philippines, 1960.

Richardson, Jim. *Komunista: The Genesis of the Philippine Communist Party, 1902–1935.* Quezon City: Ateneo de Manila University Press, 2011.

Rocamora, Joel. *Breaking Through: The Struggle Within the Communist Party of the Philippines.* Pasig: Anvil, 1994.

Rodriguez, Filemon C. "The National Economic Council, Past and Present." In *Planning for Progress: The Administration of Economic Planning in the Philippines*, edited by R. S. Milne, 38–47. Manila: Institute of Public Administration and Institute of Economic Development and Research, University of the Philippines, 1960.

Romer, Christina D. "What Ended the Great Depression?" *Journal of Economic History* 52, no. 4 (1992): 757–84.

——. "World War I and the Postwar Depression: A Reinterpretation Based on Alternative Estimates of GNP." *Journal of Monetary Economics* 22, no. 1 (1988): 91–115.

Rosenberg, Edward. "Filipinos as Workmen." *American Federationist* 10, no. 10 (1903): 1021–31.

Rosenberg, Emily S. *Financial Missionaries to the World: The Politics and Culture of Dollar Diplomacy, 1900–1930.* Durham, NC: Duke University Press, 2003.

Roxas, Sixto K. "Exchange Decontrol in the Philippines." *Philippine Studies* 10, no. 2 (1962): 183–205.

Sakai, Hideyoshi. "An Overview: Postwar Economic Development Experience in the Philippines: Thrust, Zeal and Achievement." In *Philippine Macroeconomic Perspective: Developments and Policies*, edited by Manuel F. Montes and Hideyoshi Sakai, 1–43. Tokyo: IDE-JETRO, 1989.

Salamanca, Bonifacio S. *The Filipino Reaction to American Rule, 1901–1913.* Hamden, CT: Shoe String, 1968.

Scalice, Joseph. *The Drama of Dictatorship: Martial Law and the Communist Parties of the Philippines.* Ithaca, NY: Cornell University Press, 2023.

Schumacher, John N. *The Making of a Nation: Essays on Nineteenth-Century Filipino Nationalism.* Quezon City: Ateneo de Manila University Press, 1991.

——. *The Propaganda Movement, 1880–1895: The Creation of a Filipino Consciousness, the Making of a Revolution.* Quezon City: Ateneo de Manila University Press, 1997.

Schwalbenberg, Henry. "Class Conflict and Economic Stagnation in the Philippines: 1950–1972." *Philippine Studies* 37, no. 4 (1989): 440–50.

Serrano, Cecilia P. *Beating the Odds: The Life, the Times, and the Politics of Diosdado P. Macapagal*. Quezon City: New Day, 2005.

Sharma, Patrick Allan. *Robert McNamara's Other War: The World Bank and International Development*. Philadelphia: University of Pennsylvania Press, 2017.

Shiraishi, Takashi. *Empire of the Seas: Thinking About Asia*. Tokyo: Japan Publishing Industry Foundation for Culture, 2021.

——. "The Third Wave: Southeast Asia and Middle-Class Formation in the Making of a Region." In *Beyond Japan: The Dynamics of East Asian Regionalism*, edited by Peter Katzenstein and Takashi Shiraishi, 237–71. Ithaca, NY: Cornell University Press, 2006.

Sicat, Gerardo P. *Cesar Virata: Life and Times; Through Four Decades of Philippine Economic History*. Quezon City: University of the Philippines Press, 2014.

——. "The Economic Legacy of Marcos." In *UPSE Discussion Papers*, Vol. 2011–11. University of the Philippines, School of Economics, Quezon City, 2011.

——. *Economic Policy and Philippine Development*. Quezon City: University of the Philippines Press, 1972.

——. "A Historical and Current Perspective of Philippine Economic Problems." Philippine Institute for Development Studies, 1986. https://dirp4.pids.gov.ph/ris/ms/pidsms86-11.pdf.

——. "A Memoir of the Young UP School of Economics." *Philippine Review of Economics* 54, no. 2 (2017): 151–77.

Sidel, John T. *Republicanism, Communism, Islam: Cosmopolitan Origins of Revolution in Southeast Asia*. Ithaca, NY: Cornell University Press, 2021.

Silver, Beverly J., and Giovanni Arrighi. "Polanyi's 'Double Movement': The Belle Époques of British and U.S. Hegemony Compared." *Politics & Society* 31, no. 2 (2003): 325–55.

Soberano, Jose D. "The Fiscal Policy Controversy." In *Patterns in Decision-Making: Case Studies in Philippine Public Administration*, edited by Raul P. De Guzman, 321–84. Manila: Graduate School of Public Administration, University of the Philippines, 1963.

Spang, Rebecca L. "The Rise of Inflation: Bursting the Bubble." *Cabinet*, no. 50 (2013). https://cabinetmagazine.org/issues/50/spang.php.

Stanley, Peter W. *A Nation in the Making: The Philippines and the United States, 1899–1921*. Cambridge, MA: Harvard University Press, 1974.

Steinberg, David A. *Demanding Devaluation: Exchange Rate Politics in the Developing World*. Ithaca, NY: Cornell University Press, 2015.

——. "Developmental States and Undervalued Exchange Rates in the Developing World." *Review of International Political Economy* 23, no. 3 (2016): 418–49.

Steinbock-Pratt, Sarah. *Educating the Empire: American Teachers and Contested Colonization in the Philippines*. Cambridge: Cambridge University Press, 2019.

Storer, James A., and Teresita L. de Guzman. "Philippine Economic Planning and Progress." In *Planning for Progress: The Administration of Economic*

*Planning in the Philippines*, edited by R. S. Milne, 5–37. Manila: Institute of Public Administration and Institute of Economic Development and Research, University of the Philippines, 1960.

Stuckler, David, and Sanjay Basu. *The Body Economic: Why Austerity Kills*. New York: Basic Books, 2013.

Studwell, Joe. *Asian Godfathers: Money and Power in Hong Kong and South-East Asia*. London: Profile, 2007.

Sweezy, Paul M., and Harry Magdoff. Introduction to *The Lichauco Paper: Imperialism in the Philippines*, by Alejandro Lichauco, vii–xv. New York: Monthly Review Press, 1973.

Tadem, Eduardo C. "Beyond the Grains: The Political Economy of the Rice Industry in the Philippines, 1965–1985." In *The Marcos Era: A Reader*, edited by Leia Castañeda Anastacio and Patricio N. Abinales, 244–76. Quezon City: Bughaw, 2022.

Tadem, Teresa S. Encarnacion. *Philippine Politics and the Marcos Technocrats: The Emergence and Evolution of a Power Elite*. Quezon City: Ateneo de Manila University Press, 2019.

Takagi, Yusuke. *Central Banking as State Building*. Singapore: National University of Singapore Press, 2016.

—. "Politics of the Great Debate in the 1950s: Revisiting Economic Decolonization in the Philippines." *Kasarinlan: Philippine Journal of Third World Studies* 23, no. 1 (2008): 91–114.

Thomas, Martin. "Albert Sarraut, French Colonial Development, and the Communist Threat, 1919–1930." *Journal of Modern History* 77, no. 4 (2005): 917–55.

Thompson, Mark R. *The Anti-Marcos Struggle: Personalistic Rule and Democratic Transition in the Philippines*. New Haven, CT: Yale University Press, 1995.

Timberman, David G. *A Changeless Land: Continuity and Change in Philippine Politics*. Armonk, NY: M. E. Sharpe, 1991.

Tooze, Adam. *The Deluge: The Great War and the Remaking of Global Order, 1916–1931*. London: Allen Lane, 2014.

Valdepeñas, Vicente B. Jr. "Turning Points in Central Banking: A Retrospective Essay." *Bangko Sentral [Central Bank] Review*, January 2009. https://www.bsp.gov.ph/Media_And_Research/Publications/BS09_A1.pdf.

Valdepeñas, Vicente B. Jr., and Germilino M. Bautista. *The Emergence of the Philippine Economy*. Manila: Papyrus, 1977.

Wade, Robert. *Governing the Market: Economic Theory and the Role of Government in East Asian Industrialization*. Princeton, NJ: Princeton University Press, 1990.

Wagner, Kim A. *Massacre in the Clouds: An American Atrocity and the Erasure of History*. New York: PublicAffairs, 2024.

Williams, Raymond. *Marxism and Literature*. Oxford: Oxford University Press, 1977.

Wolters, Willem G. "From Silver Currency to the Gold Standard in the Philippine Islands." *Philippine Studies* 51, no. 3 (2003): 375–404.

Wongsurawat, Wasana. *The Crown and the Capitalists: The Ethnic Chinese and the Founding of the Thai Nation*. Seattle: University of Washington Press, 2019.

Ybiernas, Vicente Angel S. "Governor-General Leonard Wood's Neoliberal Agenda of Privatizing Public Assets Stymied, 1921–1927." *Social Science Diliman* 8, no. 1 (2012): 63–82.

——. "Philippine Financial Standing in 1921: The First World War Boom and Bust." *Philippine Studies* 55, no. 3 (2007): 345–72.

# INDEX

www.ingramcontent.com/pod-product-compliance
Lightning Source LLC
Chambersburg PA
CBHW051728260326
41914CB00040B/2018/J